NIGERIAN KALEIDOSCOPE

Memoirs of a Colonial Servant

by
SIR REX NIVEN

C. HURST & COMPANY, LONDON

ARCHON BOOKS, HAMDEN, CONNECTICUT

First published in the United Kingdom by
C. Hurst & Co. (Publishers) Ltd.,
38 King Street, London WC2E 8JT,
and in the United States of America by
Archon Books, an imprint of
The Shoe String Press, Inc.,
995 Sherman Avenue, Hamden, Connecticut 06514
© Sir Rex Niven, 1982

ISBNs
Hurst: 0-905838-59-9
Archon: 0-208-02008-X

Library of Congress Cataloging in Publication Data

Niven, Rex, Sir, 1898–
   Nigerian kaleidoscope.

   Bibliography: p.
   Includes index.
   1. Niven, Rex, Sir, 1898–   . 2. Nigeria––
Politics and government––To 1960. 3. Colonial
administrators––Great Britain––Biography. 4. Colonial
administrators––Nigeria––Biography. I. Title.
DT515.77.N58A35 1982   966.9'03'0924 [B]   82-16295
ISBN 0-208-02008-X (Archon Books)

Printed in Great Britain

NIGERIAN KALEIDOSCOPE

At the laying of the foundation stone of the New Legislative Building, Kaduna, in 1959: (*from left*) the Sardauna of Sokoto; the Emir of Gwandu, President of the House of Chiefs; H.R.H. the Duke of Gloucester; and the Author, as Speaker.

*In grateful and admiring memory
of my wife Dorothy*

PREFACE

This book covers the forty years between 1921 and 1961, when I served in the various ranks and offices of the Nigerian Administration. These years also covered the political and economic development of this great country (especially the North, which I knew so well) from the dawn of a general peace to the high noon of general elections, parliaments and ministries, of factories and local airstrips – in a word, of Independence. In 1921 there were 'punitive patrols' dealing with villagers who, not unreasonably, greeted tax-collectors with flights of poisoned arrows. The peace was kept, with only five African battalions.

There were eventually twenty-four Provinces and four capitals. I served in five Provinces and two of the capitals and travelled extensively in all of them. I was in many curious situations, and odd incidents, which happened on the way to the scene of important decisions. Life was made up of the solemn and the absurd. Nigerians laugh a lot and we laughed with them. They thought we were mad in our strange antics, official and social, but they looked on amiably.

My own history before 1921 can be briefly stated. I left school in 1916 aged seventeen, and went to Oxford where I was received into the warm but attenuated war-time society of Balliol College. The next summer I joined the Army and was trained swiftly as an artillery officer. At the age of nineteen I went to Italy and joined the 120th R.F.A. battery; then on to France, where I remained with the same battery through the heavy warfare of 1918. When the Armistice was signed I was still not twenty, and went back to Oxford and took a degree. No one would employ me in the United Kingdom at a salary above £200 a year, so, after taking a three-month course in 'Colonial' subjects in London, I went to Nigeria. The salary that started when the mail-boat left Liverpool was a princely £500 a year, with an advance of £60 to pay for essential equipment.

This book has been rewritten more than once, and I am much indebted to my friends for their advice and help, especially Anthony Kirk-Greene of St Antony's College, Oxford, for his careful revision of the text, and those who typed it – from Elizabeth Taylor, long ago in Kaduna, to Gladys Newsom and Kate Kerwick more recently in London. Finally I thank my wife Pamela for her patience and guidance in what is to her a new field.

Finglesham, Deal, Kent   REX NIVEN
March 1982

CONTENTS

Sketch map of North-Eastern Nigeria

I. Lagos, 1921

Arrival

On a dull, drizzling May morning in 1921, the mail-boat from Liverpool to Lagos lay rolling in the swell waiting for the pilot. The decks were damp and the rail wet to touch. A group of passengers in dressing-gowns stood looking at Nigeria. It was not an inspiring sight. The old hands knew what lay within; we, the thirty or so newcomers, could not picture it at all. Indeed a preconceived notion of the tropical capital of Nigeria had already been dispelled by the dreary view.

The palms gave a ragged outline to the thin strand of shore. The only building in sight was the white lighthouse, conspicuous, backed by the palms. There was no sign of life whatever. On our right we could just see, when our attention was drawn in that direction by the experts, two grey lines of stone pushed out into the open sea. Between them we could by now catch sight of the white and red pilot flag on the life-boat, – the only boat which they said could ride that sea. Then we got under way and the arms of the two great moles embraced us and led us into the smooth waters of the Lagoon that gave its name to Lagos. The moles were not then complete: it was to take years for the great granite rocks (from Abeokuta, 50 miles inland) to be extended a mile and a half out into the deep sea.

From inside the Lagoon, Lagos looked a little more inviting. White houses stood among great trees with flaming tropical shrubs and neatly-cut green lawns. There were canoes in the harbour – as the water was usually called — and people were moving about on the shore. We slipped silently past the mass of Government House, white and impressive, and the twin towers of the Secretariat, to the Customs Wharf. There the damp heat of Lagos hit us.

The ship was the *Elmina*, an Elder Dempster boat of some 7,000 tons: it was a 'popular' boat at that time and, they said, had 'the lines of a yacht', though I could never see them. There was, however, an unusual feature. When you went below to the passenger deck, you came into a big open space from which little alleys led to cabins, two on each side. This arrangement was that of the early passenger ships when there was only a central 'saloon' and no lounges or smoking rooms, bars or libraries. It had the effect of making the ship cooler than its successors, in which this space was taken up with the upper parts of engine rooms.

We had about a hundred passengers of all kinds; of whom only three or four were women. Off Accra, on the Gold Coast, the Purser put up a telegram from the Nigerian government on the notice board.

1

This gave the 'postings' of all the official passengers, telling them the places to which they were to go in Nigeria. The old hands, of course, knew where all the places were, and some were going back to where they had served in the previous tour, while others, to their dismay, were going to strange territory. The newcomers anxiously asked the old hands about their postings, what kind of places they were and how you got to them. When the boat went on from Lagos to Port Harcourt in the Niger Delta and Calabar, those posted to 'Eastern' stations stayed on board for another two nights.

My posting on this list was Okigwi. They told me it was a good station – many in the East were not by any means 'good'. There was a detachment of the Nigeria Regiment there as well as the ordinary government staff. There would be about twenty white men, they said, and it was hilly and pretty. In fact, I did not reach it till twenty years later.

Lagos people poured on to the mail boat and greeted their friends. Some just sat down to their fortnightly 'good English breakfast'. Passengers with friends went off with them: others were, in due course, taken off by kindly hosts detailed for the purpose. I remained on board, with the remnant of those going on to the Eastern ports.

I was not a little surprised later in the morning to be accosted by a reddish-faced man who said he was His Excellency's Private Secretary. His name was Alan Burns. He explained that there had been a crisis in what was then called Yola Province, the remotest Province of all, and that this had involved changes in postings. A fellow-passenger, Robert Logan, posted in the first list to the Secretariat in Lagos, was now changed to Yola and I was to take his place in Lagos. The 'crisis' was quite simple. Two young officers had been playing tennis and one of them, between games, 'flicked' a ball over the net without looking. The ball hit the other chap in the eye and did it serious injury. It was, therefore, necessary to get the injured man away as soon as possible. They were short of staff in that Province and it was vital to send Logan to the relief of Yola, a journey which then took three weeks. Thus, by that simple incident, the careers of three men were affected. Burns said he hoped I would not mind staying in Government House until quarters could be found for me.

I was astonished; in my innocence I thought that a posting was a posting. I had been looking forward to this place Okigwi; I wanted to rough it; I wanted to get on with learning my proper job as soon as possible. I had been, and felt I still was, a fighting soldier with the soldier's feelings, not usually friendly, towards the 'gilded Staff'. The last thing I wanted to do was sit in a Secretariat. I had, of course, heard the uncomplimentary things the old hands said about Secretariat 'wallahs'. Had I gone to Okigwi my whole life would have been quite different. I would have been ignorant of the machinery of government. I might have become one of those who became wedded to a tiny area and were miserable in any other. I should almost certainly have been seriously ill from time to time. On the other hand, I would possibly have been Governor of the Eastern Region in a particularly trying period. I did not realise that there were a lot of people in the country who would have given their eyes for a spell in the Secretariat.

So I went off and packed my belongings. This did not take long and I found myself in one of Lagos' few cars, sweeping past the scarlet sentries into Government House grounds.

The building had been built for the original Southern Nigeria Government, replacing a very poor house which still stood further along the Marina. Sir Richard Burton described it as a 'corrugated-iron morgue containing each year the body of a dead consul'. The present 'palace' must have been far too large for its original purpose, for it has served adequately – with little change, and no extension except for an unsuccessful ballroom built for the Prince of Wales in 1925 – until the present day.

The rooms were very fine and there was an elegant central hall two storeys high. To the left, as one entered on the ground floor, was the great dining-room that would take fifty at table, and above it was the drawing-room. To the right were the offices and above them the Governor's own suite. On the floor above were the lovely guest rooms, looking over the harbour and out to sea, with staff rooms in the centre. A great staircase rose behind the lofty hall all the way up. The house was so built that almost every side could be opened and the breezes poured through. It was seldom hot inside the rooms. Character-istically, for many years the Governors of this immense territory contented themselves with a little office in one corner of the building.

Although the building itself was never actually changed, each Governor messed about with bits of it. I remember, rather later, a Governor saying to my wife: 'Let me show you the improvements we have made to the drawing room.' She replied, very casually: 'Every Governor has asked me to see his improvements, especially to the drawing room.'

When I arrived in Lagos, the Governor, Sir Hugh Clifford, was on leave and Donald Cameron, the Chief Secretary, was acting in his place. He preferred to live in his own comfortable house, from which he could easily reach the Governor's office and staff through a door in the garden wall. The great house was, in fact, empty save for Alan Burns, the man who had taken me off the boat: the ADC must have been across in the Chief Secretary's house. Burns and I had our morning tea and orange slices– then a Nigerian ritual – on the flat roof over the billiard room and car-porch. It was half past six and the best time of the day. The air was clear and fresh and the harbour before us looked like highly polished silver: the fishermen in their tiny canoes were black inlays on its surface. There was no traffic and the world was still.

I must say a word about Burns. He came to Nigeria in 1912 and passed the time of the war in the country, when he was prominent in the Lagos Defence Force, a force I belonged to myself twenty years later. He had never served in the 'bush', as up-country stations were invariably called: regardless of their size and importance, to Lagos people they were still the 'bush'. Burns was, however, a sympathetic and intelligent man and he appreciated sincerely the kind of life that was lived in the 'bush'. He was much older than I and, being imaginative as well as experienced, he was a real help to young officers.

Among other things, he realised that there was a serious lack of printed matter about Nigeria. So he set to and wrote his *History of Nigeria* which for years was a best-seller. I have also written a history of Nigeria, which differs from Burns's in that mine sought to be a history of the whole country from the African point of view in so far as a European can achieve that. Burns also produced a *Handbook*, which was brought up to date almost year by year. It contained a mass of valuable information on an amazing number of activities, with many statistical tables and maps. In the end he sold the copyright to the Government, but thereafter it was never the same without his hand on it. Anyhow, he could hardly continue its supervision for he went to the Bahamas, on his way to becoming Governor of British Honduras and then of the Gold Coast. Later he was assistant Under-Secretary of State at the Colonial Office. When in British Honduras he wrote to me to say that they had just opened a small museum of Maya remains and inscriptions. He went on: 'Whenever I receive the official despatches from the Colonial Office, I walk across the lawn to the Museum and look at the Maya writings; I don't understand them either.' (He died, aged ninety-three, in 1980.)

That first evening I was taken across to dine with the acting Governor. Cameron was what I have always thought of as sardonic in appearance –sometimes in mind as well. Very thin, with a slight stoop, clean-shaven, and with metal-rimmed glasses on a thin beaky nose, he had a harsh and rather nasal voice, which sounded misleadingly bad-tempered. He also had drooping eyelids. He was keen on golf and bridge – like many other people in Lagos. His brain was first-class and his wit was quick, but not of the amusing kind.

For example, there was at that time a great deal of muttering about quarters, and this was not astonishing as the standard of official accommodation was deplorable. Many were the letters and complaints on this subject, but nothing could be done about it at the time and there was little that could be said to assuage the feelings of the injured parties. One day a particularly long-winded petition came in and, being a petition, it had to go to the Governor. A competent minute was put up giving a possible line of reply, but all that Cameron wrote on the minute paper was 'Surely there are two m's in accommodation?'

Anyhow, this was a run-of-the-mill dinner-party of about a dozen people including myself and Logan, the man who was being sent to Yola. Cameron received me in a friendly way and apologised for changing my posting and hoped that I would be happy and find the experience useful. After that I could only say that I was a little disappointed but would do my best.

The Secretariat

Two or three days later I was allocated a house. This was one of the 'Jericho Buildings', so called because the 'sound of a trumpet' would cause them to fall down. They had been condemned for some years, but as things were there was no alternative to using them. They were semi-detached, and made entirely of wood, they had been assembled in sections bolted together many years before. The roof was corrugated-iron, painted red which was now depressingly faded. A wide verandah in front was the sitting and dining room. A single square room occupied the centre of the building, while the verandah at the back was the pantry and scullery, with a corner walled off as bathroom and lavatory. I think there was a real bath with one tap. The lavatory was an earth closet. The kitchen was a separate building outside. The floor was of plain wood and the whole was raised three feet off the ground. All this was standard Nigerian practice for many years.

The furniture was as plain as the house. Four locally-made dining chairs, one with arms, a dining table of sorts and two 'easy' chairs in which it was almost impossible to sit with any degree of permanence or comfort. There was an iron bed with mosquito frame, a dressing table and chairs. Cutlery and china I had to buy for myself locally. I never dared to entertain because my equipment was so primitive.

The best feature was the view, for the house was on Five Cowrie Creek, a wide sheet of water with a good view of the Harbour across to the moles on the right. There were some fine trees along the road at the back and up the creek to the left.

After a few months, we new officers of various departments were offered some 'bush houses' built on what is now the golf course at Ikoyi, south of Bank Road. They were of palm-leaf stems with palm-leaf roofs, steep-pitched and quite high, the whole completed with a thin concrete floor. You entered a semi-circular open space in front (under the roof) and then a room and a bathroom. They smelt very good and clean and we liked them. What is more we were even paid £5 a month 'bush allowance' for living in 'sub-standard' quarters. The only drawback of these houses was that white ants semed to like them as much as we did. Being some way out of Lagos we had to have transport: that could only be motor-cycles. For this too we were paid an allowance. Streams of young men swept into work on shiny B.S.A. machines bought for £40.

After the first week-end, I was introduced to the Office by Burns. The Secretariat was a charming looking building: mellow red brick, with snow white corner-blocks and mouldings. It was in an open square around neatly cut grass with a huge tamarind tree inside the great wrought iron gates, which had been specially imported from England. They always stood open – I doubt whether they could have been shut. Across this lawn from the gates was the centre feature, a projecting block, between two surprisingly elegant towers, with spotless white cupolas. One of them had a fine clock with four faces lit up from within at night. In this block was the Legislative Council Chamber.

The individual offices had a door on one side and a window on the other, and by a maddening quirk, the doors and windows alternated, so that if you wished to speak to the man in the next office you had to shout through his window or walk round the whole block to reach his door. There was a verandah on each side and this was the only means of communication. Behind the main block of the building lay Broad Street, which was always noisy. Across the road was a large Methodist mission school, whose numerous children sang hymns fortissimo or shouted in the playground. The two projecting wings were quieter, but hotter as they did not get the 'through breeze', an essential of Lagos life.

The Nigerian Secretariat, as it was officially called, was on the left as you entered the compound. The Chief Secretary's office was at the end of one wing, and in the opposite wing was the Treasury, with the Treasurer occupying the end office. To the right of the towers were the Attorney General, the Solicitor General, and a Crown Counsel or two. On the ground floor there were similar offices, housing the

Medical Headquarters people, the Surveyor General and his staff, and several other departments. Works and Post and Telegraphs had their own headquarters elsewhere, as did the Police. In the far corner, facing Broad Street and connected by a bridge, was the Government Press. Burns introduced me and another new arrival, Humphrey MacMichael, round to a great many officials, black and white. It was months before I came to know all of them and their jobs. They were as mixed a lot as you would imagine, but were universally kind. The Secretariat was manned by select people and many of them went far in the Service. Of those serving there in my first tour, four became G.C.M.G.s and another five were knighted.

When we had finished going round the offices, Burns sat down at his desk and opened a drawer. From it he took a large bundle of red tape. 'This', he said, 'is what we tie things up in, as you have no doubt heard.' Then he delved in the drawer again and took out an enormous pair of scissors: 'and these', he added, 'are what we use for cutting the tape.' He was a very fair man. He went on: 'You will sometimes find that red tape is invaluable, if you have to stall off some impossible request or suggestion, or if you have a tiresome fellow who won't take "no" for an answer. But usually we keep the tape in the background and use our common sense. However, it can be really useful for tying a bundle of files, where you have to keep them together for reference.' I never forgot his advice and often wished that others had had it said to them on their first arrival. Some of them used red tape as a refuge for their unsureness, its worst and most damaging use.

Burns then gave me two large bound volumes to read and the office orders that he had drawn up himself. He got on with his work, writing in a large firm hand. I don't think he ever erased or changed a word. I wondered whether I should ever reach such mastery. Oddly enough it did not take as long as I had feared, though I always changed words and made a mess of good clean drafts. The two volumes contained 'despatches', bound chronologically. The Governors of all Colonial territories and the Secretary of State for the Colonies corresponded with each other by 'despatch' in the most formal and indeed stilted prose. The despatches from London were bound in red leather and those from Lagos in green.

One complication in all this interested me at the time. The Secretary of State and the Governor were never superior or inferior to each other except when the one was in the territory of the other. The Secretary of State represented not only the British Government, but also the Sovereign, who personally appointed the Governors and saw the more important despatches and cables. The Governor in his own territory was almost physically the Sovereign. He had the Crown on his stationery, cars, equipment and furnishings. He had precedence over everyone: he not only went in first to all meals but was served first. He was received with the first six bars of the (British) National Anthem and with the Royal salute on ceremonial visits. Thus when they wrote to each other as they did in considerable bulk by every mail all this had to be borne in mind.

Some were long and interesting, especially Sir Hugh Clifford's tremendous descriptive despatches (running to two or three hundred paragraphs) recounting, in a sonorous diary form, the events of his great state visits in Nigeria. Again, there were the papers dealing with the setting up of the railway construction organisation for the Eastern line (which had stopped at Enugu in the war), the reorganisation of departments, the reasons for recent legislation, and so on.

I was to realise before long that I had arrived at a crucial point in Nigerian administrative history. The government of Northern Nigeria had been set up on 1 January 1900. At that time 'Southern Nigeria' extended from Calabar, which had been its capital for many years, to a point north-east of Lagos. The 'Colony of Lagos' covered the island and its hinterland: these two territories were only combined in 1906. In January 1914 the Northern and Southern Governments were amalgamated. They were completely different, not only legally but in principle, and even in ways of thought. Apart from that, the time chosen for such a complicated adventure could not have been less fortunate. The European war started only seven months later and it monopolised everyone's thoughts and daily life to the exclusion of almost all else until early in 1919. By then Nigerian staff had dwindled seriously and it was bound to take time to find new staff for all purposes, and get them settled and then trained up to concert pitch. Departments had to be combined and new common and acceptable policies worked out. By the time I arrived this process had been going on for less than two years.

When the amalgamation took place under Lugard, he appointed a Central Secretary to be head of the new combined administration at Lagos. This was Cameron, who at the time was Provincial Commissioner, of the Central Province (Warri). Whoever had been chosen, there was bound to be trouble and difficulty with the Lieutenant-Governors of the two Nigerias now united as one, for they had been Governors in their own right.

Lugard, the Governor General, left on final 'retirement' (if such a word could be used of such a man) in 1919, and Clifford succeeded him. The position then reverted to a plain Governorship. He was faced with grave difficulties. Besides administrative problems, there were others of great complexity, for example the combination of two different and sometimes conflicting sets of laws and courts. Clifford created a new constitution, but the most important claim on his attention was the central office of administration. Something worthy of Nigeria had to be set up and something impressive enough to deal with the Lieutenant Governors, correctly balanced with able staff, not only from the North and South of Nigeria but also from outside, that is from other colonial territories on promotion. This office he called the Nigerian Secretariat, under a Chief Secretary to the Government (C.S.G.) with a Deputy, a Principal Assistant Secretary and two Senior Assistant Secretaries.

I just happened to debouch on the Nigerian scene when all this was happening. The new Deputy, John Scott (from Malaya) and one of the S.A.S.s had arrived, and the Principal Assistant Secretary came shortly afterwards, all of them strangers and all very able. The last was Shenton Thomas, possibly the ablest officer we had at that time. The second Senior Assistant Secretary, H.O.S. Wright, was a man from the South. The third was from Somaliland (Douglas Jardine). Inevitably they were called the 'Three Wise Men'. Further, there were two Northern officers as Secretary and Deputy Secretary for Native Affairs, positions at first given special prestige and importance.*

Until this time most of the movements in the Nigerian Service had been internal and there had been few importations. Now it was laid down that all officers as far as possible should have an opportunity of serving in one of the three Secretariats (Lagos, North and South) in their early tours, then going back to their bush jobs and later, if they showed promise, returning to one or other of these offices in a higher Secretariat post. Hitherto Secretariat officers had remained in headquarters almost indefinitely and had, without any fault of their own, developed a specialised 'office mind' and outlook. This did no one any good.

There was another point. Pre-war Nigeria had obtained many of its staff from officers who had served in the South African war. Most of these were retained in Nigeria throughout the 1914–18 war; they

---

*It is worth recalling the salaries of these distinguished officials. The Governor received £6,500 plus £1,750 'duty pay'; the Chief Secretary and Lieutenant Governors £2,400 plus £600; Deputy Chief Secretary £1,400 plus £280; P.A.S. £1,200 plus £240, and S.A.S. £1,050 plus £210. Residents in the Provinces received £1,200 plus £240, and Senior Residents £1,400 plus £280. 'Duty pay' was a form of entertainment allowance paid only while in Nigeria. Heads of Departments fitted in between £1,200 and £2,000. Other officers were paid, according to seniority, between £450 and £960. These levels remained in force for twenty years.

suffered a good deal of discomfort and some hardship, and indeed an unusual proportion died of disease in the country. Quite a number served with the Nigeria Regiment in the difficult and unpleasant Cameroons campaign against what was then a German colony. After 1920 there came a veritable cloudburst of officer-veterans of the 1914–18 war, full of their experiences and war stories, often boring, which they inflicted on all and sundry. (The old Coasters too could produce tiresome stories.) A special resentment arose from the extreme youth of some of these war-stained veterans, of which I was not the least tiresome.

One of the more exasperated of the old Coasters was Nugent, my own immediate boss, who was bitter in several ways. The 'new importations' made promotion less likely for him, especially considering his position in the Service. He was also I feel sure never physically well. He did his best to make life unpleasant for me and to keep me firmly in what he considered my place. Once I had written a letter to the Director of Marine remonstrating with him over some matter I have now forgotten. He was cross about this and complained to my master. The latter sent the offending letter to me – I was in hospital at the time – and on a turned-back corner a scribbled note that was unnecessarily offensive. The point was that a very junior officer should not have signed such a letter to a Head of Department; we two newcomers had not been warned about this. It is now enshrined in the Office Rules.

Office procedure

I was sworn into the Nigerian Service by the Lieutenant-Governor of the South, Colonel Harry Moorhouse, a huge charming man whose office, though very important, was physically very humble, being a part of a largish bungalow on stilts, just up the road from Government House. I then really belonged to the Nigerian Administrative Service. The Southern Secretariat was at that time still in Lagos – off the Race Course, along with so many other institutions and officials. The commercial people lived 'over their shops' a misleading phrase, for they lived in great luxury and comfort that put the senior government staff to shame.

It was always a principle of the Colonial Office, although officials were appointed, in the first instance, by the Secretary of State, that once they were appointed to a territory they were on the staff of that territory. They were paid entirely by that territory, at rates agreed by the Secretary of State, from the territory's revenue. Transfers of officers from colony to colony were a matter of agreement between the receiving colony and the Secretary of State and, to some extent also, of the colony the officers were leaving. This principle continued until shortly before Independence, when officers became actual employees of one territory and transfer was difficult.

In 1921 I was No. 210 in the administrative list, a list which eventually built up to nearly 400 men, in addition to the senior officers. Although theoretically it was a single list for the whole country, in practice officers returned to their original group of Provinces, i.e. North or South, tour after tour. Transfers from one group to the other did occur but were rare. Of those 210, just over 100 were pre-war officers. The most unfortunate of this group were those appointed in August 1914, when everyone thought the war would be over in three or four *months*. They went on with their Colonial Service training in the U.K. and sailed to Lagos early in 1915. Then they had the chagrin of seeing the war extend year after year, with no chance of their taking any part. Psychologically, they suffered, and a lot of mean and unjustified things were said about these '15ers', especially as some of them were younger than those who came out after war service. It did not make relations any better to realise that they were almost all men of exceptional talent, intellect and efficiency.

Perhaps I should explain the *raison d'être* of a Secretariat, for there are many who cannot see the need for central offices. They were the Governor's (or Lieutenant-Governor's) offices and as such communicated his instructions and endeavoured to see that they were carried out. All correspondence, either way, passed through them. The Governor only signed despatches; all other official letters were signed by the C.S. or for him by his staff.

When a letter came in, it went to the junior secretary in the Section which dealt with that particular matter, say Native Affairs or Public Works. It was 'put up' in a file with any previous correspondence and precedents. The junior then read through as much of all this as necessary. Sometimes it was terribly complicated, as letters might run into scores of pages over the years. I was at times forced in bewilderment to take the papers to my senior to ask what line I was to take. Later, I instilled into my juniors the rule that they must not waste time in worrying over matters they were not expected to understand, when there were people who were paid much more and who were expected to justify their salaries. I found that when difficult matters were put aside and ignored for a few days, some cranny in the brain would worry over them, all by itself, and would produce a draft all ready to be written out when the file was next opened.

Normally, matters were easy. If he felt strong enough, the junior might send out a stock answer. If he did not, he would either put up a letter for his senior to sign, which conveyed what he took to be the right answer, or he could send up a minute, written on a sheet in the file, suggesting the action to be taken, or the reply to be given, or both. The senior could either accept this or send it up for the next man to express his opinion. Then it came back for the approved action to be taken. A number of matters obviously had to go to the Governor himself, and the minutes were written accordingly from the start so that H.E. could make up his mind, with all the facts clearly in front of him as well as the office's suggestions for action. Anyone could add to minutes as they went up, but sometimes a gratified junior would find that his original minute had been initialled by everyone and approved by the Governor without comment. This was a matter for some personal jubilation. We prided ourselves that a reply on anything normal went out in two days; and on complicated matters within a week.

It all depended on getting a letter into the right file at the start. For this there was a card index of subjects, but it did not go far enough. However, we were saved by human means, as in so many offices. There was a Mr Turton, a small impeccably dressed Yoruba who was never flurried and always smiling and courteous. He was an assistant chief clerk and was head of Records. Worried Assistant Secretaries would ask him to come along. They would explain that they could not get papers on, say, the sale of infected skins in Bornu – a matter which might fall into a variety of categories. Turton would close his eyes in thought and then say, '15,342 is what you want, sir, and I think page 23 is pertinent.' It always was.

Seniority was a matter of more than passing interest. While our tables of precedence never reached the refinements of those of the Indian Empire, they were adequate. Everyone's salary was clearly shown in the Staff List, and that was by itself a key to seniority, together with date of appointment. Those whose salaries were equal to each other were covered in the precedence. You might think this would only apply to formal dinner parties, but you would have been gravely, indeed dangerously, wrong as some found out to their cost.

At dinner, however humble, the seating was arranged according to the correct plan. After all, they had to sit somewhere and it was easier for them to sit in the correct order (and much safer from the hostess's point of view) than to sit 'anywhere'. You could never be quite sure that even people you knew very well would not 'cut up rough' if they were placed 'below' someone of possibly inferior status. All this, I am

confidently assured, also applied after dinner when the wives
arranged themselves upstairs in order for going to the single lavatory.
Pressure of necessity did not override that of precedence.

Later, in senior posts, one came up against visitors from overseas
and they, of course, were fitted in on a reasonable basis. A catch was
that the precedence table only applied to officials. 'Unofficials', as
they were called – members of firms and mining companies and the
like – had no official precedence and on *real* official occasions trailed in
like tail-end-Charlies, however important they might be in their own
worlds.

In those days there was no daily paper in Lagos. There were a
number of publications which came out irregularly and confined
themselves to long articles, usually highly critical of the government
and its alleged prejudices and injustices. They did not interest themselves in foreign news, for that had no appeal to their readers. There
were many local advertisements, among which was this classic:

COFFINS COFFINS COFFINS
COME AND TRY OUR FAMOUS COFFINS
ALL SIZES AVAILABLE

The production was awful, the newsprint very poor and the type-
setting light-hearted. The editors did not think much of the
Europeans in Lagos – this was reciprocated without rancour – though
the said Europeans by their subscriptions largely helped to keep them
going. On one occasion I produced a shock by saying in conversation
to an African editor, that I could see no reason for the government to
continue to pay for quite a number of copies, when all the editor did
was to revile the government without bothering to check his facts.
They did not concern themselves with 'up-country' events.

Foreign news came in daily by Reuters telegrams, expressed in
highly condensed telegraphese – I recall one about an air accident
which, in its original form, read 'PLANE DISSED AIRMEN
PULPED'. It fell to me to disentangle all this and issue the news in
comprehensible form. The result was then set up by the Printer and
issued late in the afternoon. The same, or maybe an abbreviated
version, was telegraphed to Provincial Headquarters and the larger
stations, where it was circulated. If there was no telegram, a blank
sheet with 'NO TELEGRAM' was issued to save people from getting
worried. After a run of these for three or four days in succession, the
Printer, a playful fellow, once added, 'BUT MR BURNS IS DOING
WELL' (he was responsible at the time).

It was very easy to make mistakes. Sometimes a little humour was permitted. But one day I dropped an unforgettable brick. The Reuter telegram had said that the (so-called) Mad Mullah of Somaliland had died. There had been a number of false reports of his end, which, as in the case of the Peking Embassies, 'proved to have been greatly exaggerated'. In a rash moment I added the words 'It is understood that this is for the last time.' What I had not realised was that the new Senior Assistant Secretary, Douglas Jardine (later Governor of Sierra Leone), had served for years in Somaliland and had only recently written and published a book on the Mullah, a subject near to his heart. He sent for me and gave me a sharp reprimand.

Checking the proof of the *Gazette* also fell to my lot once a week. One learned a lot about the country from this unusual angle. In general people in Lagos knew very little about what was still called by the German phrase *Hinterland*, though 'bush' was more common.

Within two months of my arrival, I developed a carbuncle between my shoulder-blades and went into hospital. I read to my dismay in the Royal Geographical Society's '*Hints to Travellers*', that 'sufferers from this painful complaint should at once leave the tropics and seek skilled medical attention': After that I was never really sick again till 1942. Lagos hospital was poor and austere, but it was a change from living alone.

After recovering from the carbuncle, I developed boils, great nasty things, very depressing. The two worst of them coincided with the important occasion of the Governor's return from leave. This was quite a show, with guards of honour, and booming guns and waving bunting – the 'streets were gay with banking' said a newspaper. It was the first time I wore the very undistingished khaki uniform prescribed for us juniors, complete with our war medals; we did not qualify for the full white civil service uniform, with its obliterating 'Wolseley' helmet, until we had completed seven years service. I added to the gaiety of these proceedings by wearing a bandage round my forehead: this failed to disguise the fact that my eyes were so swollen that I could hardly see. I should not have been there, of course, but I was not going to miss the show.

Cameron, who was about to hand power back to the Governor and so had plenty on his mind, happened to notice my condition. (Little escaped him.) Next day he sent for me – I was still on duty – and he asked me about the boils, and what action was being taken to treat them. I explained the facts to him. He picked up the telephone and got through to the Director of Medical Services, a crony with whom he frequently played golf and bridge. 'I have here', said Cameron, 'a young officer who tells me, on my enquiry, that he has been suffering from boils for some time. Your people do not seem to have been very successful in their efforts. Either you are a band of charlatans, as I have always suspected, or you are a professional service. I shall look forward to seeing evidence of which you are'. The next day, when I went to the hospital for my daily 'dressing', there was a little group of white-coated people from the Yaba Research Institute. They took smears of my pus and in two or three days produced a serum for injection. Before long the boils disappeared, and although I still had the serum when I left Lagos, I never had to use it again.

From a health point of view, Lagos was not well looked after. The 'African' hospital had originally been built for African staff only, and by the 'twenties was hopelessly inadequate. A large hospital was built on the Marina for the general public, but it was already out-of-date and too small before it was finished. The town was insanitary; with open drains everywhere; 'night soil' was carried off in great open drums and loaded on to a train. Nicknamed the 'Ghost Train', it steamed its stinking way out of Lagos in the early hours, crossing Five Cowrie Creek by a bridge built specially to carry it, and terminating at 'Dejection Jetty' just to the seaward of the present Federal Palace Hotel, (then a swamp).

Talking of Cameron, I must not forget the incident, which I have always reckoned one of the turning-points in my life, which took place while he was still acting Governor. After the Governor had seen the copies of recently arrived despatches from London, they were sent round the office. I noticed on a personal despatch, about the sailing of a new officer called Russell, that H.E. had scribbled in the margin 'Mr Niven to speak'. In the despatch there was an unusual second paragraph saying that this officer 'had expressed a desire to serve in a Secretariat'; 'while the Secretary of State had no wish to interfere. . .perhaps you might be able to see your way, etc.' I have said these despatches were pompous and very formal.

I went to Government House the next morning, and Cameron said, 'I seem to recollect that when you first arrived you were a little upset at being posted here. Now you have been here for a while, do you still feel you would like to go to a Province? From our point of view we would be happy for you to stay – but it is entirely for you to make up your own mind. You will have noticed that this Mr Russell is not of your mind and that he actually wishes to join us here, misguided as you no doubt consider him to be' (Cameron actually talked in this stilted way). I said I would still like to go. I do not know why, for I was beginning to settle in.

Cameron replied, 'Very well, I will arrange accordingly, but you will realise that you must stay here until this Mr Russell arrives to take your place.' Then he went on, 'I see that you were posted to the

Southern Provinces. Where would you like to go?' I played the simple-minded chap and said, 'You know the country, sir, and I do not, I will be very content with whatever you say.' He thought for a moment and said, 'I think you should go to the North: there you will get a good professional political* training: you would not be likely to get that in the South.' These were indeed astonishing words.

Settling down

Being poor at games, I spent much time walking in the evenings – at first only short distances, then longer till I reached the seashore about two miles away. There the casuarinas formed a solid forest all grand and dark. Beyond them the surf thundered – it really did thunder, with waves often ten or twelve feet high crashing on to the beach. There was a very poor road through the swamps to the shore, largely to keep touch with the east mole signal station. Occasionally brave people bathed, but it was dangerous: some roped themselves to trees before venturing into the water. Now the swamps are drained and the whole area is built over.

This 'bar beach', as the Lagosians still call it, is an island, very thin and about a hundred miles long. It cuts off the lagoon from the open sea. Lagos is itself an island, about six miles by one, with the mainland at Ebute Metta half a mile away. It is divided into two by the Macgregor Canal, the eastern part being called Ikoyi, from a small village at its extreme eastern end. When I lived in a bush house there, I walked over most of the island, through the short grassed dells and the thick clusters of trees, there were many cashew trees and the mangroves in the swampy shores, often solid with crabs. It was very pleasant and quiet.

Lagos (then a town of under 100,000 people) had about 5,000 police, a third of the entire Force of the Protectorate. Mostly the people were friendly and well-behaved. For example, when the people were upset by the introduction of water charges for the new supply, a 'mob' of some hundreds arrived at the Secretariat headed by the Inspector General of Police on a bicycle. 'We are the rioters', they said politely when the Lieutenant-Governor came out on to the verandah of his office. 'All right', he said, 'I'm busy now but come back to-morrow afternoon and I'll see two or three of you." The people of Lagos were gay and full of laughter, however adverse the conditions of life might be.

*In the early 1920s we were changing from a 'political service' to an 'administrative service' – the word political here means 'dealing with government'. For many years we were often called 'political officers'.

The police were always calm and smiling: most were old soldiers and, though mainly illiterate up to the 1940s, they had plenty of common sense. They were armed with rifles for patrol work and batons for civil duties. The prison warders had carbines or Greener guns. I once heard a warder say to a prisoner who was doing some inept digging, 'Take my gun, let me show you how to do it'. Prisoners did a lot of outwork, especially clearing verges. This they enjoyed, especially the chance to chat up the girls.

Surprisingly perhaps, there was no real 'garrison' in the capital. Just across the Macgregor Canal stood the barrack of what we called the 'household troops' – the single company of the Nigerian Regiment (officially part of the West African Frontier Force) that furnished the guard for Government House. Their battalion was stationed in Abeokuta, 60 miles away. At that time all the officers of the Regiment and of the Police (as of most other departments) were British. In the Secretariat we prided ourselves in sharing our work with a charming and able Nigerian Assistant Secretary, called McEwen. These Scottish names were common among Coast people, not necessarily for reasons of paternity, but often from admiration of some notable local white man.

There was a lot of entertainment among Europeans, and young officers, especially talkative ones, got invited as fill-ins. Many parties were all-male, of course, as there were so few white women. There was some dancing on Saturday nights. There was absolute and very strict equality and no form of colour bar, but that did not mean that there was any genuine mixing. There was some 'careful' entertainment by Europeans of Africans and their wives – lawyers and doctors, some of them later knighted – while old Henry Carr presided in Tinubu Square, the heart of old Lagos, as Resident of the Colony. A gentle man of great culture and vast knowledge of West African affairs, he was in charge of the strip of coast on either side of Lagos which formed the old Colony of Lagos. In his courtesy he treated the most junior of colleagues as he would the most senior. The Government eventually gave him a C.M.G., it should have been a knighthood. British colonial history is a long tale of lost opportunities woven conspicuously into the web of its successes. It was notable that the Nigerians, however wealthy, seldom entertained white people.

Many of the Nigerian intelligentsia were rather 'political' and were dubbed 'nationalist' by nervous Europeans, and so came to be regarded automatically as hostile and therefore to be shunned. This again was a mistake. While insincere fawning would have been wrong, honest attempts to get together and discuss each other's point of view over a drink would have done no harm and might have done good. As it was, a rather dubious white element cultivated them and fanned grievances many of which were imaginary. One of the most striking facts about Lagosians was their ignorance of the rest of the country: it semed to me that almost any white man with a few years' experience knew more of Nigeria than these people who were born there.

I was fortunate to meet Henry Harman, Principal of King's College, and his wife. I often went in to supper with them. This relationship had one important consequence for me. While in Lagos I wrote a few short stories about ancient Wessex (my family then lived in Dorchester). When they were finished I let the Harmans read them. They were polite, as people are, and I put them aside. Ten or twelve years later a Mr Higham of Longmans Green, the famous publishers, wrote asking me to call on him when I was on leave. He said that Harman (who apparently was doing work for them) had mentioned a book I had written and wondered whether I could write a geography of Nigeria for them. I said I would, and in due course started to write.

When I was back in Lagos a year or so later, Higham came out on a visit and dined with me. Just as he was leaving he said, 'By the way, you were going to write a geography for us – do you think you could make it a history?' It appeared that someone else was doing the geography. I said I would, but asked for something in writing. A contract was signed, and so started my happy relation with Longmans. The book was written in Lagos between the hours of six and seven every morning, and was published in 1937. It went through thirteen editions and sold about 140,000 copies, mostly in Nigeria.

We had an excellent library in Lagos. This was another of Burns's achievements: he got together books out of some existing small libraries, from the estates of people who had died, and from sales on departure, and with grants from the Carnegie Trust bought a large quantity of reference books as well as light reading from the U.K. He was chairman of the library committee, a post in which I followed him years later. The books were housed in a charming building in the corner of Government House grounds.

Nearby stood the colonial church, St. Saviour's, which had been built by Government in a pleasant kind of Gothic, as had two others up country. Until Clifford came as Governor, there had been a government grant towards its upkeep and the salary of the chaplain. Clifford quite logically said that if this Anglican church was to be maintained there would have to be one for the R.C.s and therefore for the Non-Conformists as well. And so provision was struck out of the Estimates. This disestablishment had a stimulating effect. The

Church Council raised enough money to meet all the expenses, including the padre's salary. In later years the church was doubled in size but a tower, for which there was a base, was never added. While this church was in essence for white Anglicans, as time went on Africans would attend and be welcomed. Lagos was full of churches, most of them very denominational, and I doubt whether some of them would have welcomed white faces in any number.

Behind King's College (which stood at one end of the Race Course) was the new Roman Catholic cathedral, designed in concrete by a gifted priest, as so many of them were. Bedecked with decoration like icing-sugar and flying buttresses that were probably unnecessary, it was eye-catching. The Anglican cathedral stood on the waterside, in brick of an uncertain texture. Much too small for its purpose, it had little room for expansion. It had a splendid organ, and an organist of international repute, Felo Sowande.

Besides these there were cathedrals of subsidiary sects. One was purely Anglican but differed by permitting polygamy to its members – it was a prosperous church! – and many parish churches, like the well-known missionary church St. Paul Breadfruit, so named from the huge tree that grew beside it. Baptists proliferated into churches, daughter-churches and grand-daughter-churches, all differing from each other, with Methodists and Congregationalists and Seventh Day Adventists, not to mention the Cherubim and Seraphim, who from time to time dipped in the wild ocean waves. No wonder the good Muslim – there was a big mosque in the middle of all this – looked on in respectful dismay at this splendid plethora. On Sundays all Lagos streamed to church in their best clothes: important men in striped trousers and black morning coats with shining silk hats, the ladies in splendid European clothes bought direct from Paris (or the local dressmaker, via the fashion plate).

The distinguished Africans lived in fine houses with their families and dependants in some considerable state. Many were very wealthy; being a lawyer was not without its material benefits, and business was most rewarding. The Yoruba (and most of these people were Yoruba) have always had the gift of trade, an 'eye to the main chance'. Many of them had degrees from British universities, and their daughters went to good schools in England.

Nevertheless, the Union Jack flew from the high mast in Government House grounds, as it had flown since 1864, the year in which the Island was annexed to the Crown. This was after a spirited naval action in the harbour. Most things that could go wrong with the Royal Navy went wrong that day: sailing ships had their drawbacks in confined water, especially when those waters were powerfully defended with stockades and determined shore batteries. However, the island was taken. The cause was the suppression of the slave trade, a trade that took 5,000 men and women at a time in the baracoons of Lagos, people seized in the wars of the hinterland and then traded to the great profit of entrepreneurs, black and white alike. The Island was taken to stop the trade; we had tried other ways and knew there was none. The British did not want Lagos! The British Parliament were against taking any more overseas lands.

As I said, the Union flag flew supreme in 1921: there was no question as to who were the masters in Nigeria. Democracy might have been possible in administering Lagos itself and a few towns, but for the whole country it was not even thought of. The British Governors, in the King's name, were the supreme rulers. They held a most difficult position, for only the brave ventured to disagree with them. If they had good Chief Secretaries and Lieutenant-Governors they were lucky, for these were big enough to answer back; yet some of them did not do so. Governors seldom heard the whole truth. The vast size and complexity of Nigeria made it almost impossible for them to have a good knowledge of the country. They were appointed for five years, which meant that at the end of their Nigerian service they had worn the purple for ten years (having come on from at least one other governorship), during which period they had not had a reasonable discussion with anyone, except on leave. It was not their fault: they were most amiable and would have liked to be friendly but it was hard for this to happen.

The first Governor I knew was Sir Hugh Clifford. He had been in the Malayan civil service, who considered themselves a class apart compared with the rest of the Colonial Service, and had been Governor of the Gold Coast before he came to us. He had the almost impossible task of following Lugard who was then unique. There was no one in the Empire with his prestige and reputation. Kitchener in his time had been an exception, and indeed there were considerable likenesses between them.

Clifford was physically a large man with a large red face and bright blue eyes, and a large voice too. In every way he was large: his gestures, his manner and his conception and conduct of official ceremonial. There was nothing mean or insignificant about him, and he was observant and shrewd.

A master of English, he wrote books about Malaya which are still worth reading. His minutes in our official files, on even the simplest subjects, were couched in rolling tones, more worthy of a proclamation. Here is one addressed to the Chief Secretary, which became well-known among those who served in Nigeria in those days:

'We have been honoured by the gift of two fine portraits of their Majesties [King George V and Queen Mary] and these have recently arrived and are safely lodged in Government House. I am, however, at a loss as to the Department to which should be entrusted the delicate task of hanging these gracious pictures. I am reluctant to confide this task to the Public Works Department, a department which since my arrival in this country has lost no opportunity of convincing me of its astonishing incompetence in executing even the simplest of tasks that should normally fall within its ambit, tasks which one might expect to be carried out without apparently inevitable disaster and consequential inconvenience to those who look to it for technical aid. After much reflection I have decided that this important responsibility should be assigned to the Railway Department and would be glad if you would kindly instruct the General Manager accordingly.

A copy of this minute should be transmitted to the Director of Public Works.

H.C.

When Clifford gave parties or balls at Government House, all the men had to wear full evening dress, with starched shirts and collars, white waistcoats and tails. A stiff collar did not last long in the damp Lagos heat and we always took a spare one with us; some actually took two and needed them. The ladies were more fortunate in their evening dresses, but damp patches on their backs were not unknown. I remember one ball at which the great staircase was lined on each hand by soldiers wearing scarlet and gold zouaves and fezzes while the Governor received at the top.

After Christmas the long-expected Mr Russell was said to be on the high seas and I got ready to leave. When he came, we found him strangely unimpressive; perhaps he had been over-anticipated. I handed over to him with some apprehension.

During my stay in Lagos I had learned a lot. I knew how the government machine worked at the centre and now knew personally a large number of heads of Departments and senior officers, some quite well. I knew how they worked and what their departments were capable of doing and what they were supposed to be doing. I knew a good deal about the laws of the country and how they were meant to be administered – I had sat on the bench sometimes with FitzGerald (my first neighbour; later Chief Justice of Palestine). To some extent I had got used to the climate. I knew about Government finance and how it all came to account. I had, in fact, a considerable advantage over my contemporaries. Perhaps most important, I knew how careful and conscientious were all those who handled matters of government in the Secretariat and Treasury: I also knew what good people they were, with a great sense of fun and fair play. Yet I still had much to learn in practical administration.

II.   Kabba Province

Koton Karifi – taking over

I left Lagos in January 1922, and went into the 'unknown'. I went by the ordinary train (that is, not the Boat Train), officially the 'Down Mixed'. It left Lagos every alternate weekday at noon.

After my conversation with Donald Cameron, the North was told that I would be available and I was then posted to Zaria, a lovely place to live in. But because Russell's arrival was delayed, my posting was changed. In the course of my service I was posted to Zaria three times, but never served there, although I visited it often enough.

I was eventually destined for Kabba Province which no one I met in Lagos seemed even to have heard of. Admittedly it was a new Province, being the eastern half of Ilorin Province plus a thin slice across the River Niger, nevertheless, this ignorance was ominous. In the Lagos view, Kabba Province was the end of the world, and I learned later that so far as the rest of the North was concerned, it was also regarded as little short of a penal settlement. This feeling continued almost until Independence. At one time a confidential document was issued sternly denying this supposition and adding that the word 'Stellenbosch' should not be applied to it (in the South African war, to be posted as Town Major of Stellenbosch was a particularly unpopular assignment).

Lokoja, the new Provincial Headquarters, had once been the centre of the world in these parts. Now it was reputed to be somewhere far away and difficult of access (true) set in the Niger swamps (not true). It was not the fault of the officers posted there that the place had this reputation; they did their best, but being tucked away it did not get its proper share of development funds. The Native Administrations were small and poor and not well-staffed, compared with their great Northern counterparts. The climate was supposed to be bad. This was true of Lokoja but not of either Kabba or Okene. The people were fascinating and very intelligent and the country in parts was beautiful. When Independence came, these people filled many important posts, for their education was more advanced, thanks to the missions, than that of the Northerners. Meanwhile I had to get there.

The train from Lagos was 'mixed' because it carried goods and passengers, which made its progress slower than it might have been. The entire population of the area would come down to the station to see their friends and make an honest penny or two. The people sold food wrapped in leaves which appeared horrible to me, but obviously

22

it tasted good for the lady vendors were soon cleared out of their supplies. There was fruit and meat on skewers, and local cloth and mats were bought. The noise was deafening. There were no platforms.

On the train there was a restaurant car, not as grand as that of the boat train but serviceable and as clean as they could manage; the food was uninspired but eatable and cheap. At night small but respectful crowds would gather to see the Europeans eat, brilliantly illuminated in the electric lights of the train, or unwise white women, who thought that blue glass made them invisible by night as by day, while they undressed in their cabins to go to bed.

The first part of the journey is through high forest. There are Yoruba villages with palm-leaf roofs and mud walls, square in plan, and banana 'trees' in the streams below them and cocoa trees in the clearings. We passed through the big towns of Abeokuta and Ibadan with roofs of corrugated iron or beaten oil-tins, rusted to a rich red, with great trees riding above the houses.

The first station in the North was at Offa, in Ilorin Province, and to arrive there was always an emotional moment for the white officers serving in the region. This simple platform was the threshold of 'home'. The policemen were Northerners. It was not the same for Northern Nigerians: their threshold was Minna, and in some cases Kaduna. That was the veritable North. The Northern officer had a patrimony that was never shared with his Southern colleagues: a sacred loyalty, like that felt to a good regiment. Curiously Ilorin, 50 miles further north, had no emotional appeal, but the Niger river, crossed at Jebba, again raised a lump in the throat. Jebba itself was a poor place, but the two great bridges and the Juju Rock had their own message: there was history here.

On this leg of the journey my immediate destination was the junction at Minna (created in 1912) between the original Baro-Kano railway and the Lagos railway, which then made its tortuous way across and along the Niger Valley. After the Niger the journey was tedious, and apart from the rocky Kaduna river at Zungeru there was little to see. The country is 'orchard bush', small trees and fairly high grass with high forest confined to the stream beds. The villages and railway stations were mostly small, consisting of round grass-thatched huts, mud-walled. The people are Nupe, with some Gwari. The costumes of the Nupe women are mostly blue of various shades; they are very prim – the Gwari are not.

The train reached Minna after dark. Here I descended and my voluminous baggage was taken out of the van and piled on the platform. I had about fifty cases, my 'free' two and a half tons. I was met by a dignified person in a long white gown who handed me a note from the Station Magistrate which said he was sending me fifty labourers, his messenger, his horse and his welcome. I would be expected at his house for dinner when I had cleaned up; my loads would be taken to the rest house.

The railway station was lit by electricity and it was no trouble to get the loads counted, signed for and put on the carriers' heads. My three boys looked on with some astonishment and dismay. One had been to the North but the other had not. The straggling column set off into the night. The messenger headed the party with a hurricane lamp and I followed on the horse. We went along a wide 'road' and gradually started to climb in total darkness. As we got used to the darkness I could see that the ground fell away to the left and rose to the right. Below us now, the bright lights of the train snaked away through the night and the engine's great headlight picked out points in the bush far ahead. The stars seemed just above our heads.

I had no idea how far we had to go or whom I was going to meet. The title 'Station Magistrate' meant nothing to me. It was not in fact very far, and in about twenty minutes I could see dim lights – not like electric ones. I was taken over to the S.M.'s house by a boy with a light: it was a criminal offence to move about in a government station without one, unless there were street lights.

I went into a large, high room with a raftered roof, huge cushioned chairs, colourful mats and skins on the floor and animals' heads on the walls. A pressure lamp flooded this apartment with light. Here were the S.M. and a police officer whose names I have now forgotten. After a few drinks we had dinner, waited on by silent Northern boys. There were no white women in the station. After a few perfunctory questions about the journey and my past history, the conversation turned to local affairs. It was clear that these men were not only uninterested in anything to do with Lagos, but that there was a definite hostility to it and those who worked there. I picked up quite a quantity of thoughts different from those I had become used to.

After dinner I was illuminated back to the rest house, a fine mud house with thatch roof. There I found an air of inaction. No bed had been made, there had been no preparations for the night, and there was no hot water for the bath. The rest house had only a table and a couple of chairs. Very tired after the long train journey, I was far from happy.

The first thing was to locate my camp-bed in the great pile of wooden cases and then the case had to be opened, the mosquito net had to be located; the travelling bath had to be relieved of the many articles that had been stuffed into it in Lagos, and bed linen and blankets had to be found. It was cold. The Harmattan wind was blowing to our discomfort; while its dry dust was not as bad as further north, we were not used to it.

Then it was clear that the boys were not accustomed to erecting a camp-bed. After strenuous efforts lasting about an hour, all was complete and I had a bath and went to bed. The next morning I was determined to train the staff in this exercise. By my own example – not that I was an expert – we eventually got the time for putting up the bed and net down to four and a half minutes, and the same time for making the bed itself.

Fortunately I was eating with the S.M. which I found to be the amiable custom of the country; otherwise I would have fared ill indeed. The next morning, as I left the rest house, I observed that I was almost at the top of a great granite hill, with some large trees and dried grass and withered shrubs. There were three or four large thatched houses nearby, and in the cleared areas round the houses were plants of various kind, obviously well looked after. All the high roofs were of grass on thick mud walls, with small verandahs round them, except in the front where they formed a place for sitting. The Nupe were fine builders and their thatching was particularly good, nearly as good as that of the Zaria people. Beyond the houses, and the small round houses for the boys which belonged to them, the ground fell away and one could see for many miles across country.

The Station Magistrate's house had a terrace and a sitting verandah on the edge of the steep slope down into a narrow valley, some 400 feet below. Here the single line of the railway gleamed as it twisted and turned, seeking the best gradient, before disappearing behind a shoulder of the hill we were on, for its gradual climb to the 2,000-foot plateau of the North. Beyond the rails the ground rose quite steeply to a long whale-back hill that was higher than our side. This hill was partly covered with the tiny grass-roofed huts of a biggish Gwari village. It was here that Byng-Hall, my future Resident, was said, some years before, to have been made king of the Gwari, owing to his intervention in a gravely disputed succession. His arrival in headquarters with numerous cattle and sheep and nubile damsels, pressed on him by a grateful tribe, caused a good deal of official embarrassment, as he later told me.

I found that the Station Magistrate was in charge of the so-called Government 'station' that included the railway area, the hill top and a rather new native town on the other side of the rails. He was personally responsible for *all* that went on in that area (except the railway itself) and had judicial powers, not exalted, but effective. With him was a white policeman, whom I had met the previous night, and a doctor. The railway had an engineer and a white senior station master, who was in charge of a number of other neighbouring stations.

I had to spend two days on this summit awaiting the departure of the train for Baro, on the Niger. These days were not wasted, for I found out quite a lot and my boys settled down to a new kind of life. The strain was as great for them as it was for me, though I did not appreciate it at the time. They knew the drill of running a white man's house, but had little initiative.

The train travelled thither southward on alternate weekdays. Leaving at 8 a.m., it managed to traverse the 111 miles of fairly flat country by six that evening. I was the only first-class passenger and at the end of the day felt far from first-class. The other classes were crammed full – the Nigerians certainly enjoyed railway travel. There was no restaurant and by mid-day sandwiches were dry, drinks were tepid. Eventually it became cooler. The monotonous country did not change, but the ground rose round us into flat-topped hills.'

The arrival by the great river – and it is indeed a great river – was not spectacular. There was a small native town of standard Nupe appearance, then the train ran along a bank and there on one side was the Niger. It did not look a mile wide. The other side was swampy, and in the far distance were more flat-topped hills. We saw some corrugated iron warehouses and barges and a Niger Company boat. The train pulled to a halt, below the ruins (invisible to us) of mud buildings of the old township of Lugard's time – offices, a hospital, West Africa Frontier Force lines and quarters. Baboons now wandered through them. Here Lugard had planned his River port for the opening up of the North in the early 1900s and ocean-going ships, could still tie up and load their produce direct for the open sea.

Schönn, the chaplain on board H.M.'s tiny ship *Kwarra*, wrote in his diary one morning in 1843: 'By God's good grace we are permitted to open our eyes on another day.' There followed the names of those who had died in the night. The Niger did not look menacing that evening as the sun set in glory and the labourers moved my many loads down from the train to the smart wood-fuelled Marine launch, called the *Manatee*, which had been sent to meet me. Forward, behind the helmsman, was an excellent but unfurnished cabin: the deck and fittings were of best teak, and the traditional brasswork gleamed. The electric lights were soon switched on. The boys with astonishing speed and efficiency erected chairs and a table and then the bed and netting, and before long dinner was being served.

Until that time my orders were to go to Lokoja, the Provincial Headquarters. The African captain of the launch gave me a note from Geoffrey Izard in the Provincial Office that I should stop off at a 'sandbank' on the way and take over the Division on the east bank, called Koton Karifi. There was no further explanation or information but it did turn out to be my definitive posting.

Before dawn the launch cast off, with the mail on board. By the time I woke up, we were out in midstream moving swiftly with the current. The blue ensign with the device of the Nigerian Marine flew at the stern under the plume of wood smoke. The waterside villages were anonymous to me and very similar to each other, each one a ragged line of huts on the riverbank, stacks of measured firewood; canoes drawn up, some quite large, some tiny. The morning mists swirled in little eddies; the water was pearl grey and dead calm.

I had a good traditional English breakfast. Then the furniture was folded up and stacked away in convenient carriers' loads. We watched the shore and wondered what lay before us – I speak for the boys and myself. There indeed was the real unknown, behind the line of great trees beginning to emerge as we neared the eastern bank. As we looked we saw a high thatched roof and some small roofs beside it. I recognised it as a rest house – so this must be Adaha, the 'port' of Koton Karifi. Beside the rest house were some wretched grass huts and a ragged line of labourers with the usual white-robed messengers in charge. As the launch tied up a note was handed to me from Campbell-Irons, whom I was to relieve. It merely said welcome and that the labourers were waiting for me. I went ashore, the loads were landed and taken up by the labourers and the launch gave a joyful hoot and swirled off into the main stream.

Our very odd column set off along a high causeway into the forest of great trees soaring a hundred feet and more above out heads. They said that at 'high' river the embankment we were using would be under many feet of water, and we were duly impressed. After half an hour we came out of the forest into the open, and in front of us on rising ground stood neat houses, mud and thatch in the Nupe style; behind them rose a flat-topped hill, scrub-sided. As we approached the view opened and on a low hill to my right a small Union Jack hung despondently from a twisted pole. I should have been cheered by this emblem of my country, but it conveyed nothing but dejection.

The path from the town went up the hill about 500 yards. At the end of it, set back in a large open space behind a vague avenue of jaded jacarandas, stood a large square mud house, with whitewashed walls and green window-frames closed with wooden shutters. The area round it was cleared of grass, without flowers or any trace of decoration, save whitewashed regimentally-arranged stones. On the right stood a small round house which I found to be the Divisional Office, a splendid name for an insignificant place. On the left was another round house. That was the rest house and I saw my loads trail off in that direction.

Captain Arthur Valentine Campbell-Irons came out to meet me. To my eyes he was incredibly old and worn, although he cannot have been more than forty-five. He was a District Officer of some standing; he had come to Nigeria in 1906, having fought in the South African war, and had married rather late in life. I was astonished to find that Mrs Campbell-Irons was a dark-haired stunning beauty, as friendly as her husband was awkward. She wore a short frock and under it pyjama trousers tucked into mosquito boots and on her arms were home-made 'sleevelets', for want of a better word, of blue linen, all to keep off the mosquitos and sandflies.

They had not enjoyed their sojourn here and it was painfully obvious that they were anxious to get away. The mosquitos and isolation had troubled Mrs Campbell-Irons. My arrival had made that possible and so I was welcome. They gave me the usual lunch of roast chicken, and I was taken down into the town in the evening and shown the 'institutions', such as they were. I knew nothing whatever of the working of Native Administration, the basis of Northern government, and I had to learn. I did not even know what the phrase 'Enay' meant; Campbell-Irons said in answer to every question that such-and-such was a matter for the 'Enay'. It was obviously so essential a matter that I did not like to show my ignorance by asking what such a word meant.*

The word did not of course mean the Chief of Koton Karifi, who was not a particularly dynamic person, or even his council of somnolent old men; it really meant the whole 'machine', the Court, the prison (the first thing the British built, they said, was a prison), the so-called police and, most important, the Treasury and the tiny 'central' office.

The organisation was very rudimentary but the theory was easy to grasp. The point that did not occur to me until later was that this machine, with its ramifications in the big Emirates, was supposed to be operated by the Chief and Council (or by the Chief alone) and not as the private tool of the District Officer – a point that escaped some of my colleagues.

The Campbell-Irons fed me that day and on the next day I did my unaccustomed best to give them lunch before they left. He had been posted to Kabba Division, many miles inland on the other side of the Niger. They were delighted at the prospect.

In the morning Campbell-Irons handed over the office to me and

*'Enay' = 'N.A,' = Native Administration or local government.

opened the quaint strong room to count the cash there – about £2,000, mostly in shillings. The routine was to count out two or three bags and then weigh them against the others one by one, the receiving officer hoping that the other bags were not filled up to correct weight with pebbles. One of the habits was to gum coins on to the inside of the bag and then fill it with anything handy that gave the right 'feel' to the bag — something I did not know at the time. As it happened, the figures were correct, for I did not find a dud bag. In general dog did not eat dog, which again I did not know. There were a number of things that had to be signed for, and the clerk Mr. S. Oruama had everything in order. He kept the cash book and store record, made out the monthly returns, and filed and typed letters. He had no assistance at all. Mr Oruama was a very correct man, which was just as well for my sake. He never, so far as I know, made a mistake. It must have been pretty dull for him living in this strange place (he was a Niger Deltaman) but it was just part of the deal. His time would come, as it did. (Years later I found him as an Assistant Chief Clerk in Kaduna).

After lunch the numerous loads of the Campbell-Irons were brought out and taken up by the carriers, who then disappeared down the hill. Mrs Campbell-Irons got into the official hammock and, borne aloft by four men, went down into the high forest, with her husband on foot.

Alone in Africa

I was then 'alone'. Alone, that is to say, apart from about 30,000 people who looked to me for support and assistance and sympathy, but with whom I could neither communicate nor have ideas in common. There was so much to be found out and so much to be learnt that there was no time to feel lonely. I was in sole charge of an area about 50 miles from north to south by about 15 across. It was then the smallest Administrative Division in the North.

To the romantic there was fascination in the fact that the extreme south-western corner was on the exact Confluence (with a capital C for historical reasons) of the Niger River and its great tributary, the Benue. Just opposite the Confluence was Lokoja, the best-known town in the North. It lay along the river bank beneath the steep slope of Patti (Nupe for a hill), 1,000 feet of red ironstone and green trees rising to a flat top, part of an ancient plain. Lokoja town was about four miles long and very narrow. At its southern, downstream end stood the white bungalows and houses of the Government station.

To me the smallness of Koton Karifi was a great advantage: it gave me something positive to get hold of and to understand. Had I gone to a Province further north I should have been in a subordinate position, under a senior man as District Officer, doing the tasks and carrying out the duties apportioned to me by him, according to local tradition or his own personal whim. I would have only received a limited picture and experience of the work – so much depending on the personality of the District Officer. Some, of course, were excellent and knew how to train staff, but others scarcely understood the principles on which they were supposed to be working. Later, when in a senior position myself, I spent some effort making sure that new arrivals were receiving the introduction and instruction to which they were entitled. But sometimes I was more than a little doubtful. As it was, only once thereafter was I not in charge of a Division, unless on a special job.

The District Officer's house was surprisingly large inside. Two great square mud pillars held up a ceiling of bush timber with mud on top. A wall by one of the pillars cut off a bedroom section, which occupied about one-third of the floor space; the remainder formed a sitting and dining room. The floor was made of broken potsherds laid on damp mud, hammered flat by the village damsels with wooden bats. When dry, the whole was polished with palm oil and really looked good. Another fashion was to lay palm kernels as a flooring: they took a fine polish but were expensive for a large area. There was quite a quantity of furniture of very heavy mahogany, leather cushions and poufs in bright colours. On the floor lay locally woven grass mats of various shapes. In the bedroom was a big iron bedstead and wooden chests of drawers and wardrobes, rough but effective. All the walls and ceilings were whitewashed. The pantry was in the back verandah as was the bathroom – rather, the bath area.

The rest house and office were round and large and very simply furnished. The former was so near to the main house that I later joined the two under one roof and put a large sitting room between them.

I have mentioned messengers and must now say a little about them. They were the backbone of the administration. They remained in the office while District Officers came and went. Many were ex-soldiers. The older ones had survived many years of the strangest administrative vicissitudes, and they were mines of information, much of it not only unreliable but definitely coloured according to their personal inclinations or the feelings of their supporters in the town.

A messenger wore on his breast an embroidered gold crown about three inches across. Their monthly salaries were small but no one knew how much they received, either as retainers from the chiefs or in direct bribes from litigants. They were careful not to be ostentatious in their clothes and housing, but at the great Salla Festival they were quite unrecognisable in the splendour of their apparel and their great turbans, and in the gaiety of their horse furnishings.

Messengers had to be taken with more than a grain of salt. If you made allowances for their prejudices and the highly-paid recommendations that were gently pushed in your direction, they could be most useful. But there were officers who accepted all that they told them and based their own policy thereon, sometimes with awkward results. My two messengers on Koton Karifi knew between them thirteen distinct languages, and would change with effortless fluency from one to another – yet they were more or less illiterate. Any kind of public meeting in that Division required at least three launguages for everyone to understand what was being said, and for my benefit English, which was probably their weakest tongue.

After a fortnight Geoffrey Izard, the District Officer in charge of the Provincial Office at Lokoja, was sent out to see what sort of chap I was and how I was getting on. Izard was a barrister and had a very tidy mind. He helped with a lot of problems and sorted out much that I had not understood. He stayed the night and went back to Lokoja, having arranged for me to visit him a week or so later.

It was on that visit that I at last met Captain F.F.W. Byng-Hall, the Resident of the Province, and lord of all he surveyed. An old regular soldier, he had come to Northern Nigeria, like others, after the South African war: a short, rather plump man, slow both of movement and of speech, but very shrewd and understanding. He was never properly appreciated by his superiors, who looked for agility, forgetting that the battle does not always go to the swift. He usually wore a monocle in one of his watery pale blue eyes. He had a curious mannerism, holding one corner of his handkerchief between his teeth, clutching the other end with one hand. When he was not doing this he was smoking a cigarette. Later, when I knew him better, he would spend hours telling remarkable stories, some of which I was told had been published in *Blackwood's Magazine* under the name of Captain Felix (his actual Christian name). All right-thinking officers took this magazine monthly and eagerly awaited its arrival. I did not subscribe to it, though I sometimes read the stories if copies were left lying about.

To go back to the visit to Lokoja, I stayed with Izard, then a bachelor, for a couple of nights and met all the people I would have to deal with. Lokoja has a wonderful setting at the foot of its 1,000 foot hill, with the great expanse of water below it, 10 miles wide at high river. It was very much a backwater. There was no new building and although only twenty years had passed since it was Lugard's capital, already it had an old-world air. The European houses formed a wide circle round the 'golf course' and tennis courts below the Residency. They were all wooden houses, built in the U.K. and shipped out in sections. The area was called 'Blackwater Crescent', in playful allusion to the disease then so common and so inevitably fatal to Europeans, though it later became quite unheard-of. There was a gap in the ring where a house, haunted by a man who had hanged himself, had burnt down and never been rebuilt. (All things considered, we were surprised that so few people took their own lives.)

Later a club was opened here, but in my time people used to gather at each other's houses for their evening drinks. There was some bridge and occasional poker, but I do not believe it was common. There was only one white woman, the wife of the John Holt Agent. Besides him there were several other trading agents and among the Officials the two I have already mentioned; Le Chard, the Commissioner of Police, as the post was then rather grandly called; a doctor, two or three Marine officers, and the officers of the 2nd Battalion of the Nigeria Regiment.

On a memorable day in March 1922, Sir Hugh Clifford gave the Battalion its new Colours. As I have said, Clifford was a great man for ceremonial, and I can never forget the sight of those lines of scarlet zouave jackets and khaki shorts and puttees and glittering bayonets, the faultless manoeuvring and the counter-marching of their splendid band, on the green polo ground beneath the sheer face of Patti. Clifford, in blue uniform and feathers, was at his best and his well-turned speech was subsequently published in a Gazette Extraordinary. By his special command that day (St. Patrick's Day, as it happened) was forever to be the Regiment's feast-day.

Shortly afterwards the troops were taken away to Kano and the mess – the largest building in Lokoja, standing on a conspicuous ridge – became a hospital. This move was considered by the old hands to be the end of the world, but in fact the troops were now much more conveniently placed both for themselves and for the Government.

I used to go by canoe to Lokoja, about twenty miles downstream from K.K., in a couple of hours: it took ten or twelve to get back upstream. It was so boring that I would take a hand with a paddle. The crew thought me quite mad – why work like that when you have people to do it for you and you could sit in a deck-chair and watch them work? I remember, years later, passing behind a small group of peasants watching white people play tennis on a very hot afternoon in Kano. They said among themselves (in Hausa): 'What do you think they get paid for all that running about? See, they are important people, surely it must be a large sum?

When I first arrived in Koton Karifi, I asked, not unnaturally as I thought, for a map of the Division. After some research by the clerk, I was given a piece of very faded tracing linen, with names of villages here and there and some 'caterpillar' drawings of hills and a few lines to indicate paths. The flies had used it for their own purposes and there were so many dots that one could not distinguish between fly and village. Anyhow, it was so small as to be useless for practical purposes. I set myself the task of making a new one. The job was finished on 16 November 1922, as I see from the original which hangs on the wall behind me as I write. So it took about nine months, less time when I could not map because of work in the office or rain. Fortunately the paths between villages were kept clear to a good width, and you could get long 'sights' on the compass. At each corner a new reading was required. But the only way to measure the distance was by counting the paces, and that can get tedious when one reaches 20,000 in a day. It was not possible to map more than ten miles in a day. This included sketching-in nearby hills, taking readings on a barometer from time to time, to get the height, climbing up the nearer heights and taking 'rounds of angles' for intersection, and then drawing it all in in the evening while it remained clear in the mind. The result was not bad – indeed it remained the standard map for over thirty years until they brought in the aerial surveys.

My other ploy in Koton Karifi was the writing of a detailed report on every aspect of life in the Division. For example, my African staff and I counted the people attending the larger markets. These were held every four days, some of them attended by as many as 4,000 people, mostly women. We weighed the loads carried by different kinds of people and found that even old women would carry as much as 90 lb. on their heads (or on the shoulders among the Gwari), whereas the 'official' load was limited to 56 lb. We enquired into the fertility of the women, which differed slightly from tribe to tribe, and into the survival rate of the children. We were shocked to find that only 47 per cent of the children born managed to live till seven or eight years of age.

We measured their farms and weighed the produce and calculated the wealth of the farmer and his family – at about £15 a year. We estimated the incomes of the village craftsmen, the blacksmith, the carpenter, the dyer, the weavers, the pot-makers (who made jet-black pots, like Roman ones, by hand and eye without a wheel). No one was 'poor', no one was hungry, and no one was rich. The farms yielded their fruit in good quantity.

The Report was one hundred pages long, and I hopefully and formally presented it, along with the new map, to the Resident, who sent it on to the Lieutenant-Governor in Kaduna. Some months later a comment was received – but no word of appreciation, let alone of interest. His Honour 'thought that 110 lb. of corn to the acre was rather low'. Of course it was, being a casual crop grown by the homestead; the main crop was yams on which the people lived. I did not feel encouraged to write long reports again.

All this meant that my staff and I spent a lot of time on tour. The area was small, but there were good simple rest hours. I improved the roads and put in simple bridges of bush-timber covered with matting and earth, which would take my motor-bike and which helped the women with their heavy loads. They never seemed to mind carrying awkward loads on their heads over what were almost 'obstacle' courses. I tried to learn Hausa (one had to pass a language in three years for 'confirmation') but no one in the Division spoke it well.

Behind the D.O.'s house the ground rose steeply 300 feet to the flat plateau of the ancient plain. Here were glades of shorter grass on the deep red ironstone, and small antelope and bush fowl were to be found. It was pleasant to walk there in the evening and there were charming, as well as grand, views. From the edge of the plateau you could see into little valleys and hidden dells: from the western edge the immense vista of the Niger opened up, from 20 miles north to 40 or 50 miles south. At low water the river is difficult to see, but in high water it is spectacular.

On the eastern boundary, where the ground rose higher was Tawari; with the grave of David Carnegie, a District Officer killed in the early years. Here the highest points were 1,400 feet above the sea. The country was very pleasant. Where my boundary reached the Benue river at its southern end, there appeared a choice example of officialism. From our side a fairly wide road reached the bank of a small tributary and entered on a flimsy but adequate bridge. The stream was about a hundred yards wide. Exactly half way across our bridge ended and a flimsy ladder took the traveller down into the water to complete his crossing as best he might. The other Division would not allocate money to build its side of this amateur structure.

When I was in Lokoja, I would climb Patti in the afternoon. There was an excellent 'permanent' house on the top for week-ends, I could get there in twenty minutes from the Residency. One day in the Rains, when the grass was high, I had the shock of my life. For I trod abruptly and heavily on a large soft thing; which rose suddenly, yellow and speckled, and I thought it was a leopard. It went very fast in one direction, as I did in the other. It was, in fact, a huge hyena.

In Koton Karifi there was, however, a leopard that disturbed people at night. As it passed through the Government staff lines the messengers ineffectively threw stones at it. After it had taken a number of goats, I felt that something should be done. Being very young and inexperienced, I set out to shoot it. A rather grand feeling – I would not have done it in later years. I went down to the small prison – I had heard that its nightly route was past this place. They brought a goat; which was tethered in a small open space before me. We sat in the prison porch and waited. I had a messenger with me, though he could not have done much good. The night wore on and the goat got bored. The bleats became less, and after a while it went to sleep. So did my messenger. In the end, after about four hours, I gave it up and went home.

When you looked across the Niger to the flat-topped hills on the other side, you were actually looking at a District of Kabba Division, whose headquarters were some sixty miles to the west. The Native Authority was at a place called Agbaja, about twelve miles from Koton Karifi, and in its jurisdiction were two other small chieftaincies, upstream, the further one being tiny, just the area round a small water-logged town called Eggan, opposite Baro. Those two had hardly ever received any visit by a white man, even though it was not difficult to get there by river.

It came to pass that approval was received for this riverain area to be handed over to the D.O. Koton Karifi. My area and population was thereby more than doubled and I was to be given some proper work to do. I took over as soon as I could get there. It was in the rains and the country was wet. The plan was to sleep in the awful rest house at Adaha on the east bank and go across the river at dawn. There carriers were waiting (which one of the messengers had gone over the night before to arrange) and as soon as they were loaded we set out up a steep track that zigzagged through a wide clearing from the river to the summit, about eight hundred feet up. As we climbed the view below and behind us opened out like a map: my white house at Koton Karifi looked infinitely far away.

The top of the hill was absolutely flat, ironstone with glades and low trees and rocky pools. There were all sorts of animals about but I seldom had time to go after them. However, there was a large roan antelope which was always in the same place every time I went that way. A roan is about the size of a horse and the range was barely three hundred yards, but although I am a reasonable shot with a rifle, I could never hit him, and he just shambled away into the bush. I always had a Mannlicher-Schaunauer rifle on trek, as well as a double-barrelled gun. There was often something to shoot for the pot.

Agbaja was a very dull place, with no view and poor housing. The little town looked miserable when I saw it first in the rain, and even in the sunshine it was little better. I found the people rather depressing, too. However, that first afternoon I made a friend. In the prison, I saw a tiny bundle of grey fur sitting disconsolately by a smokey fire. This was a monkey, which came to be called George. He was so small that he could fit into my hand, and, being of a nervous disposition, he then wrapped his very long tail round my wrist. He had unfortunately burnt the tip of it and this made him even more miserable. I took him away and he remained a constant companion for a year or more. He soon grew into a handsome monkey with a maliciously glinting eye. George used to sleep on the top of my mosquito net and when anything came near the house he would wake and make a fiendish noise. In the morning, when the tea came, he would slide down the pole and put out a tiny hand for fruit.

From Agbaja there was a winding path that went down the southern escarpment – not so high as on the river side – and from there it was about twelve miles to Lokoja. In the dry season I opened up this path and constructed a zigzag path wide enough for a hammock to be carried. The hillside was steep and we had to cut out on one side and fill up on the other against a rough embankment of stone. This taught me much that came in very useful when we built the road in Kabba three years later. I had to teach the local people all about road-making, even how to use a pick and shovel. It was a big moment when the Resident drove to the foot of the escarpment on a very rough road and than came up the hill in a hammock. The first of that high rank, possibly the only one, who had ever been there, he seemed to appreciate it, but I felt he was glad to get away after lunch.

I had a hammock with me on tour, with four special bearers that were allowed by the Government. I was always scared of falling and breaking a bone miles from anywhere, and the hammock, though far from comfortable, would have been better in this situation than nothing.

Problems started almost as soon as I took over this new area. I invited the two chiefs of the northern areas to come in and have a conference. As they came in I discovered that a lot of tax from the previous year, ending in March, was still outstanding. This seemed surprising, as the Koton Kafiri tax on the other side of the river was all in. The amount per head was very small, about three or four shillings, and there should have been little difficulty in collecting it. I received a hint that in fact it had been collected and that it had been invested in trade goods which were by then on their way to Yola, 400 miles up the Benue.

When the chiefs arrived they had quite a party in the town, for I doubt if they had been there before. I discussed various other necessary matters and then raised the question of tax, pointing out that they were in arrear and that if they were not careful they would be running into the collection for the current year which would not do anyone any good. They agreed that this would be bad and said it would be only a matter of days before it all came in. If that were the case, I said, they would naturally want to get it all cleared up, and the Agbaja Chief, the Olu, would be delighted for them to stay on with us, at the top of his horrid damp hill, until it came in. At first they did not take me seriously, but soon were convinced that I meant business. I said that all they had to do was to send reliable people home to get the tax and bring it up to Agbaja. The last thing they wanted to do was remain in the rain and wind on this inhospitable plateau, but did not dare say so. There was only one thing to do and they did it. And they learned an expensive lesson. They sent down into Lokoja and borrowed the money from the sharks of that town. The interest probably exceeded the profits they hoped to make on their Yola venture. I heard later that one of the canoes had sunk with all the trade goods. I was not very upset.

One of the advantages of having this new area was the assignment to me of a steel barge for my own use. About fifty feet long and eight feet wide and flat-bottomed, it had two rooms, a kitchen and an earth closet, with room for the boys and crew on the two fore-and-aft decks. When the camp furniture was put in, it formed an excellent mobile rest house. I could go up and down the river in comfort and also up the wide Gurara river which constituted the western border. It was moved by six or eight polers but with luck it was possible to get a tow from a Company boat going upstream, which was the most boring part of the journeys. The river was always fascinating, although the sudden storms could be awkward; we dared not have the side screens down for fear of overturning.

There was very little real crime in the area, with the result that my six police had nothing to do save mount guard on the strong-room and go on tour with me, which they enjoyed. This absence of crime was just as well, for the N.A. police, or *dogarai* as they were called, were hopeless. This was not their fault, for three reasons: they should never have been chosen, they had no training and they were grossly underpaid. There was no case of homicide or even of wounding in my time there.

My tour ended early in 1923. I handed over Koton Kafiri and never saw the place again. I was sorry in a way, for I had been happy there, although there was little to induce such a feeling. Over four months' leave were due to me, plus the duration of the two steamer voyages and odd days in travelling in the country. I had a reasonable bank balance: there had been little to spend money on.

The voyage was uneventful and the sea calm. There were a few ladies on board and at each homeward port everyone hung over the side to see who was coming on board for the rest of the trip. All women are goddesses on shipboard: let us not forget that Aphrodite appeared on the waves. I was taken aside by a man who seemed to me incalculably ancient. He had noticed me talking to one of the ladies and wanted to give me some advice. He said, 'Just try and imagine what she will look like in a third class carriage at home.'

It was exciting to get home to Dorchester (in Dorset), where my father was Rector of St. Peter's. I told stories of Koton Kafiri and no one believed them.

Kabba division – roads and maps

My return from my first leave was normal and, oddly, without change of posting. I had had a good leave and had bought a car of a long-extinct make, a Clyno. It cost about £100 and would go at 30 miles an hour. I sold the car at the end of the leave, having enjoyed four months' motoring for a few pounds.

From Lagos I travelled by boat train after receiving the usual hospitality in the capital. There was no difficulty in Minna though I again had to wait for a train to Baro; they never seemed to manage a proper down-connection.

I went out shooting round the Government Hill at Minna with Major J.A.G. Budgen, a senior District Officer, a very handsome man who had gained undying fame in the East African campaign against the Germans by a remarkable exploit. One evening he heard a commotion in the camp and went to investigate: he found a large leopard standing on a prostrate black soldier. Budgen only had a double-barrelled gun. The leopard came at him, and leaped with its fore-paws in the air to tear him apart. Budgen stood calmly with the gun pointing upwards from below his waist. As the leopard closed he thrust the gun under the animal's neck and pulled both triggers, blowing off its head. He was that kind of chap.

I found that I was gradually going up in the world. There were forty or more officers now junior to me in the country, and before long a man was posted to Kabba Province who was actually my junior in service. There were no adventures on my journey to Lokoja, where I had a few days to catch up with developments, read the circulars and

Gazettes. I had brought out with me enough supplies for the eighteen-month tour, in a general way, but there were stores to be bought locally, like biscuits and cereals which take up space and might lead to excess baggage payments on the ship. Soda and a few drinks were also required.

I picked up George the monkey again. He had grown bigger and acquired a taste for beer. He had been not a little spoilt while I was away. He was also very strong: he could arrive on the dining table from the verandah, grab what he wanted and bound off with it on to the other verandah. In fact he became a nuisance and I persuaded an unsuspecting colleague to accept him as a gift.

It was a little odd that I was worse off 'socially' in Kabba than in Koton Karifi. There I had been able to go into Lokoja quite frequently, specially when I was on tour on the opposite bank. From Kabba it was three days' trek each way to cover the 52 miles, which meant that a short visit to headquarters took more than a week. I once did the 42 miles from Kabba to a point where a motor could pick me up, between dawn on one day and 10 a.m. the next. I was in a hurry, and did not notice the fatigue.

The country traversed on this route was quite empty of people and I could do no useful work on the way. The same applied the other way round, and officials were loath to come from Lokoja to visit me, except for the policeman and the Forest Officer (we had Forest Reserves in the division). From Koton Karifi you could send a chit by a trading canoe for stores from Lokoja and get them back the next evening, but in Kabba that was out of the question.

At that time there was only one motor-car in the Province, belonging to the Resident in Lokoja. A favoured few were taken for an afternoon drive. There was only one possible direction to go – south – and ten miles out there was a bridge under construction, so that was the end of the 'run'. I got a lift for those ten miles on my way to Kabba and then set off along the broad, well-worn 'trade route' for the rest of the journey. This being the wrong kind of country for horses or donkeys, everything had to be carried on the human head. What could be carried was remarkable. Once, an upright piano landed (in a wooden case) at a remote river 'port' on the Benue. Forty miles away a small group of Europeans were sitting over their evening drinks discussing how it could be brought up – there was no road. They heard a great thump on the ground near them, with musical reverberations; then an old woman came into the lamplight mopping her brow. She said she had brought up a big load from the river – she did not want payment then, because there were other loads to bring and she would be back for her money. There was the piano in its case.

The carriers would always compete for the lightest loads. They often got it wrong, for a large clumsy load could be quite light and a little box, over which they pushed and shoved, might be a heavy box of ammunition. Sometimes it was necessary to make adjustments, but by the second day things had usually settled down. We kept the same men as much as possible. I always liked to have at least one spare man in case of accidents. They were all paid for by the government – via myself – for each journey at statutory rates. The route had been through empty country with isolated villages dotted along it every few miles, and nothing whatever on each side for 50 or 60 miles, not a living person and not a farm. The great slave raids during the hundred years before the British occupation had cleared the country. On our first trek we reached Kabba on the morning of the third day. In its latter stages the path opened out, and well before the government station one was walking along a ragged avenue with lines of pineapple plants edging the road. The fruit was never much good – the skilful attention it needed was lacking.

The centre part was undulating, the so-called Choko-choko switchback. This section covered a major climb of about 700 feet. The country was picturesque with fine but empty views. There were always travellers on the road, traders carrying merchandise, but no markets and no real movement of people. As you came over the last rise into Kabba you could see the grey juju hills behind the town, not high but striking in a strangely Chinese way, spikey with broken granite slopes; great trees grew in unlikely fissures. In the dry season the trees turned scarlet with the huge flowers of the cotton (kapok) and then to white as the lint broke out. Away to the left were other granite hills, some quite near and in the background the 1,000-foot sheer face of Okorogidi.

Kabba was about 1,500 feet above the sea, i.e. at least 1,000 feet higher than Lokoja. This made it noticeably cooler, specially at nights, and generally more comfortable. It was little higher than Okene, 25 miles (or two days trek) away to the south, where the nearest D.O. was stationed.

The so-called Government Station at Kabba consisted of three bungalows. As it was one of the first places to be built in the early years of the century, government spent some money on it. The houses were on concrete plinths three feet above the ground. All were of the same design, built of local burnt clay brick, with thick walls, glass windows and red-painted corrugated-iron roofs on steel-rafters. In the D.O.'s house, there was adequate furniture and an iron bedstead, in a mosquito-proofed room on the corner of the wide verandah that ran right round the house. The 'mosquito-room' guaranteed that any insect getting in, could not get out again. Two other corners formed a bathroom and a store-cum-pantry. The sanitation was external, a neat round mud hut about twenty feet away from the house. This was all right in good weather, but in the rains you had to dress up as for an important expedition. There was a bucket under a wooden seat which the prisoners kindly removed each day.

The first of these houses, as you approached, was the divisional office. Behind it and some distance away were the police lines and messengers' quarters, and three concrete cells with barred doors, one of which was the 'strong room'. Into this was received the government share of the tax collected by the chiefs, from which all government payments were made. If a large surplus developed, you asked for a police escort and a group of tough chaps appeared with a senior N.C.O. to take it away to Lokoja. This did not happen often.

The office was like the D.O.'s house, with mats on the floor, a big safe and tables and chairs. Most of the floor space was empty, for in those days everyone who came up to see the D.O. sat on the ground and would have been most unhappy if invited to take seats. On the verandah, but walled in, was the clerk's office, with the stationery store in one corner. The centre building was the rest house – it would have been used by a second officer if there had ever been one. Further on the road began to descend, and about half a mile away was the town of Kabba. It had wide streets, grass-lined with jacarandas and flowering shrubs, and the hills rose behind it. At one end was a little group consisting of N.A. buildings, a serviceable small prison, a court house and an office for the treasurer – all in mud and thatch. Two schools existed, one Roman Catholic and the other Protestant. These were mission schools, but no white face was to be seen. Occasionally, they were visited. Otherwise government activities were noticeable by their absence.

There was, however, a man called a 'dispenser'. He had a few bottles of medicine (thinned with pond water), filthy dressings and repellent-looking unguents, all in a dirty little box. So dirty was he himself that one felt a touch from him might well prove fatal. No doctor ever 'inspected' him, and indeed no medical officer ever came to us. It would have meant being away from his hospital for at least four days, probably more, which would have left Lokoja without an M.O. at all. The local remedies, though no doubt often successful, were certainly not inviting. And, of course, there were no pain-killers or disinfectants.

The Native Authority maintained vaccinators, who were numbered among the wealthy of the Division. Theoretically all vaccinations were free, but the unofficial schedule of fees was one shilling for the scratch or two shillings for exemption. Once when I was having lunch in a rest house overlooking a popular market, a tremendous commotion suddenly broke out below me in the crowded area and people gathered up their wares and fled. I asked what it was: perhaps a leopard had appeared? 'Oh no', said my boys, 'it is just the vaccinator.'

Kabba was well situated as headquarters. Almost in the centre of the occupied part of the Division, it had a net of paths and trade routes branching out in every direction. The head-waters of a number of quite large rivers rose in the Division, which made road-making easier than if there had been large rivers to cross. A road had been cut and levelled from Kabba south to Okene and culverts had been put in, for there were only small streams to be crossed. Just before I came, heavy rains had washed out many of the culverts. The southern section, in the Igbirra Division, descended a long valley and had to negotiate a couple of quite wide streams. It seemed to take a lot of effort to replace these when they were washed away, which happened at least twice in my time.

My Lagos motor-bike was brought to Kabba, slung between two long poles and carried by a team of three men. I used it for going down to the town, but one evening I thought I would be more adventurous and tried it out on a 'good' section of the southern road. It might easily have been my last run. I came round a corner and over a small hump: immediately in front of me a culvert had gone, the gap was ten feet wide and six feet deep, sheer-sided. By good fortune a single nine-inch plank lay loosely across the gap – I could not stop, nor could I turn aside; the only thing was to take the plank. When I had crossed it, I stopped, feeling faint from shock. There was no one about: the countryside was empty. Somehow I managed to get the heavy cycle back across the gap.

I used to walk for exercise in the evenings. I had started the habit in Lagos and carried on in Koton Karifi, at least five miles before sunset, which of course took place at 6 p.m. with that regularity common in the tropics. Most of Kabba was only passable on foot and I worked out that in my first ten years' service I walked at least 25,000 miles.

When I reached Kabba I found, as in Koton Karifi, that there was no usable map, so I settled down to making a new one. Mapping from Kabba outwards in every direction and joining up the 'spokes' by cross-webbing, I completed the map on the western side of the Niger. This was a much bigger undertaking than the previous one and took two years — covering about 5,000 square miles of country, including the whole area inside the great bend of the Niger, i.e. the Igbirra Division, to the south, which seemed never to have been mapped, and the western half of Koton Karifi, recently transferred to it.

We got into difficulties with high grass, dense forest and narrow winding paths, and work was sometimes slowed down to two or three miles a day. This was too slow and in the end a method of sighting on to a drum-beat was worked out. There were complications in this, but it answered the problem and made it possible to go up to ten miles a day.

This work was helped by a number of factors. First there was a 'measuring wheel' which allowed me to dispense with counting paces. Then there was a very straight path, about twenty-five miles long west from Kabba, which in a rough way formed an excellent 'baseline'. The eastern area, by the Niger, was traversed from end to end, about sixty miles, by the north-south telegraph line, much of it dead straight, with a wide cleared area beneath the wires. And thirdly, all over the place were well-defined hills, mostly granite, overlooking broad valleys. From them I could take 'rounds' of angles, so I fixed not only my own position but that of many landmarks to which I did not have the time to walk.

These evening climbs were social occasions led by the youths of the village and followed reluctantly (but not in any way compulsorily) by the more elderly. There were men carrying the stand of my invaluable heavy telescopic theodolite (a war surplus artillery relic) and the big wooden box with the optic part, the inevitable messengers with rifles, a policcman or two, a man with my big camera, and swarms of children who raced up and down in front of the straggling column of their elders.

When I did the Koton Karifi map, I fixed the positions of the rest house at Adaha and that opposite Lokoja, so that I could 'tie' the two maps together. They agreed reasonably well. I was not a trained map maker and had to rely on common sense. The map, and checking village censuses, took me – always on foot – into every village in the two Divisions, places that had never been visited by a white man and which, in some cases, had had no previous existence on the map or in the tax lists. From the hill tops, in the late afternoons, the blue smoke of the evening meal often gave away the presence of a village: compass bearings and estimated distances would show whether or not the village was known. The map was finally completed on 22 January 1925, just before I went on leave. A copy was deposited with the Royal Geographical Society, who expressed some interest.

There was one place in a remote corner of the hills which seemed primitive beyond belief. Unusually for that area, the women were naked, but when they addressed the A.D.O. they put on a narrow piece of cloth. I talked to the people for some time and made a lot of notes, then thought I would try the classic question, which might be appropriate, in such a place – how did they make fire? They said, 'This fire outside the chief's house never goes out.' In the extreme disaster of the fire going out, could they kindle a new one? 'Oh yes', they said, obviously thinking surely you can't be such a mug as not to know. 'How?' I asked. They said they would show me. The head wife came out of the house with a ball of cloth the size of a football. Solemnly they unwound it – there must have been a hundred yards of bandaging so it took a long time – and then handed me a box of matches.

All administrative officers had powers as magistrates under what was then the Provincial Court system – a system which worked excellently for many years, and none the worse for the prohibition on the appearance of lawyers before it. In the end it went in the first of the modernisation actions around 1934, and the people got more law but less justice.

We did not hear many cases, for the Native Courts had parallel powers, but from time to time they put cases before us. I never knew what the word 'litigious' meant until I served in Kabba. The office compound was often filled with optimists, hopefully striving to upset the judgment of a Native Court. Sometimes, and often nearly too late, one discovered that cases which were raising much apparent passion were not their own at all but, say, their grandfathers' and had already been settled on appeal at least once. They would trot out cases each time a new D.O. arrived, and it must have cost them a lot to square the messengers to get their names called. Was it worthwhile?

One day I was sitting in a Court listening to the evidence. It was a Native Court, with powers adequate for petty theft and the like. A woman was suing a man for loss of produce. What had happened was that the woman was going along a bush path to market with a big load of produce, when she met a man who was an old boy friend. She said, 'Hello, it must be years since I saw you.' He said, 'Yes, what fun we used to have together,' and she said, 'Didn't we just!' And he said, 'You still look pretty good to me, what about another go?' She put her load down beside the path and they went off into a guinea-corn farm near at hand. When the woman came back to the path she found to her fury that her load had been stolen. The man had gone off by another path and knew nothing about it. Mad with rage, she issued a summons against her lover. At the back of the court a man was laughing immoderately. I asked my people who he might be – he was the husband. The lover had to pay.

Quite unwittingly I committed an injustice in a case I was hearing. A man was charged with burglary in a long room, a sort of lodging-house, where he had been seen in the middle of the night walking with a lighted lantern in his hand. In my simplicity I thought that this was a sign of innocence, for a guilty person would surely not be so blatant. But according to all the local experts, I had been wrong in acquitting him, as the fact of the lantern showed his guilt. The first thing a good burglar would do was to blow a magic powder under the door and give it time to do its work. Then he would enter with his lantern and rob at leisure. The powder would be sleep-inducing and everyone would be in a deep sleep. The police used to find these powders when they arrested people, also a wad of cotton-wool, which was for invisibility, and a little pot of grease to get out of handcuffs. When these had been placed out of reach, they would say 'he is now helpless', and he certainly was.

Another case was more puzzling. Kabba was badly split into factions regarding the succession to the chieftaincy. One day members of 'section A' came streaming up to my office in great agitation. They said that the leader of 'section B' had been seen placing a stone in the thatch of the biggest roof belonging to the leader of 'A'. The stone was produced, a smooth piece of granite shaped like a spearhead so that it would stick in the thatch. This stone, they all swore, would attract lightning – for which the area was notorious – and so set fire to his whole compound and with luck burn him up with it. Unfortunately British law, thorough and painstaking as it is, had never categorised attracting lightning with intent as a crime. I could have fallen back on the old charges of intent to commit a breach of the peace and the like, but the 'crime' was too nebulous for that. So the only thing was subterfuge.

I got out the impressive leather-bound Record Book, huge and heavy, and a pile of legal volumes. The leader of 'section B' was then charged with attempted murder – it seemed better to do the thing properly – and the rest of the day was spent taking down depositions, reading them over and getting them signed or attested.

The Court (myself) then explained to the assembled public that the accused had so far not actually done anything. The stone they gave me was solemnly wrapped up and sealed in the presence of all, marked 'Exhibit 1', and locked away in the safe. The accused was bound over and warned that all that had been written would be taken into account should another squeak come out of him. They went away very thoughtful and no further trouble arose. The loose sheets on which I had written the depositions were put into an envelope – I had written nothing at all in the great Record Book. I wondered sometimes what my successors thought of that stone. Maybe it is now in some museum.

We were expected to take anthropological notes on the people we visited and some of the matters turned up were very interesting. Some of our officers went in for the subject seriously and eventually became professional anthropologists. In the end we had an official Government Anthropologist, C.K. Meek, who published valuable books based on the officers' findings. With the hundreds of different peoples in Nigeria the field was all but limitless.

In Muslim areas it was difficult to penetrate far under the Islamic reserve, but, if you did, there were clear strata of pre-Islamic tradition. Most tribes seem to have some sort of story of creation – very different from each other – and from our own Jewish one – and a conception of an omnipotent God. In general they were what is loosely called 'animists', worshippers of in-dwelling spirits. Every rock and tree, and every glade and hill, had such a spirit, and they varied in their disposition according to their appearance: sinister trees had sinister spirits and happy glades had happy spirits. Sometimes there would be a miniature grass hut and sometimes just a small pile of farm produce or a calabash of palm oil or wine. Whatever happened, you had to keep the spirits sweet and if possible on your side.

Riots came easy in Kabba. In my next tour there occurred the most exciting and dangerous one, between the Roman Catholics and Protestants. I have forgotten the cause but an elder son of the Chief came up to the house after dinner. Apologetically he explained that there was trouble in the town. He said in English: 'My father tells me to say to you that the Christians are killing each other.' I mounted my motor ʒike and roared off down the hill. The powerful headlight was a valuable asset as it dazzled the contestants, but the sight was an alarming one. When I arrived on the scene they were going for each other with great cudgels and heavy sticks. The noise was alarming. Four elderly N.A. police appeared and we managed to part the combatants and make them sit down in opposing rows. All their sticks and clubs were taken from them and burned. Then I preached a sermon – it was not difficult to find a text! Silence prevailed and shamefacedness overcame them. The pagans in the trees and on the big rocks laughed immoderately, and they all went home. Considering the uproar, there were few injuries.

Down on the green in the centre of the town was a stocks for feet and hands. They were not historic souvenirs. The Native Courts were very fond of them, and often on a market day they would be in use. The quarrelsome drunk or the screaming termagent from the market would sit there for an hour, and their tantrums would die away. No one threw anything; a few people laughed at them; and small boys came and made rude remarks. They learned the very simple lesson of live and let live. Unfortunately a Labour Government in London discovered this practice and stern orders came suppressing it. This was almost impossible to explain satisfactorily to the Native Courts. The Nigerian form was humane and in its own way a civilised arrangement. A fine, even if summarily inflicted, never had the same effect.

In the same way the prisons were reasonable. They were not in any way comfortable, but there was no isolation and all the prisoners mixed in the great courtyards and under the trees. The food was good and the roofs were watertight. The warders were friendly, in fact rather too much so. It used to be said that the only thing a prisoner really lacked was the society of women, and even that was not always so.

I once visited a remote prison in Kabba, very neat and tidy. There were about fifteen men prisoners, mostly theft or assault cases. To my surprise, I found three women prisoners sharing the communal dormitory and facilities. I had not come across this before, for usually there was a tiny women's compound with a few cells and the kitchen arrangement for the prison. The women were middle-aged by Nigerian standards – say in their early thirties. I asked them if the men were a nuisance. Oh no, they said, they were very nice and helpful, but, they added, they did have rather disturbed nights. However, what did that matter, for they could sleep when the men were out working? Probably it all got tidied up by some conscientious D.O. but I left it alone.

I have mentioned the office safe. One morning I was checking cash at the end of the month – for I was the local accountant as well as everything else – and, thinking of some deep point, went off to breakfast. Shortly afterwards my steward came in to say that I had left the safe open in the office. The safe was indeed open, but in front of it stood a policeman in his blue uniform holding a rifle (loaded) with a fixed bayonet. He would not let me approach the safe until he was marched off by the Corporal!

A District Officer in Nupe Province, 'Dolly' Edwardes, once wrote a booklet about practical road-making, based on his own experience. It aimed at destroying the belief that the subject was in any way esoteric and confined to trained engineers, and that even bridge-building – shorn of technicalities, and on a small scale – was within the capacity of the average chap. Its simple twenty-odd pages inspired me like Holy Writ and I had a look round to see what could be done. Funds were, of course, a consideration but the Native Authority had some hundreds of pounds in its Works votes and could raise more; so long as expenses were kept down, there was no difficulty.

I formed the determination to build roads outwards from Kabba as soon as possible. The Kabba part of the Okene road was good, but the rest were trade routes, cleared and bush-bridged but not motorable, even in the dry season. Just behind the town was a stream about forty feet wide, which was a serious obstacle to anyone coming in the rains, with the result that the Kabba market lost trade in bad weather.

There was a big town called Aiere about 12 miles to the south-west, and beyond that was the Southern Provinces' boundary and a populous area. This line seemed to be the first one to tackle. The immediate problem was the stream, the headwaters of the Osse River, which reached the sea west of Benin. We had excellent masons available, who had worked on railway construction and there was any amount of granite, in six inch slabs, and mahogany, which had to be felled. Locally, the mahogany had no particular value.

We built a three-span bridge over the stream, each span of twenty feet, with six timber beams, twelve by six inches in section, resting on solid granite piers fifteen feet high. At first the masons did not quite realise what was wanted and slacked; I pushed over part of a defective pier with my own hands and stood there until they had rebuilt it correctly in the flaring light of bonfires; they had grasped the position and the work went forward like magic. They brought my dinner down to me that night at the site. Beyond that point and its substantial embankment, there were few obstacles and the road was easily completed at a ridiculously low cost. This was during my first tour in Kabba.

Of course, I had to lay out these bridges myself, with pegs marking all the work. The masons planned and arranged the culverts themselves once the centre and width had been pegged.

The Attah of Igbirra

Meanwhile Byng-Hall had been pushing on with the road to Okene, forty-five miles from Lokoja. It was obvious that road construction was vital to any kind of progress. No government or commercial activity can be carried out if you cannot get about. Trekking by horse is enjoyable and going on foot can be tolerated so long as your feet do not succumb, but it is a severe limitation and is impossible for inspections by busy technical officers. The Government gave us no encouragement of any kind with our road construction, and the Public Works Department, after beginning the Okene Road, fell out with Byng-Hall and gave no further help for several vital years. There

were some awkward bridges on the road and exactly in the middle
was a substantial river which required an elaborate work where there
was only a poor car ferry. The Public Works eventually built a good
bridge with fifty-foot timber girders on lofty piers to replace the ferry.

Just after this road was finished, the firm of John Holt imported a
30 cwt lorry for sale. The Attah of Igbirra, the Chief of Okene, had a
small canteen in the town which he kept supplied from John Holt. He
saw this lorry, liked it and offered to buy it. The Company were only
too pleased and offered reasonable terms. On every load of produce he
sent in to them in Lokoja, they would credit him with, say, ninety per
cent and set ten per cent against the cost of the lorry (in those days just
over £200).

The operation began. He sent in a load of local produce and at the
same time an order for goods to be sent back to approximately the
estimated value of the produce. Holts, in their simplicity, fulfilled the
order, and this went on for some time. After a while – possibly as long
as a year – they had recouped not a penny towards the cost of the
lorry, so they decided to mention it to the Attah. That astute poten-
tate expressed keen astonishment and even dismay. He had, he said,
sent in goods regularly and must be well towards paying for the lorry.
'How much', he asked 'is still outstanding?' The agent said that all of
it was. The Attah said, 'But the arrangement was that you would
deduct one-tenth of the value of all produce and set it against the lorry
and you do not seem to have done so.' The agent pointed out that the
Attah had always sent in orders of equivalent value, which the
Company had fulfilled.

The Company then made a fatal mistake and sent a lawyer's letter
demanding payment. The Attah not only stopped dealing with them
himself, but instructed the 100,000 people of his tribe to stop as well.
In a very short time the Company faced complete disaster and finally
begged the Attah to accept the lorry as a present. This he did, and
later sold it to the Etsu (Chief) of Nupe for £300.

Byng-Hall went on leave and Budgen (already mentioned) was
sent from Bida to take over the Province – we had no one on our staff of
the right standing. Budgen was a most conscientious and, within his
own limits, upright man. There was no District Officer in Okene, and
the Resident had it under his wing. Budgen naturally went there to
have a look round. He had a tendency to avoid using existing messengers who, he rightly said, were already in the pay of some influential
person. He co-opted a youngish local Igbirra man called Chukura
with a good manner and some English and Hausa – possibly an old
soldier. Budgen himself had attained Higher Standard Hausa.
Chukura's paymaster was certainly not the Attah. He at once started

a train of accusations against the Attah, and produced a stream of people to testify against him. Witnesses were always pretty cheap.

Budgen came over to Kabba and discussed the Attah with me at some length. I thought he was a good and an efficient chief, but of course my experience was very small compared with Budgen's. I was interested but only gave my impression. Budgen told me in general about the various tricks that could be played: for example, always pay labourers yourself and not through the head-man, whom you should keep with you till the labourers were well out of range. Where people were called up from villages for work, as was then the custom, make sure that they were properly relieved at the end of the fortnight and did not appear again on the next list. Where a man made a complaint, let him bring a friend with him who could speak English or Hausa – do not use him as an interpreter, the messengers have that job, but watch his face and that will tell you whether the messenger is playing straight or nor. These and many others were invaluable tips.

Meanwhile things were hotting up in Okene and Budgen kept me informed. Eventually he thought he had enough to go on and wrote in to Kaduna recommending that the chief be suspended. He took a tremendous risk, for after all he was only 'acting' in Byng-Hall's absence and if anyone was to make allegations about an important chief it had to be the Resident of the Province. Kaduna reacted far too quickly and sent down the most senior Resident in the North, E.J. Arnett, then Resident Kano. The Attah was suspended and I was told to look after Igbirra, as well as my own quite complicated Division. I was seeing high-powered administration at work with a vengeance.

Arnett came to Okene and listened to the complaints marshalled by Chukura. My own messengers did not conceal their opinion that a great mistake had been made: yes, they said, a chief does do things that the white man thinks are odd but the black man accepts them as part of the perks of the job. One or two points, they thought, were going a bit far, but a few words would soon settle that. Arnett sat day after day and wrote down many pages of evidence, some of it extremely flimsy. I kept things going in the two Divisions as well as I could and listened to Arnett's conversations in the evening. He was rather a precise and stilted man, thoroughly imbued by the Holy North, and completely lost so far south in the Kabba landscape. In the end he finished and went back to Lokoja.

It was then that Byng-Hall came back from leave. He was furious at finding all this going on and did not mince words. He sent for Arnett and asked him what he was doing in his (Byng-Hall's) Province: Arnett went back to the rest house and returned with his commission and terms of reference. Byng-Hall read them and at once put his finger on the weak spot. 'Mr. Arnett', he said, 'you have kindly conducted an inquiry into the conduct of one of my chiefs, who I see has had little opportunity of seeing the allegations and answering them, but so far as I can see you have failed in the second part of the commission.' (Byng-Hall told me this afterwards.) The second part was an accusation that the Attah had directed against Budgen, that he collected and kept in his compound young Igbirra virgins for his own purposes. Arnett was expected to investigate this also. Whether this was true or not was never known, but there had not been, so far as I knew, any investigation. Shortly after that he went back to Kano and Budgen went on leave. My own relations with Arnett had been good throughout his stay, unusual as his position was. All the time, this kind of event had been most instructive for me. I learned never to interfere with the *status quo* unless one was quite sure of one's facts. Budgen had not done this and it was not within Arnett's scope to do so.

The Attah remained suspended and Kaduna decided to try him on no less than fifty-three counts, varying from accepting money from those attending his court to illicitly keeping prisoners in his own household. The trial was heard in Lokoja before Chapman, the Station Magistrate (he happened to be a lawyer) who was given special powers. I held Okene in rather troubled peace. Whenever I felt irritated or ignored, I would write in and say that the peace was getting more tenuous, and they would then send me more police and N.C.O.s and boxes of ammunition, until I had the greater part of the police available and felt very safe!

It was by now the height of the rains and Okene was cold and damp. However, we had our fun. Byng-Hall, who was very good company, would drive out when he could and stay a night or two. He stayed in one of the rooms in the big Rest House and I had the other: they both opened on to a wide verandah and at one end of the building, still under the great thatched roof, was an open space where we had our meals and interviewed people.

One night we got a secret message from the town that an attack was to be launched that very night on the Rest House, which was to be set on fire. Byng-Hall would then rush from the building – such was the plan as recounted – and he would be shot in the stomach with poisoned arrows. He was very upset (the target was a large one) and went on muttering 'shot in the stomach. . .' I finally calmed him by ordering doubled guards (we had plenty of men, as I have said). That night we got little sleep, with the guards marching about and being relieved every hour.

In the morning, we received news that the chiefs wished to come up. Byng-Hall readily agreed. These were the old men, members of the council, who were carrying on the adminstration in the Attah's absence, and they were received in the open part of the house. They came in and, being of low grade, sat on mats on the floor. Byng-Hall's own messenger invariably carried an enormous silver cigar box for the Resident's use. This he put on the table.

Byng-Hall asked for the box to be opened. He said in his solemn way in poor Hausa, which was translated into Igbirra, 'I understand that you wish to burn this house down. I do not like it very much and wish to build a new one. I would be very glad if you would be so kind as to burn it *now* so that we can all enjoy the fun.' A squad of police in the background leaned forward, eager not to miss anything.

Out of the great silver box he took a box of matches. He handed them to his messenger and said, 'Here are matches: now set the house alight.' The messenger, with a poker face, said just that in Igbirra and handed the matches to the senior chief. He took the box in his hand for a moment and then dropped it with a great cry, as though it had been red hot, and prostrated himself in abasement. The Igbirras round about started to giggle and then a deep bay of laughter arose as the thousands who had come up to see the show got the point. They rocked with laughter till they could scarcely stand and tottered off home to spread the good news. We heard no more about trouble in the town. I learned the valuable lesson that laughter, if properly used, can move crowds.

In the end the Attah, by skilful defence and calling in his old District Officers (who had sometimes been a little indiscreet, to say the least), was acquitted on all but two counts, and on those he was sentenced to small fines. I have sometimes wondered if they were ever paid.

He fathered a distinguished family. Two became ambassadors in Europe after Independence; one at least was a senior medical officer and a consultant of marked ability; but the greatest (a Balliol man), was Permanent Secretary to the Ministry of Finance, Abdul Aziz. He took the country safe and sound through the civil war in 1967–70 only to die comparatively young. A daughter was the first Nigerian nursing sister and would have gone far had she not gone in for a series of adventures of her own.

The Igbirra were noted for their powers of controlling rainfall. The old men wore black feathers in their scant hair – this was regarded everywhere as a sign of rain-making. I had to travel frequently between Okene and Kabba. The Divisional boundary was half way, where it was possible for a kit-car to reach a point short of the boundary. On the Okene side, the valley was often impassable. It was

August, at the very height of the rains, when the water seemed to descend like a cascade for days at a time, and I wanted to get to Kabba quickly and, if possible, dry. Having heard of the powers which the Ohindashi had used for the Resident on the Lokoja road, I thought I would try my luck.* I asked him to come up and this he did.

The Ohindashi was a very old man: a shabby grey gown hung loosely round him, and in his black skull cap was a feather, the black feather of a goatsucker. I told him I wanted to get to Kabba on the following day, quickly and dry. He thought for some time. Then he said, 'It is the worst time of the year, but I will see what I can do.' He thought a bit more and finally said, 'You won't get wet until you reach our border. After that I have no power and can do nothing.'

I set out, with labourers with camp loads and my own staff, early in the morning. It was very cold and the clouds sat low and menacing. We entered the long valley, and there was not a soul to be seen. The clouds loured on us, and swirled ominously up and down the side-valleys. The air was full of water, not just damp, but it did not rain. When we came to the head of the valley, things looked much worse. In the flat country, a mile or so from the boundary, the rain was clearly falling heavily from the low cloud right across our path. Soon the noise reached us. Just past the boundary we literally walked into this great cascade and continued in it soaked through in a second and frozen. The kit-car looked like a launch at its moorings, but it was a relief to get into it and eventually we reached Kabba. The old man with the black plume in his hair had indeed kept his word.

What the Ohindashi could do was not unique in that part of the world; even the messengers, with a coy smile, would put a coil of grass beneath a stone to avert rain. I once wanted to look round in an area in the heart of the Olle forest to the north of Kabba, where I had noticed some black crystals, believing them, wrongly, to be associated with tin. The clouds overhead were black, and it had consistently rained in the afternoons for a week. The village head said, 'You will get wet, unless I send a boy with you with my own juju medicine.'

A lad appeared with a thin staff, six or seven feet long. At the top a thin string held up a round mass of what seemed to be vegetable matter mixed with mud, about the size of a tennis ball. We set out. After a while it started to rain gently. The boy twirled the stick and the ball flew out on an orbit. The rain diminished. In the forest it got stronger but we did not get wet. When he slackened his efforts the

---

* 'Ohindashi' was a title of great distinction among the Igbirra. In this case he is said to have stopped rain falling *upstream* of the numerous crossings, and let it fall downstream. The Resident was therefore able to get through.

orbit sagged and the rain spotted around us.

It is perhaps striking that in my four years in those parts, only one case of homicide came to my notice. A hunter was out with his 'Dane gun' – a shockingly dangerous kind of trade gun. Anyway, he went after what they called 'meat' – any animal, undomesticated, that was available. He heard a noise behind a bush and fired. Unfortunately the noise was a young woman picking up sticks. By a terrible stroke of ill-luck she dropped dead. I was sufficiently interested to hold an inquest as Coroner (very rare in those parts) and went into the matter carefully. I could find no reason for the death other than the one given, and there was no trace of any stranger. It was definitely accidental.

It was miraculous that there were no killings. There were plenty of fights, and with a great number of palm trees about and the consequent instant availability of heady palm wine, these fights were sometimes serious and produced nasty wounds. They had to trust to 'native' remedies, which mostly worked: there was no skilled attention except in the close vicinity of Lokoja.

Many of these fights broke out over boundaries, the simple ones between farms, the graver between villages. A very awkward one actually involved only two hundred yards of the 'sacred' boundary between the Northern and Southern Provinces. This had to wait for an A.D.O. from the South to come and meet me on this disputed line and we spent a day listening to fantastic stories from each side: very convincing, with a wealth of corroborative detail, but perhaps rather lacking the essential merit of truth. We sat and listened and marvelled, and found that it really boiled down to the possession of certain trees. In most of Nigeria every 'economic' tree, that produces something edible or useful, is owned by someone. This is even true where the land itself is commonly owned – the trees are personal possessions or perhaps more often family ones.

We did not hesitate long and persuaded them to a compromise, but even this meant an actual alteration of this boundary, which in turn meant each of us referring it back to our Resident, then to the Lieutenant-Governor, and finally to the Governor and the Surveyor-General. A year or two later a little notice in the *Gazette* indicated in heavy Survey language the final approval of this great act.

Another source of trouble was the appointing of village headmen, who were entirely responsible for the peace within their villages and, in the North, for the collection of the taxes as apportioned to them and not what they thought ought to be collected for their own gain. They were people of local eminence and the posts were much sought after – the tiny salary was no inducement. In many places the succession was in a certain family, and in others between two or more families.

In one large village, feelings ran high over the appointment of a headman by the Chief of Kabba – it was his right and indeed his duty to make it – and the people refused to accept it. One morning a large crowd came up the road to my office in Kabba. A small group came in and sat glaring at each other in chilly silence. I listened to a short version of their cases, which I already knew, and then I gave my decision in support of the Chief.

A man leaped to his feet and rushed to a window and shouted two or three words in Yoruba. In an instant a mass of men swarmed over the verandah rails and into the office from all sides. The place was crammed with shouting gesticulating people, angry and almost out of control of themselves. In the distance I thought I could hear police whistles. I was much too astonished and scared to do anything but sit quite still behind my fortunately rather wide office table. My very stillness was not what they had expected and the first rank slowed their arm-waving and their shouting died away. Gradually the noise abated and as the police filtered in from the clerk's office, the crowd was silent and looked not a little deflated. I motioned the police back and addressed the crowd on the merits of good manners in securing one's objectives. I then told them they could go and we would say no more about it.

I had learned two valuable lessons: first, that silence and immovability will quieten a rough crowd (save in peculiar circumstances), and secondly, that it was necessary to have a desk so deep that a man could not stab you across it. Wherever I went in Nigeria, if there was not such a piece of furniture, I either had one specially made or had extensions fitted. I hope that some of my creations are still the prized possessions of certain offices.

In this vein I recall a nasty situation that once developed in Lokoja. The Lieutenant-Governor, Sir William Gowers, came down from Kaduna on a rare and very formal visit. He took his seat in the Court House to receive the assembled chiefs. Before they could start to enter in their ponderous way and make their greetings, some hundreds of the people of Lokoja rushed the Court House, screaming and yelling for a chief of their own. We had no government police on duty – an odd omission. Another A.D.O. and I managed to slip out behind the crowd, and brought in the N.A. police whom the chiefs had with them – a motley gang – through windows and a back door. With this advantage they forced back the crowd from the rather alarmed seniors on the dais, and eventually cleared the room. The sight of G.S. Browne, Secretary of the Northern Provinces and a massive man, brandishing a chair remains in my mind. These men were used to the courtesies of the Emirs; and our rough ways filled them with horror – which did them no harm.

Meanwhile the need for a 'motorable' road from Kabba to Lokoja (52 miles) became more and more pressing. It occurred to me that before we started we should be sure that we had enough money and that we were working on the right geographical line. I got approval for the vast sum of £500 in the N.A. Estimates, but the second pre-requisite was not so easy: we had to go and look. The existing so-called 'trade route' went in a great arc to the north: was there a feasible route along the chord of the arc which would save distance and labour? An important consideration was the difference of about 700 feet between the height of the Kabba plain and the Niger valley: was the existing road, a rather dramatic and tiring series of switchbacks, the best place for the descent?

A small column of carriers with a tent and camp equipment and food, two messengers, two government policemen (who insisted on coming, theoretically to protect my person but really for the fun), two or three hunters and a couple of chaps from the last village, we set out into the unknown. This country, completely uninhabited after the great slave raids of the nineteenth century, had little hills and streams, and was covered, as usual, with low 'orchard bush'.

At first we did pretty well: the hunters knew the country and I surveyed as we went along. Then the carriers and the others got separated. We ran into elephant trails that looked very like ordinary bush paths, some leading in one direction and others in different ones. In the end I was alone with a messenger and a policeman. We climbed a granite hill and saw a camp fire about a mile and a half away. We made for it and found the tent and most of the loads by a stream. The rest came in later.

The next day progress was slower. By now we were off the Kabba plateau, and the elephant tracks were more confusing. We found traces of elephant only a few minutes away from us; we found their footprints in the sand of a small stream, with the water just seeping in, and moved swiftly through the thin fringing forest, but we could see nothing: the huge beasts had vanished. From hilltops we could see bush fires here and there, clouds of black smoke, blowing at a brisk speed.

In the evening we formed a camp. Just as we had done so we saw the nearest plume of smoke we had been watching turn suddenly in our direction. The dried grass went up like tinder. We had just had time to burn a control circle round the camp when it was on us and we were invaded by swarms of small creatures, insects and snakes. Fortunately, they were none of them really dangerous, and we per-

suaded them to go on their way when the fire died down. The speed of
a bush fire is terrifying if you are in its way: we were covered with ash
and burning grass, but the main fire passed by.

Then it became dark and the lions got wind of us. There must have
been several of them – exactly how many was the subject of heated
argument for days – the ground was too hard to show what, in
Anglo-Indian, are called pug-marks. We set up bonfires at the corners
of the camp and hoped for the best. Our armament of two police rifles
and my Mannlicher would not have been much use in the dark; our
only hope would have been to attack the lions with burning brands
from the fires. Then, to complete our discomfort, a great storm of rain
burst over us and nearly carried away the tent. However, it dis-
couraged the lions, who went away. Lions were quite common in that
area. Later, when we were building the bridges, I asked the masons
on a very remote and isolated site whether they were a nuisance. 'No',
they said, 'the lions are all right – the flies are the trouble here.'

Early the following morning we started off in the direction of a
granite hill which we knew to be near the existing trade route. One of
the hunters, very mysteriously, led us aside a mile or so off our line.
The grass here had not burnt and we were hemmed on to a little track.
Then suddenly and unexpectedly it all opened out and we were on the
edge of a huge grassless area. There were trees but the lower branches
and the bark had gone, and the trunks were worn smooth and
polished. Here and there were mounds of elephant droppings. We
were in an elephants' dancing floor. I had always thought it was one of
Kipling's tall stories, and yet here it all was. There was no doubt that
great feet had hammered out that floor and that by night the area
would be filled with huge grey shapes.

After that we had a sudden adventure, which could have been fatal
for us. There was a distant sound of hounds baying, and everyone
stood utterly still and waited. The noise grew louder and then a pack
swept by a hundred yards or so away. It was terrifying and we felt
very exposed standing there, for they were wild hunting dogs and
anything unlucky enough to become their quarry had no chance.
Even leopards get smartly out of their way.

Soon after this we found the wide track and the village we sought.
The whole bush trek had been about twenty-two miles. In the end I
decided to stick to the general line of the trade route.

When it came to the actual building of the road, I knew that the
descent could be contained in about 5 miles of road. The existing
'switchback' route was more or less straight: if the new road was to be
properly graded the line would have to go in and out of little valleys
and round spurs. This would make it longer and the grade could be

reduced. In the upshot I decided to take a 2° slope as the line to be maintained. As soon as the ground started to fall, working from the Kabba end I set my level at 2° depression (roughly a 1-in-33 gradient) and started pegging the centre line. We soon went off the existing track, and the people with me thought I had gone mad. The road headman pegged the correct 22-foot carriageway and the ditches, outwards from the centre. All went well on the flattish ground but we soon found ourselves running along hill-side, rapidly getting to steeper slopes. Here the experience I had gained at Agbaja (see page 36) came into its own and I could show them how to cut on one side and fill on the downside, with proper rope 'profiles', giving the level of the roadway out to the top of a peg, and pegs getting taller as the ground fell away with slots cut into the hill to carry the level.

As we pegged, this gradual descent followed the hillside and round a projecting spur. For the first time we realised that we were on one side of a valley running east and about 300 feet or so above a good-sized stream. As the track followed the hill shape we came out again from time to time on the side of the valley.

After I had done about half the pegging, I thought I would have a change and went off for a shoot. Leaving early in the morning I went down into this valley with a hunter and climbed the other side. We found any amount of game tracks, old and new. I followed a hartebeest for some time and eventually got a shot and killed it. Our activities must have been under close scrutiny for it was not long before this utterly deserted place had filled up with hungry people, who strung the body to poles and carried it back to camp. All I got was an unchewable steak and some good liver.

However, I had not had enough of hunting and walked on for a while away from the road. This was a mistake. One has seen pre-historic drawings of cattle and bison, or something like them – we came over a rise and there they were. The glade was about 300 yards across and on the other side were five splendid bush-cow, as they are called in West Africa, grazing quietly. We should have merely admired them and gone away. But foolishly I fired. I must have nicked one of the big ones, for there was a great commotion and they charged.

I made several instantaneous discoveries. First, we had not time to get back into the trees; second, there was no cover in front of us save for a clump of grass; third, I had only four cartridges left. We fell flat behind the grass and prayed. The hunter, who thought I was omni-potent, was for my going on shooting: I had to hold him down to avoid giving ourselves away. They came at a great speed, their heads down. The earth shook and so did I. Our prayers were answered, for they did not see where we were and charged past with a thunder of hooves and great snorts into the trees and circled in a huge arc. I feared they were coming again, but they thought better of it. Very humbly we got up and retraced our steps. The lesson we had learned was not to over-reach oneself.

Lesson two that day was startling but fortunately it too involved no damage. As we came over the last rise and saw the valley I have mentioned at our feet, I looked across at 'our' side. There I could clearly see the line of our pegging. It looked fine, the slope was steady and exactly what we wanted, and in fact it looked as if it had been drawn on the landscape. Then I looked along to the left, where we had not done anything, I could see sheer rock face and observed with dismay that our line would go right across it. This would have been impossible to work. However, I noticed that just above the next section to be done, and before the cliff face, there appeared to be a low col: this might give us our way out.

The next day the first thing I did was to walk on and up to the right and sure enough there was a col and on the other side a gentle slope. So instead of continuing the trace we swung a little upwards and over into the next valley, and the situation was saved. This was the only section of the descent which went upwards, and no doubt it does so still to this day.

Most of the road excavation was fairly straightforward but every now and again we came across rock. If we could not go round it or build over it, we tried Hannibal's old trick. Bush wood was cut and piled on it and then set alight. When the rock was hot, we had water poured on it and attacked it with sledge-hammers. The rock could usually be broken up quite quickly. Hannibal, of course, had used vinegar – we found it difficult enough to find water.

In the end we finished less than 50 feet out at the foot of the descent and there was therefore a short steep rise at the Lokoja approach to the climb. In that hill section we built just more than a hundred granite culverts. After that the road presented no difficulties except for bridging. Further on there was one large bridge that had to have 30-foot spans and we had to bolt mahogany beams together to span it, but that was easy.

Married

My leave in 1925 was a decisive one. Having been confirmed as an officer of the Colonial Service in Nigeria, I could now marry if I wished – and I certainly wished. In June Dorothy Mason and I were married in St Columba's Church, Pont Street, London. She was the daughter of D.M. Mason, a Liberal Member of Parliament: her mother was a beautiful American and they were well-off without being actually rich. She had, therefore, been brought up in comfortable surroundings, and naturally had gone to the toughest of girls' schools, St Leonards, in St Andrews, Scotland. She had a good idea of what lay before her for I had spared nothing in my regular letters during the previous tour; but the reality was, of course, impossible to describe.

We sailed in July and the journey was uneventful. With us were our full two-and-a-half tons of luggage, indeed rather more. All our clothes and personal things were in four steel 'uniform cases', black enamelled in the standard manner, with names in white script. Fortnum & Mason had made a long steel case with a hanging bar at one end for use as an air-tight wardrobe – something they had never done before. It contained a full-length mirror. Besides this they had made a mirror for the dressing-table with two hinged wings, curved at the top and set in good plain elm, which today is still as good as ever.

After four years I had a fair idea of the kind and quantity of stores required, together with luxuries – like puddings and crystallised fruit. Specially for the lady was a gallon container of medicinal paraffin in case of difficulty and a gross of packets of sanitary towels (the old kind), as well as a full medicine chest and bandages and the like. Toilet articles had to be bought in quantity, bottles and jars and packets. On the whole we did not do badly. All this came from Fortnum & Mason, and the linen from John Barker. Fortnums packed those of our wedding presents that we were taking (excluding the electric lamps misguidedly given us), as well as a 'Dulcitone' piano which was supposed to help Dorothy to keep up her singing.

Lagos turned on its hospitality and we were taken in for the day by Shenton Thomas* and his wife and then put on the boat train. Dorothy saw all the strange new sights, some of them still strange to me. We changed at Minna on our way to Baro, and it was at Baro that our first contretemps occurred. We were met there by a much bigger Marine boat than the old *Manatee* and just after dinner on board a white man came on board whom I had met once before. He was an Administrative Officer a little senior to myself: he said that a serious matter had arisen and would I come and advise him. He was going on leave and was staying the night in the rest house up the hill. I

*Shenton Thomas was then acting Chief Secretary, possibly the ablest man we ever had. Later, he was Governor of Singapore at the time of the disastrous surrender to the Japanese in 1942.

therefore reluctantly left my bride on her first night on the edges of civilisation.

The matter was worse than I thought. This chap said that two 'boys' had come to him and laid a homosexual charge against their white master, someone in the Railway Department in Baro. He felt that we should take action about it.

He then set himself up as a Court and summoned this wretched man before him. The man was horrified, as well he might have been – the penalty if he were found guilty would have been fourteen years in jail. My senior proceeded to hear and take down the evidence of the two boys. It was not at all convincing and the demeanour of the accused man was excellent throughout. Time was getting on and the officer obviously believed every word of the evidence. I was determined that nothing precipitate should be done and was also going to take good care that I was personally not involved in any official way. On the other hand he was senior to me and that could not be laughed off.

I pointed out – it occurred to me rather late – that, while we were both members of the Provincial Court, we were not on the staff of the Province in which we were then sitting; the District Officer of that Division would be far from pleased to learn of what we had done in his territory. Secondly, he was going on leave and could not therefore complete the affair; thirdly, we had no way of securing the man if he were sentenced; fourthly, there was the question of whether he should have access to counsel in the face of so serious a charge; and fifthly, I was not going to have anything more to do with it and, as it was by then midnight, I was going to bed. He saw the point after a while and I left the two white men drinking whisky with some degree of amiability.

Meanwhile a great tornado had come up and my wife had to endure a mighty thunderstorm alone on the strange river Niger. The lightning had been bad, though we in the grass-roofed rest house had not noticed it particularly. In the end we got to sleep and woke to find ourselves on the bosom of the great river. It glinted in the sun and birds were flying swiftly over its waters; the herons were standing motionless watching their faithful reflections until their beaks flashed down into the water; and the crocodiles as usual looked like shapeless logs.

We passed Adaha with the high water lapping its rest house. We could see the roof of the Koton Karifi house over the trees, and we thanked God that we were not going there. And then round the last bend, and Lokoja lay before us: Patti was very green and very red after the rain. On the pier stood the Resident, Byng-Hall, and two or three others. He came forward and said the immortal words, the first addressed to her in our own Province, 'Mrs Niven, this is no place for a white woman.' After that he could not have been more kind or friendly. There was only one other white woman there at that time; she had been out for some years, but even so was not very helpful.

Two days later we set out for Kabba. The N.A. there had bought a new Ford kit-car and it seemed that the road to Kabba was open for the time being via Okene, Our heavy loads were entrusted to carriers and sent off by the direct road, while we with our own personal things and a boy or two went by the kit-car.

While it was true that the Okene road was *usable*, we were to discover that that word had a special meaning. After lunch at peaceful, lovely Okene with George McCabe, a recent cadet, the last section to Kabba proved awkward. Parts of the road had washed away; although the bridges were passable, some surfaces had gone and on the steeper slopes we had to do a lot of pushing and walking.

A few days later the kit-car fell over a steep embankment and never looked the same again, though it would go if nursed. Then a sudden and violent storm washed away the essential bridges near Okene, in spite of which our loads duly arrived. We said farewell to the man I was relieving and we were alone.

I shall never know what Dorothy really thought during those months in the rains, but she never complained and took everything with great good nature. Only once, after a night in a rest house, when there was heavy rain and we had a mighty invasion of ants, did we come near to breaking-point but that soon passed.

Mail from home took a long time to get through – this added to the strain. Official mail came once a week by a so-called 'runner' from Lokoja. It took him at least two days, sometimes three to get through. He brought parcels as well as mail, and if necessary a friend came to help him. The mail was well wrapped and only spoiled if he actually fell into a river. Theoretically, home mail came every other week, since the mail boats were fortnightly; sometimes there might be a bonus mail by intermediate boat, but we never counted on it. Parcels had to be assessed for customs duty in Lagos and therefore arrived later. The mail bags had to travel in the boat train, were taken off at Minna, then came by rail to Baro and finally by boat to Lokoja. After sorting, the mail came on to us *via* the Provincial Office (where the Chief Clerk kept a running account for customs fees). It arrived therefore at least a week after the boat had docked. If we answered at once we could only catch the boat after the one that had brought the latest letters out. We used to reckon two months as the minimum for a reply to get home. You could cable, of course, but that was expensive and not satisfactory. Neither of the Kabba Divisional Headquarters had a telegraph office.

The newspapers and periodicals came by the mail and made quite a parcel. In a station where you were with other officers, it was easy to circulate papers and magazines, but we were alone and had to rely on our own resources. *The Times* came in bundles of six issues.

We all had our different ways of dealing with these newspapers. Some glanced through all of them and studied the latest with the greater care; others like ourselves, arranged them in date order and started with the oldest reading one every day so that we had a daily paper until the next mail came in. There was no form of radio – we did not get that for years – and Reuters telegrams, by the time they reached us, were virtually useless. The Times Bookshop sent us the most recent novels, four at a time, and 'heavy' books. It was essential to have the latter as the novels were soon read — history and bio- graphy took longer.

We had the same cook as I had had on my last tour. He was not a good cook, but was passable and had not poisoned me. The steward was new, a friend of the cook, while the 'small' boy (the most junior of the staff, who did most of the hard work) had been picked up in Lokoja. He was the first cause of trouble. Although very young, he had an eye for the girls. One night after dinner, the steward came in and said that the boy had a girl with him in his hut – rather an important girl. I went with him and looked in the hut: there was no girl inside his mosquito net. When I told him to lift the back of the net, there, between the net and the curved hut wall, was a naked damsel of obvious charm. She was one of the Chief's daughters and since I was not looking for trouble from that quarter, she was sharply sent off. The boy left us rather abruptly.

Then we found that sugar and some stores – after all, we had enough for eighteen months – were disappearing fast: 25 lb of sugar and tins of flour went in a week. This we traced to the cook and he left. The steward said he could cook and set to work, and indeed we found that his claim was justified. We later discovered that he had been trained by a most exacting white woman in Lagos – he had even been taught a different sweet for every day of the month; that was a change for us, after a diet of baked caramel and boiled yams. His name was Sally Porbeni: he came from Warri, and he stayed with us for thirty- one years, till 1956. He soon whistled up relatives to help in the house and we had an organistion which not only lasted out the whole of our Nigerian service but also became a by-word for excellence in the North. His family prospered with us: the first son born to him in Kabba, Freeman Porbeni, retired recently from a high post in the

Labour Department, and another is a chief pilot in Nigerian Airways. He died in 1980, aged nearly ninety.

Life was no sinecure for anyone, for we kept up our touring and were out of station for nearly three weeks in each month. The touring routine, to which my wife readily adapted herself, was that the cook and his 'mate' set out at 5 a.m. with the cook's large wooden box, a table and two chairs. We had our tea at 5.30, the carriers came up at 6, and we set out at about quarter past, just after dawn, walking a good three miles an hour. About 8.30 we would sight the cook's fire and come to a selected place usually by a stream, often very picturesque: the table was laid with a cloth and cutlery, and the delicious smell of frying bacon and eggs and fresh coffee pervaded the air.

After breakfast we went on with the messengers and left cook to clear up: meanwhile the carriers and the other boys had gone ahead and when we reached the destined rest house at about 10 or a little later, the furniture would be laid out, the beds up and the bath ready. The hot water was boiled up in four-gallon kerosene tins – ample for one bath. Sometimes the water was so 'thick' that it had to be allowed to stand to clear.

We depended largely on the village people to bring up fire-wood and water, chickens and some eggs, and fruit (if any). This was a traditional obligation, to be paid for on departure. The rest house was free.

I went off to inspect the village nearby and have a discussion with the chiefs, and my wife wrote letters or did her own chores till I got back. The village headman would of course always be in evidence, and there were the inevitable litigants to be listened to. After lunch one had a rest, and then a walk in the evening. The map was finished by then but there was usually something to look at, even in apparently dull areas.

Sunset was always at 6 p.m., and then a bath and drinks and dinner and bed. Sometimes we went on the next day, sometimes we stayed two or more days, depending on what there was to be done. In Nigeria it generally rains (in the season), if it is going to, after 5 p.m. and the mornings are clear. At the height of the rains, of course, it may rain all day and all night, and in that case we would put off leaving. The bridgeless streams would be full and movement could be difficult.

Much of the travelling was done over quite narrow paths, not the trade routes that I have mentioned. Travellers used to speak of 'trackless' Africa, but in West Africa that would be nonsense: there are always tracks between villages, becoming wider and more important where the village has a market. Some white men used bicycles, but we found that the paths were too rough and often dangerous. People – local people – were constantly on the move, and there were always plenty of strangers, with their loads, many of them traders from far away.

Rest houses varied greatly. Some were quite small and it was difficult to get two beds and a dressing table in them; I remember one that took only the two beds and the net, and we had to climb in from the foot of the bed which was in the front door, having undressed on the verandah. Others were relatively large. Few had furniture: later it became policy to put in elementary things – tables and chairs and lampstands (an important article). Some were clean and some grubby, but all had whitewashed walls and usually good floors of beaten pots or beaten earth. None of them had doors or windows but a few had shutters over window openings (later, glass windows were put in the better and more frequented places). And all the time we were in Nigeria we never lost so much as a pencil through theft. The Village headmen were responsible – expenses paid – for the upkeep of these places. All the lavatories were in huts outside, often consisting of a pole on forked sticks over a hole in the ground. We created a sensation by bringing a 'collapsible' lavatory seat – a bit of real progress – but it did sometimes collapse at inconvenient moments.

My wife used to arrange elaborate booby-traps with folding chairs and the tin bath lid and the like across the doorways; but these would fall down in gusts of wind with a fearful crash, or be pushed over by a curious goat, causing much unnecessary alarm. We always carried with us rolled-up mats for the floor.

The rest houses were usually some distance from the village and the villagers could be noisy in their celebration of the visit of the great man and his wife: in their eyes we were uncanny and therefore great. They would marvel at my wife's honey-coloured hair: fair people were rare and her very fine skin astonished them. Old ladies would beg leave to touch her arm very gently and would then say, 'It is just like water.'

We both wore puttees to protect our legs. My wife wore hers over silk stockings. I wore mine over socks. Dorothy had special ladies' 'light' puttees with a khaki 'spat' over the shoes. It was said that snakes could not bite through this material. Otherwise we both wore khaki shirts of 'solaro', khaki interwoven with red thread to defeat the rays of the tropical sun, so dreaded at that time. I had a spine pad – a piece of material similar to the shirt and buttoned on to the back of it, shaped not unlike a large dried haddock. She also had a solaro jacket, which was comfortable and looked smart. Khaki sun-helmets completed the picture but before long we substituted 'terai' hats, wide-brimmed felt with double crowns. However odd it sounds, she always looked immaculate and elegant.

The bed linen was packed in the tin bath; it had a wicker lining which could be lifted out, so that the contents did not have to be unpacked whenever we had a bath. What the boys did, despite the difficulties of touring, and without comment let alone complaint, was astonishing. For example, they baked bread in the early hours, using a kerosene tin as an oven, with burning wood piled round it. They would even bake in this way in the falling rain. The boys did all the laundry and pressing of the clothes and were most particular and proud of their efforts.

I have mentioned the road that I built to Aiere in the south-west; the road to Okene existed, sometimes; and that to Lokoja was nearly finished. There remained the north-west, towards a wide and well-populated valley. For the first 10 miles or so, the route ran through high forest, a belt some 50 miles long by 10–15 miles wide. Here the quickest way to build temporary bridges was to use the timber at hand and make 'crib' piers of interlocked tree-stems (like a log-hut): granite was difficult to find and probably deeply hidden in the forest bed. We continued with it when we got clear of the forest. It was cheap, and later it would be easy to substitute proper piers.

Here we had another example of 'rain control'. There were a number of these bridges to be built round a place called Otunbedde, and it was important to spend some time there laying them out and supervising them. So we decided to spend a week in the large round rest house outside the village, at the height of the rains, in August.

The last time I had passed through this place there had been a large hole in the thatch, when we got there not only was it still there but it had grown larger. I was not very pleased, as the Village Head had promised to re-thatch the building – for which he would of course get paid market rates. He rapidly grasped the gravity of the position and said, 'How long are you going to stay?' I said that I could not finish what had to be done in less than a week. The Village Head, an oldish man in a huge and grubby robe, looked depressed by the news. Then, to my astonishment, he said, 'It is a long time and there is naturally a lot of rain about, but if any rain falls on the roof of that house while you are with us, you can cut my throat.' During all that week the rain fell everywhere, but no drop fell on the rest house roof, and indeed little fell in the surrounding compound.

All the business of rain-making and rain-stopping was quite unheard of in the Muslim areas of the North. To interfere with the predestined pattern of God's will is a thing that no good Muslim would ever contemplate: rain is part of Allah's great scheme for man.

North-west across a broad valley were some low hills and over them the road (about 40 miles of it) had to go to a large place called Isanlu. Because there was a steep bit in the middle, I took a great sweep to the north and then round again on to the old line. So we had a steady reasonable climb and at the turn a splendid view right across the Niger valley for many, many miles to the distant hills in the Nupe Province. There were several such views and from some it was possible to see river steamers at high water.

It was here that my wife was taken ill for the first and last time in her Nigerian career. She was very sick and I had to leave her while I laid out the road, but the cook sent a boy many miles to a mission station at Isanlu Makatu for a bucket of oranges. On these she lived for some days and recovered. We thought later that it must have been dengue fever, but being 100 miles from a doctor, we could never find out.

In that part of Kabba to the north of the Division, there was a tiny and scrupulously clean rest house in the Olle Forest Reserve. When I was doing the map it was on my route and I went there for a night. The people were pleased to see me – it always put a bit of money into circulation.

That night was oppressive and I woke at about 1 o'clock. I lay awake and was surprised to hear the murmur of voices and the movement of feet. It was so odd that I got up and went out on to the verandah. There I found my cook and steward looking out. The night was absolutely still: there was no movement of air: the moon was full and brilliantly clear. The space before the rest house was as bright as high noon. It was a vast sheet of quite smooth granite with a slight slope. When we had first reached the place I noticed that there were two small shrines, what we casually called '*juju* houses', one at each end of this space, maybe 200 yards apart. Across the space moved a mass of people, back and forth: 'They are visiting the *juju*', said my cook. But there was nothing whatver to be seen; not even the tiniest nocturnal creature moved in the moonlight. The movement did not approach us at all. After a while it died away and we went back to bed.

The next morning the villagers were very non-committal: they did not deny the portent nor did they agree to its existence. 'What man', they said, 'do understand the *juju* thing?' But they themselves never went that way by night.

I always meant to investigate hauntings in Nigeria – we heard of several – but there never seemed to be time. There were several places (such as rest houses) where a horse would stall and shake or a dog would bristle and whine and flatly refuse to enter the compound, but where humans felt nothing strange. There were places like Ikot Ekpene (in the extreme south-east, near Calabar) noted for its *jujus*, where to my senses a strange and eerie atmosphere could be felt merely driving through them. My driver, a stranger and not an emotional man, noticed it. 'Plenty juju live for this place', he said. There were pools and little groves. I often felt that these had their own secrets, but some would just laugh at the idea.

To give another example, the Commissioner for the Cameroons lived in British times in the old German Government House, the Schloss, at Buea, in the foothills of the Cameroon Mountain. At the time of which I am writing, both the Commissioner and his wife were musicians and there was a good piano in the house. They were having a party that night and were upstairs dressing. In his dressing-room he listened to the very fine playing of a Chopin prelude and thought that his wife was doing better than usual. When he dressed he looked into their bedroom and said with some surprise, 'Hello, I thought you were downstairs: I have never heard you play so well.' She said, 'I have not been out of this room; I thought how well *you* were playing.' There was no one else in those parts who could play that kind of music, or any other, on a piano.

But to come back to earth. When we got our new cook it was he who suggested that the lady of the house should keep a 'store ledger' like a government department. There everything would be listed and the total of articles received would be shown on one side, and stores issued in little columns, as they were issued – on the other. Thus the state of the store, and the weekly issues could be seen at a glance. She did this and it worked well. In fact, the system was carried on for years, until the War, when we had to rely on local purchases. People were amused at these precautions, but some other wives adopted it to their great advantage.

The great day came when the road through to Lokoja was open. It still took two-and-a-half hours in the resuscitated kit-car, but it could be done, and the tiresome three-day trek was a thing of the past. In the eleven months that my wife was in Kabba she saw just seven white people, none of them a woman. Visits to Lokoja made a change but they were rare: the canteens, as the trading stores were called, were poor, and little worthwhile could be bought. It is strange to think of a woman with a taste for clothes being in a place where she did not see a new dress for nearly a year.

There was one special visit. The acting Governor, Sir Frank Baddeley (he was the Chief Secretary to the Government and did not go further in the Service), came to Lokoja in the special gubernatorial yacht, *Dayspring*. He must have been one of the dullest senior officers we had and was correspondingly difficult to deal with. However, he was very polite to my wife, as he well might have been for her father, though no longer an M.P., was much involved around Westminster. Someone organised a concert to entertain the great man; local talent was conjured up and, being able to sing, she was roped in. The concert went off well.

In addition to the dulcitone (which was not a success) we had a 'portable' HMV gramophone, another, more useful wedding present. This was the kind you wound up but the tone was good and with the new electric recording process the sound was good too. The records suffered from local conditions. On one trek, for a reason I have now forgotten, we left the records behind with a Village Head. It was in the rains and he felt that he should keep them dry, so he put them in a corner of his hut near a wood fire. When we returned they were all beautifully warped. *Oh, for the Wings of a Dove* and the *Indian Love Lyrics* were our favourites.

Wherever we went one of the most important loads was the one which contained the filter: without that we could not have lived. It was set up on arrival and as soon as a kettle of water had boiled it was poured in; in due course the filtered water was ready to be drawn off into bottles. The filter 'candles', through which the water passed, had to be kept absolutely clean, also the bottles: dirty bottles could cause a lot of trouble. These were washed by the faithful boys in permanganate of potash as were also lettuces and fruit, when we could get them.

The filled water bottles were put into a jar made of porous pottery which kept water perceptibly cooler than the surrounding atmosphere. This was a well-known action, on the same principle as using a canvas bucket hung up in a breeze. Refrigerators were not available and we did not see one till about 1932. No meat could be kept, and if you wanted to eat it cold, you had to cook it for the purpose and eat it the same day.

Butter was a problem. First of all the tin (there was no other kind) had to be put into the cooler pot for a few days before you opened it. Then it was taken out fairly solid, placed in a screw-topped jar and put back into the cooler. It was taken out just before meals and put back again immediately afterwards. Similarly a packet of plain chocolate could be poured out of a corner of the packet. My wife's face creams had to be treated in the same way to keep them solid. Bacon seemed to keep slightly better, but not in Bornu. There, if you opened a bacon tin, you would probably find some strips of meat floating in thin grease. We had small sides of bacon sent out by post every six months from Fortnums. Very close rationing made it last the course, and it kept 'moist' by being packed in salt. We always had liquid quinine – we never went on to the fancy drugs like mepacrine and paludrine. Horrid as it was, it kept us well throughout our service and being a slight stimulant gave an extra kick when one was needed. We never had malaria.

It is astonishing that some people could still be careless about taking their quinine or whatever the current drug might be. They were then surprised when they went down with malaria. It could be cured, of course, but it did no one any good. Dysentery too was easy to get but hard to get rid of. We never had it, I am glad to say.

After eleven months my wife went home and I was alone again. It had been a wonderfully happy time, with everything against us. Perhaps if we had started, as so many did, in a large station, the conflicting interests and the inevitable isolation from the country and its people would have affected her whole outlook. As it was, she always identified herself with the Africans and not so much with the other white people – though we had great numbers of good friends – she was never so happy as when we were on tour. Later, in senior posts, we would arrange from time to time to get away to some place where there was no other white face, where we could walk about freely and talk to the people and admire the view.

That was in May 1926. I had not long been back in Kabba when I got a message to pack up and leave for Kaduna, the headquarters of the North – a very different kind of life. I never served in Kabba again.

III.   Kaduna: Secretariat

The place

When I arrived in Kaduna it had been a capital for only about ten years. Lugard's old wooden Government House was just up the road, and among other buildings was a quarter of a Secretariat building and half of a 'European Hospital' (as such establishments were then unashamedly called). Many departments were working in converted but unsuitable bungalows. There were only two two-storeyed buildings, apart from the Secretariat and Hospital.

Kaduna was sited in a plain entirely away from the influence of any of the great Chiefs and from any existing town. Consequently it had only a tiny and artificial African population. Within fifty years we saw it grow into a town 10 miles and more across with a population of at least eighty thousand, of all tribes and languages. We saw the Secretariat expand and then turn into Ministries; we saw the new buildings go up, among them the Legislature in its charming setting, and the great new Law Courts. The old Government House gave way to another, and through it there passed an astonishing variety of men – the post of Lieutenant-Governor became Chief Commissioner and then Lieutenant-Governor again and finally Governor, with powers that varied from high independence of Lagos to virtual subordination, and back to Regional independence in the Federation. With the best climate for white men in the whole country, Kaduna was a Mecca for the ambitious and a plague spot for the true 'bushman'. Here was the Secretariat, where service brought a man into a prominence before his seniors that might do him good – or sometimes ill. The man devoted to his 'bush' division dreaded its office hours, its procedure, its collars and ties. The work was hard and exacting.

In 1915 the site had been an empty space, sloping gently to a substantial river called the Kaduna with plenty of water all the year round, water that ran over granite sills into deep pools full of fish, yet not so wide that it could not eventually be bridged with the funds then available. On this Kaduna river was a small Gwari village, now swallowed up in the new lower town.

Sir Frederick Lugard, as High Commissioner for the Protectorate of Northern Nigeria at the turn of the century, depended on the river Niger for the transport of every person and every ton of material and supplies from the sea. The Niger valley, even 400 or 500 miles inland from the sea, is still less than 500 feet above the sea and is very hot.

His selected capital at Zungeru was on the Kaduna river, a navigable tributary opening into the Niger on its north bank. Though a little higher than the Niger itself, Zungeru was most uncomfortable to live in. For example it teemed with mosquitoes and other nasty bugs, and his staff spent much of their time being ill; too often unto death itself. A change of site became essential.

Lugard's people scoured the likely areas of the country as best they could on horseback with loads carried by head-carriers. They decided on this plain a further 120 miles up the Kaduna river. They were 'led', as they would have said, to choose almost the ideal site, with plenty of room to expand, a country rolling enough to make it interesting, yet having no awkward gradients. Two thousand feet above the sea is a reasonable height for West Africa, where we did not have altitude on the East African scale. In practice it turned out never to be really too hot in the hot season and not too wet in the rains. The soil was good and plants and trees would grow. So between 1914 and 1917 the new capital was laid out on a generous scale. The roads were planted with saplings which grew quickly into fine trees, and in ten years every road flowered differently and at different times. It looked very pleasant when I first saw it in 1927.

On his return from Hong Kong, Lugard* was keen to make Kaduna the capital of the unified Nigeria. The War made this difficult, but the real reason why it was not carried out was the timing of the mail boats at Lagos. They brought the all-important despatches from the Colonial Office and there was just time to reply to the more urgent while the ship was waiting to turn round, usually a week. To send the despatches by train to Kaduna and back would not have allowed more than say two days (at best three) for the drafting of the replies, and some officers would no doubt have died of apoplexy in the rush to produce the answers. It seemed that a delay of a fortnight i.e. till the next boat, would be intolerable.

Nevertheless, plans were produced giving sites in Kaduna for the major buildings of Government such as a Legislature, Government House and Secretariat. Some buildings were actually built with this in mind, and others were built in part. But the scheme lapsed – a great pity for the siting of the capital away from Lagos would have resulted in a better distribution of resources than actually happened.

After the Second World War the question of the capital came up again. Of course Lagos, tucked away in the south-west of Nigeria, is

---

*Lugard became Governor of Hong Kong in 1907, in the happy-go-lucky way in which the Colonial Office scattered its best officers about the world, and returned to Nigeria in 1912 as Governor of the Northern and Southern Protectorates. When they were amalgamated in 1914 he became Governor-General of the new Nigeria until his retirement in 1919.

far off-centre and is completely unsuited as a modern capital for a number of other reasons. Sir Arthur Richards considered moving it to Kaduna and ordered an enquiry and estimate. It was found that to move only the central Government and the 'Exco Departments', i.e. those like the Medical whose Heads were on Executive Council, would, together with all the necessary telecommunications, cost well over one million pounds sterling, at that time an unthinkable sum for such a project, being one-tenth of the total annual receipts, the kind of money that could not be met by loan under the Colonial Office's rigid rule of financial purity. Later all despatches came by air, and so would have reached Kaduna a couple of hours before they reached Lagos! Lagos could very conveniently have remained the commercial capital.*

In Zungeru Lugard occupied a large wooden Government House which was received in sections from the United Kingdom and erected on the spot. In 1916 it was taken down and transferred to Kaduna. Although made of wood it survived remarkably well and was a cool, pleasant building with ample room for the practical purposes of the time. Sir Richmond Palmer, Lieutenant-Governor of the North in 1930 and a distinguished Arabist, was determined that this site at Kaduna should be used for a Government House indefinitely and earmarked it, as he thought, by building an elegant water-tower, at considerable expense, exactly opposite the front entrance gates and porch. It was pierced by a huge arch for the Lieutenant-Governor to drive through, with a guard-room and a room for the official visitors' book in its base.

The water-tower was the memorial to the immortal engagement known at the time as the 'Palmer-Baddeley row'. Sir Richmond Palmer was an able lawyer, perhaps a shade eccentric, who for many years had been Resident of Bornu. He was large and kind, with a twinkle in his blue eyes. Sir Frank Baddeley was strange to Nigeria, most of his service having been in Malaya, whence he was promoted to the exalted post of Chief Secretary to the Government of Nigeria. He was also able, but we were never in a position to assess him fairly because to us he was an 'office man' and, like others, found Nigeria difficult to understand and seldom visited the 'bush'. He arrived at the tail end of a long feud which had been going on since Amalgamation, in which the Northern Lieutenant-Governors strove desperately to retain their powers against the growing claims of the Central Government of Nigeria. We in the Kaduna Secretariat did

*In 1976 the Supreme Military Government decided to build a new capital in the bush near Abuja using a vast area of empty land in the Niger Valley.

not know the ins and outs of the battle, but occasionally we got a draft sent down to us in Palmer's nearly illegible hand for factual scrutiny, and these would give us a line. At that time the row seemed to be about the issue of mining rights and leases, and rights of occupancy over land. In this Palmer won.

Baddeley put the huge sum of £25,000 in the 1929 Estimates for a new house for the Lieutenant-Governors in Kaduna. Palmer refused to plan a new house and stuck to the old wooden one on the old site. Money from the water works vote had paid for the water-tower; but Lagos spent some thousands of pounds on putting up a fence and guard house at an improbable site across the railway. Palmer could do nothing about this. Then Baddeley played his last card, a house was built inside the great fenced enclosure, but not for the Lieutenant-Governor; it was to be a rest house for the Governor when on tour from Lagos – and to be officially known as 'Government *Lodge*'. When it was finished and beautifully furnished, Sir Donald Cameron, the next Governor, came up on tour. He looked at it and said that he did not care for it, it was unsuitable and extravagant – by this time we were in the great slump of the 1930s – nor was there really enough room for large-scale entertaining. Cameron stayed on board his train in a railway siding, where he gave my wife and me lunch in nostalgic memory of Lagos.

The house stood empty for years and the wooden house became more and more tatty. In 1937 a new Chief Commissioner came – the former Lieutenant-Governorship had been thus down-graded. This was Sir Theodore Adams, another stranger from Malaya, who gave no thought to the feud, if he ever knew anything about it, and decided to move in. He created the elaborate knot-garden that enhanced the front of the house and a couple of miles of hedging and the tennis courts in the back of the house. Until then it had just sat in untilled bush.

In later years, Lagos, all peace and smiles now, offered a huge sum for a new Government House in Kaduna. By then it was agreed that the existing house was hopelessly unsuitable in size and layout, and a fine new site was suggested reaching down to the river (where Tripanosomiasis Research now stands). The then Lieutenant-Governor, for his own reasons, refused the offer, and the opportunity passed, with all the other lost opportunities.

When we reached Kaduna in 1927 it was young and undeveloped. There were only four roads crossing the long King George's Way which ran from the Zaria road on the north to the river, 2½ miles away. One of these crossing roads went round about from the Kaduna North station to the cemetery, a mile in the bush to the east, a discreet and reasonable distance to place the dead: here, as in life, the whites lay together in a tiny huddle. The Africans had no wish to be buried in so remote a place: their ideas were more cosy – they preferred burial nearer home if not actually in it.

A large railway bridge crossed the 500-foot river in four spans. Though primarily for trains, it was decked over and could be used by motor vehicles and pedestrians. Access was controlled by rather erratic gatemen at either end, uncertain of train movements. The Railway could never find enough money to build a pedestrian way outside the girders, which would have been worthwhile as the panic on the part of these people, often heavily laden, was at times alarming and often pathetic. Whether a train could actually have stopped before it got on to the bridge, if emergency demanded it, was at most doubtful; the gradients on each approach were steep and curved. Beyond the bridge was Kaduna Junction, prophetically named, for there was no other line at that time or for some years, until the track from Port Harcourt in the Eastern Provinces joined up with the main line there in 1929. This railway station had enormous platforms, like Cambridge in the United Kingdom, capable of taking an up and a down express at the same time back to back. The trains to Jos used a bay on the same platform, and were much shorter owing to the heavy climb on to the high plateau.

Three times a week, when all these trains met, the scene was beyond description. Apart from the crowds of people getting off and on and changing trains, there were hundreds of others who had come along on the chance of meeting some long-lost friend. The trains were in the station for about an hour and the din never slackened until they had actually departed in their several directions. In a class-conscious way the white passengers travelled first-class, in great comfort. At first few Nigerians did so but later the situation changed. Nowadays a huge majority of the white people living in Nigeria have never set foot in one of the country's trains. They miss quite a lot.

The headquarters of the Northern division of the Nigerian Railway was at the Junction, in houses built and maintained by the Railway in a thin curve, some of them beautifully sited with lawns sloping down to the river. Railway staff were Government officials. On the subject of railways, it should be recorded that when the track was laid into Kano in March 1911, the construction department (it was built by the Railway itself and not by contract) set themselves to break a record. On a good straight stretch they got everything ready and in one day, between dawn and sunset, laid and completed 4½ miles of track, which broke all previous records. This was done by hand – there were no machines, beyond the ordinary railway-mounted cranes.

Kaduna began its existence as a purely official town. It is true that there was one United Africa Company canteen, very poor in building and stock, and the Bank of British West Africa, but the two white men in charge merged into the 'official' landscape. On the other hand there was not more than about 100 white people altogether in the station. A dozen were in the Secretariat and the same number in the West African Frontier Force, three with the police and half a dozen, including three Sisters, on the medical staff. All the Central Government departments were represented except Customs and Marine. The Headquarters of the Nigeria Regiment was there – under a full colonel as Commandant, not a brigadier, though there were five battalions.

On my first trip to Kaduna, our house was much the same as the ones we had had in Kabba, following what was called unofficially the 'Lugard type', though I doubt whether he had much to do with their design. They were based on a single central room with a very wide verandah. In Kaduna these verandahs were almost completely walled-in, then divided up in various interesting ways. In a few cases – a matter of seniority – there were double rooms in the centre, and the Secretary's and Commandant's houses had an upper floor. The Secretary, Northern Provinces, was an important appointment with the rank of Resident; he had the same position *vis-à-vis* the Lieutenant-Governor as the Chief Secretary had to the Governor in Lagos, but he did not normally 'act' for him.

All the official houses were in good 'compounds' 100 feet each way, with a variety of trees, some the original bush trees and others flowering ones specially planted; the houses were therefore out of sight of each other. We did not do very well over flowers in the early days except for zinnias, marigolds and station masters' joy – periwinkles. We enjoyed the services of a man paid for by us personally. Called a 'garden boy', his title aptly reflected his small horticultural capacity, although he did sweep up the drive and sometimes the whole compound.

The furniture was good and sufficient. The dining tables, in fine wood, would seat six in comfort, eight under pressure. We were still primitive in some ways – carpets and curtains were yet to come. However, good floor mats were easily available. Earth closets were unavoidable, and were cleaned by a 'sanitary gang'.

The life

There was a lot of entertaining in a mild way and dinner parties were common and very popular. There was a distinguished but rather erratic Medical Officer, in charge of the 'African Hospital', a good man with many friends. One night he found his evening clothes laid out for him, got into them and walked out of the house to his bicycle. Then he wondered vaguely where he was dining. He tried the most likely house and found it in darkness; he tried another and then another; finally he gave up and went home. There he found his friends assembled waiting for their dinner with him. Fortunately his boys were not as vague as he was.

Food was easy in Kaduna – plenty of guinea fowl and ducks, and good vegetables and fruit. The canteen was poor but we could get supplies from Lagos by train – frozen butter and bacon and cheese. We still relied largely on our Fortnum and Mason cases.

After dinner people played card games, some which, like vingt-et-un, were amusing and kept you awake. There was a ghastly game called 'freeze-out' (popular on the Coast) where each player had three 'lives' and someone lost one in each round. We had a roulette wheel – a small one but with the proper cloth – and played for pennies. At that time the West African Currency Board issued a tiny coin with a hole in the middle called an *anini*, its value one-tenth of a penny. These made excellent counters. Much excitement might be worked up: winnings were eventually calculated in the actual value of the coins, and our guests found that they had had a hectic evening and had lost just sevenpence. Of the solemn bridge players some were skilled and indeed some said that they lived off it!

Needless to say Kaduna had electric light long before anywhere else, the generators being driven by coal brought from Enugu. It was cheap and covered not only the whole station but much of the native town. The water supply was good and came direct from the river. At first it was rather cloudy, but later they dealt with that problem.

For church services, for which we had quite a crowd, we used the verandah of the Masonic Hall, a wooden building. It was strange how Masonry flourished in these places and interesting to see how some of the Masons prospered. Later the original hospital, a bungalow, was 'converted' – an apt word in this context – and done up in a clumsy attempt at the gothic style. We had our own chaplain, shared sometimes with Zaria and/or Jos.

Kaduna was very formal. On one's first arrival, 'books' had to be signed and cards left, and the young officer would certainly not be asked out if this was not done. However well you had known people elsewhere, you had to call and they had to return the call. Young marrieds waited for ladies to call on them and there were tense moments when no one seemed to make a move. The Lieutenant-

Governor had a book which was kept by the guardroom, and every-one signed it as a matter of course. The Commandant of the Regiment had one, too, and so did the Secretary: others did not merit them. When we had a Chief Justice he had a book, but at that time there was no Judge in Kaduna, or indeed in the whole of the North. They came up on circuit from Lagos.

Leaving cards, simple as it sounds, was not without its risks. For example, one day I went with my little card in my hand up the drive of the house of the Station Magistrate, whom I knew a little. His wife was bending over a flower-bed and I wished her a good afternoon. She straightened herself but did not turn round, and said, '*In Kaduna* when we are calling we do *not* speak.' However there was a lighter side and sometimes fortune smiled. Once I went to call on the Staff Captain and his wife. He lived in a good new bungalow with wide doors everywhere. As I walked up the drive I not unnaturally looked at the house and was astonished to see the captain's wife, a dark-haired beauty, sitting in the bedroom doing her manicure, entirely naked. Embarrassed, I stumped loudly up the steps to the table where one left cards and out again: the vision had been warned and vanished.

His immediate neighbour, Major A.E. Percival, the GSO1 (who, as a lieutenant-general, was in command of the ill-fated defence of Singapore in 1942), had a larger modern house with a beautiful garden. Percival was a very keen gardener and his flowers and lawns were a sight for sore eyes. Every year a flower show was held on the Secretariat verandah and there were always some fine blooms; a cup was also given for the best-kept and most attractive compound. For years this had been won by the Chief Health Superintendent, but this year the prize went to Percival. It seemed a strange coincidence when a fortnight later he was fined three guineas for having a dirty com-pound. The back, we understand, was not as good as the front.

Kaduna was a good place for evening walks. The country was flattish, native paths were numerous, and there was no obstacle to going in almost any direction. The hills were a long way off, and there was nothing to climb nearby. As the place was still small, you were soon outside the station roads.

There were good hard tennis courts by the club and a rather depressing golf course. The race course contained the polo ground and the cricket pitch: there was a lot of good polo. After my experience with horses in the war I had no wish to ride and doubt whether I would ever have been able to keep my eye on a polo ball long enough to hit it: I found it hard enough to hit a stationary golf ball.

In those days there was a little club opposite the Secretariat build-ings. Not only was its low flat roof made of tin, but its walls were of the same substance, all painted official green. Nevertheless in this edifice we had dances to gramophone records and sometimes to the W.A.F.F. band itself. One evening during a polo dance in fancy dress, some excited subalterns climbed on to the roof. There was nothing novel in that, but on this occasion they persuaded the pretty wife of a senior police officer to join them. Willing hands hauled her up – rather too vigorously, because her very thin trousers were badly split. She then sat firmly on the roof and refused to move. The subalterns abandoned her at her earnest request, and went to find their partners for the next dance. Two or three ladies who had guessed what was the matter assembled to help her down. As she slid off the roof, the remains of her clothing caught on a nail. Her husband made rather light of the episode next day: perhaps he did not know what had really happened. One evening the Governor, Cameron (not noted for his sense of humour), attended a Club dance and his large car with its Union Jack flying on the bonnet, was left outside in the car porch. When the time came for him to leave, the A.D.C. flung open the rear door for H.E. and as he did so a subaltern and a married lady slipped out on the other side. Some of these apparently mentally deficient subalterns ended as excellent major generals.

After a few years the club was given up and a fine new building was built on the race course, excellent in every way, with a beautiful dance room, bar and snooker room. In the dry weather it was good to sit outside, as in the other Northern stations, round braziers under the brilliant stars: the night air could be crisp.

The Secretariat occupied the upper floor of a red-brick building, at one end of which were two great curving flights of steps, with bulbous balustrades, joining at the top. This staircase must have been planned as the centre-piece of a great hollow square of office blocks, but was seldom used. We all used a simple but obscure stairway set in a dark corner at the other end of the building, to the irritation of the Secretary (Northern Provinces) whose office was by the stair-head. The offices were a succession of simple rooms, as in Lagos, with wide and shady verandahs. There were doors on each side so that either verandah could be used. The furniture was austere and unchanging with the years. The bare wood floors did not have the high polish of the Lagos office – it would not have lasted in the grim dryness of half the Northern year.

I was posted to the Lands and Mines Section, which we who served in it said in our simple way was the training ground of the promising. Many who passed through it did indeed prosper in the Service. This office was on the ground floor beneath the Secretary's office. Beyond us was the Treasury officer and his staff. Crown Counsel had his 'chambers' in a tiny annexe to his own bungalow crammed with seldom-used law-books. The police were further along the road by their lines and the magistrates' court. Works eventually came near the Mines section. The Medical headquarters for the North was housed in a bungalow nearby.

I was bemused by the mass of completely new, unaccustomed and then unintelligible matter thrown at me in the Mines Section. I joined there a very senior man, H.B. James, but he knew little more. This Section dealt with all mining titles and the titles under which land was held by 'non-natives'. (Foreigners were allowed to hold land in the North under a Certificate of Occupancy and the first application for this title had to be made to the Administration Officer in the bush. He sent it into Kaduna or Jos for processing. The issue of Title was under the hand of the Lieutenant-Governor.) Much of this work was legal and in every official action we *had to be right*: we could not afford to be wrong, dealing with matters involving large private investments. The whole thing was fascinating and developed the mind in the most surprising way. James suddenly went on urgent leave with glaucoma, and in his place A.E. Vere Walwyn came in from Kano. We saw that something had to be done to simplify the difficulties surrounding our work. So he and I set ourselves to work out a pamphlet which would help our colleagues in the bush as well as our successors in the office on the land questions. At the same time we also wrote a guide to mining procedure. These aimed to set out the law in simple terms and showed how applications for titles should be dealt with. Thus we cleared our own minds, and guided others in their remote stations who had no one they could turn to for advice. Later the idea was developed, and I wrote quite a large book called the *Office Guide* which gave the procedure for all the routines that people in the bush could be asked to do – such as issuing licences for arms of precision.

Captain W.S.E. Warren, formerly of the Gurkhas, made a brief appearance in the Mines Section. He was an inventor of ingenious gadgets, one of which was a wooden structure to ensure that the messengers put incoming files *behind* those waiting their turn for action, rather than on top of them. He felt rather under a cloud at one time, so he took the statistics for the week and announced that an average of 173 files had been handled by him each day – which caused not a little surprise.

As the Secretariat was small, its staff could be of good quality: we had the whole of the Northern service to choose from, and they were themselves a picked service. The final result was naturally good. We did, however, have some oddities. Frank Belmar, for example, had served all his career in the same office doing the same financial routine. He had never been in a Province and indeed had rarely visited one. Then there was J.B. Welman, an ingenious and very able man, with the siege of Kut el Amara (in Mesopotamia) always at the back of his mind. He never really recovered from his badly wounded arm and the horrors of the long march into captivity under the Turks. He was a valued contributor to *Blackwoods's*, a searing wit and he was not above private feuds, which we followed with breathless interest from day to day.

Vere Walwyn himself (he finished his service as an outstanding Secretary of the Northern Provinces) was also not without his eccentricities. While he was with me in the Mines Section the office hours were changed so that breakfast was half an hour later — we always worked for two hours before breakfast. Walwyn had objected so much to the new hours that he made his cook come over to the office with a frying pan — he already had a primus stove there — and prepare bacon and eggs on the spot. The Secretary, Gordon Lethem, was striding up and down in his office just overhead singing *Onward Christian Soldiers* as was his wont when dealing with a problem. He smelled the delicious aroma rising through the floor boards and came down in fury, to be courteously offered a plate of bacon and eggs. He never ate bacon, he said, and strode away.

There was another officer who always took a file with him when he walked round the office — 'just', he said, 'in case someone asks me what I am doing.' That was an office in which no one was unfriendly or ever questioned another's motives or movements. Strangely, he finished up in prison on what always seemed to us an incredible charge. I think of him when I remember finding the important and 'difficult' files of his that had been hidden for months under a great pile of loose maps on a map cabinet. Another man had the quaint habit of hiding such files behind little-used legal volumes — his career too ended unhappily.

In the time of the very able Sir William Gowers as Lieutenant-Governor — just before he went off to Uganda as Governor — a new piece of office equipment arrived. An Assistant Secretary sent one up to Government House with a note, 'His Honour might be interested in this', adding recklessly, 'It is quite foolproof.' The answer was swift: 'Would you please say what it is *for*, and refrain from further comments on my mental capacity.'

Once at a dinner party at Government House the wife of Gordon Lethem, (then acting Lieutenant-Governor) was heard to say across the table in rolling Scots: 'Gordon, you're talking to the poor girl like a minute.' He had the Scots' habit of rather pompous utterance. Later, as Governor of British Guiana, he had a town named after him, which must have gratified him not a little, for no one could claim that he was modest. I once heard him describe himself as 'a man of no mean calibre' – a phrase which passed rapidly in Nigerian legend. When he retired he bought an estate in the Scottish Lowlands and his wife used to say 'Gordon is a little bored these days as he has nothing to administer but a thousand black-faced sheep and they are not amenable to reorganisation.' Lethem created a minor sensation one day. His private secretary – Bobby Alford, who ended his career as Governor of St. Helena – entered his office in the old wooden Government House, to find a chit in Lethem's bold writing, reading 'Private Secretary: kindly see that the sideboard is dusted without delay.' It filled a foolscap sheet.

There were plenty of people of our own age and we made many friendships which lasted throughout our service. Most of them had been in the armed services and we had much in common. Next door in a similar house was an auditor called Cusack, an Irishman with a charming black-haired Irish wife. There was only a strand or so of wire between us, so we saw a lot of them. Then in the way the Audit had, they went off to Nyasaland and we never saw them again. Walwyn, newly married, and his wife were just along the road.

At that time Kaduna was accessible only by rail. There was a rough road for about 20 miles to the south-east that ended at a village called Kagoro in some fine granite hills. Kagoro had a rest house, and when we had cars we would go there for picnics on Sundays. In that first tour we had no car and I got about by motor-bike. To the north 10 miles of road ran to Rigachikun, the first station out on the main line. This was a full standard Public Works road and was the first section of the roads to Zaria and to Jos, completed much later.

In 1928 we came to the end of our first tour and a half in Kaduna. The learning process was still going on and the student had made some progress, indeed perhaps reasonable progress. The next tour found us in Bauchi.

IV. Bauchi Province

Bauchi town was the headquarters of the Province of that name, 80 miles by road from Jos and 2,000 feet below it. The town has low hills round it, isolated granite rocks, sometimes called *inselbergs*. It is flat when you get to the Government station, and used to be swampy in the rains. An established station, it was attractive to drive into, between the well-kept houses and compounds. There were many fine 'locust trees', with the pretty 'harnessed antelope' grazing at will among them.

The old station was all mud-housing, except for a deplorable house built by the Public Works as a Residency. It was two-storeyed and rather narrow, for like so many other government works it had never been finished: completely out of place, it looked just like an English boat-house. The Provincial Office was a much pleasanter building, with a wide verandah and great locust trees about it. I was given an office upstairs with a polished wooden floor and well-used furniture.

Bauchi was 'bush', and yet not so woebegone as Kabba. It was a true 'Northern' Province with several real Emirs and all their trappings. Most of it, however, was not Hausa, and the Hausas themselves looked down on it as 'pagan' country. So it was, although there was more than a sprinkling of Islam: Bauchi in fact means 'slavery'. In the 1926 'reorganisation' Bauchi Province had lost Jos and Pankshin and had received three small emirates round Azare, which now seemed even more cut off than when they belonged to Kano. They made Bauchi a 'big' Province of about 25,000 square miles.

Going to Bauchi was one of my mistakes. I found that whenever you 'wangled' something, that is to say when it did not come to you in the ordinary way, it tended to turn sour. I had plotted when I was in the Mines Section in Kaduna to get out and do something special in the bush, and this was it. We were never really happy in Bauchi.

The official reason for my posting was to set up a section of the Mines Office there. In the Kaduna Lands and Mines Section of the Secretariat we had noticed that there was waste of time and delaying correspondence in preparing mine titles. We thought that if powers could be delegated to the Residents of the Plateau and Bauchi Provinces there would be a saving of time and what was pompously called an 'expedition of government business'. To some extent this happened: we then carried out locally all the work of preparation up to actual signature by the Lieutenant-Governor.

The greater part of the tin mines were in the Plateau Province, but there were also many on the western borders of Bauchi, as well as a few on the other side of that Province. There was ample justification for an office in Jos but less for one in Bauchi. What made it attractive for me was that the Bauchi mines were in the glorious hilly country where the Plateau breaks down into the Zaria plains.

Towards the end of 1928, I arrived there ahead of my wife. This was just as well, since they were short of houses and, being alone, I did not mind camping in the rest house, a good mud building but rather on the edge of the station.

The D.O. Bauchi Division was Captain E.S. Walsh, who had a gift for building. He planned and built a number of excellent mud-and-thatch houses, and had also finished off the road to Bornu, to the north-east. The most ingenious of his many contributions to progress was the 'drive-through' garage: very simple, just two parallel mud walls and a thatch roof on extra-strong A-frames so that it would not spread out under the weight of wet grass. There was no need for doors. You just drove in and, to get out, went straight out again the other side, with no backing – wife-proof, it was called.

There was a strange Somerset Maugham twist to my arrival. The usual practice was to spend a couple of nights in Jos, the railhead. I found that my Resident, A.C. Francis, was very sick in hospital there. He died that night, so the next day I attended the funeral of my own Resident, whom I had never met, before I reached his Province. That was not all, for he was the son of the headmaster of my school. The gentle C.A. Woodhouse became Resident soon afterwards, to be succeeded by H.H. Middleton, a very tough, efficient officer.

There were seven white people in the station when I arrived. All of them played bridge and I did not. They had an arrangement of going round each others' houses to drinks, and I was told when it was 'my day'. I did not care for this very much but I could get out of it by going on tour. When Dorothy came out, there was one other white woman in the station, Walsh's wife, who did not speak to her for ten days after her arrival. She was very pretty in a 'chocolate box' way, and did not welcome even unintentional competition from other young ladies.

Mrs Walsh had gained fame in the North in her first tour by her maternal indiscretion. At that time it was not permitted for government wives to give birth to children in Nigeria, because of the climate and service difficulties, but this lady was determined to do so. She kept her pregnancy very secret and in the end even the doctor was taken by surprise. The story was that the baby was delivered on the doctor's breakfast table. There was only a tiny African hospital in Bauchi and no nursing suster, and the M.O. had to do all the work: he was not pleased. She was sent home as soon as she could move.

There were two tennis courts in Bauchi station, and the tennis was of high quality: two of the men, Walsh and Lawrence, played for

Nigeria in inter-colonial matches. Dorothy's standard was high enough to give them a good game and sometimes take a set off them. I did not compete, although I practised a lot, and was at times allowed in to play with the others.

Every compound had its own well, and at one newish house there was difficulty over siting it. Several attempts had been made by the Works people without success, when they sent for a local expert. A ragged old man appeared one afternoon and had a good look round. He was, of course, limited by the extent of the compound. Then he stopped and said, 'Dig here.' They dug and behold there was ample water. He had no twigs, rods or other gadgets.

We were, however, advanced in some things. For example, in 1928 we had telephones in most Government stations, even if there were only two or three in each. Only important people had them in their houses; there were no 'subscribers' in the sense that anyone paid for the service, which was far from good. There were manually-worked exchanges of sixteen or twenty numbers and the 'subscriber' had a 'coffee-mill' type of phone which took a good deal of manual effort to activate. The exchange was manned by an amiable African who was not immune from confusion, and sometimes the strongest were reduced to gibbering impotence. There were no 'trunk' telephones between towns; it was many years before they arrived.

The telegraph, however, connected almost all the Government stations, and it was possible to get messages through quite quickly, though not always practicable to do so. The line ran on steel poles, usually along the main roads, but often went off on long chords through the bush. The lines were patrolled day and night by devoted and hopelessly underpaid men who were prepared for any emergency: they lived a hard life and, like St. Paul, strove with beasts. They were not isolated, however, for they carried little sets which could easily be hung over the line to enable them to speak with the nearest post-office.

Lugard, in the early years, used the telegraph service like a telephone, and would summon an unfortunate Resident to attend at his headquarters post-office and stand by the instrument answering Lugard's questions as best he could. I have seen the transcripts of some of these conversations, which could run to two sheets of foolscap.

Once I had settled into my new office it was obvious that there would not be a great deal to do, so I helped the D.O. Bauchi with his touring. On his behalf I set out on the trail of a murderer somewhere north of Jos — where the Bauchi border ran only about 10 miles from the town. I followed him on foot for about 60 miles right up the boundary with Zaria, at which point he disappeared in the direction of Zaria city. At the same time I visited the mining camps on the route. One of these, a French camp, was so dirty that even the least clean of my servants felt moved to do some sweeping. He showed prescience, for all the four white men in it died within a few months.

As I had plenty of time I went up the road to Bornu, to us as romantic as the road to Samarkand. It runs north-east from Bauchi and I was to superintend the surfacing of the last part by the border, a section recently completed by Walsh. The Bornu section had been built some time before by Pierre de Putron when D.O. Bornu.*

Some forty miles out from Bauchi, one crosses the last bridge, there being none in all the remaining 245 miles; and 56 miles out from Bauchi, there is a large elephant-shaped rock by the roadside which is the last rock or stone to be seen by those going north along this great road. Further on there is no local word for stone: the nearest is that for a hard sun-dried brick. The elementary schools kept pieces of quite ordinary stone in glass fronted cupboards as samples.

In most of the North of Nigeria there is a fine form of red gravel known as laterite: easily dug up, it spread well, and once it had been rained on and rolled it made an excellent hard surface, for our light traffic. The Bornu laterite was not of this standard, indeed I doubt whether it was laterite at all. All it did after rain ws to produce mud into which wheels sank easily and disastrously. I spent weeks on the job at various times and discovered that the so-called road drainage often actually ran in the wrong direction. The ground was so level that you could only tell that the slope was wrong by using a professional level: even then there was nowhere for the surface water to drain away. So we dug deep sumps and hoped that they would keep some of the water off the road. I stayed in the numerous rest houses on this road, one every ten miles, built in the old days of trekking up by horse.

When my wife came out we bought our first car, a second-hand open Morris two-seater, for £60. In it we could get to Jos (80 miles away) in two and a half hours, sometimes a little less. One day we came round a corner among the rocks that then fringed the road, to find a huge leopard asleep in the sun, lying full length across the road. We hooted, and it rose languidly and wandered off into the bush. The car only had a canvas folding roof and no side windows.

Many years later a pet leopard broke loose in Jos and ran up a street full of people, who vanished at remarkable speed. It was chased by its owner (a labour officer, who later became head of the Civil Service) and a couple of policemen. Ahead was a granite outcrop with no

*This well-known character achieved distinction, after his retirement, as a *Jurat* of Jersey during the German occupation.

houses on it, and here the leopard took refuge under a huge slab, round which a powerfully-armed force collected. When the leopard was scared out from his hiding place he jumped on to, and then held down, a white police cadet. No one could shoot for fear of injuring the young man. Finally, an American missionary pulled the leopard off with his bare hands, and the animal was shot. The police cadet escaped with a torn ear.

One morning outside Bauchi, an ancient man came to the rest house where we were camping, and unrolled a great leopard skin, ten feet long from nose to tail. He said it was a present for me. I offered him money in exchange but he would not take it. He said, 'I don't think you understand the position. You see,' he explained, 'this leopard was my enemy, it stole my chickens and my goats. I lay in wait for it with my sons and when it came I speared it. You see, I hated it, so I am not going to take a penny.'

So much for leopards.

When my wife arrived were were given a house and moved out of the rest house. It was different from any other in Bauchi, being built on a high plinth to clear a ridge of stones. You entered it through an arch with double doors, and ahead was a huge mud fireplace. There was no normal ceiling and the apex of the thatched roof must have been thirty feet above the floor. On the left was the dining room, which was even larger and had a semi-circular end. The walls of the house were four feet thick at the base, tapering to about fifteen inches at the top. The bedroom was as vast as the dining room, and looked rather ridiculous with plain camp furniture and rough tables. In its doorway was a subterranean nest of driver ants – which, fortunately, seldom worried us. Only once, on tour and stopping in a remote rest house, did we get mixed up with a real column of 'drivers'. The column came on to the verandah – as is well known, they will strip small animals to the bone in quite a short time, and are therefore given a wide berth by everyone. The boys put down wood-ash round the house and especially in their path: this was the standard protection, but it didn't work. They then sent off to the village for help. An old man, with a cunning eye and in dirty rags, came up. He had a matchet in his hand and with its point he drew a line in the earth right round the house. The ants baulked at the line and, even stranger, those that were already within its perimeter, crossed outside it again. We were not troubled inside the house at all. It took them a day to pass by.

To go back to Bauchi, the trouble about the bedroom was not the ants but the snakes. Snakes were commoner there than in other places. One afternoon I was reading from a Hausa book to a Mallam (scribe) sitting on the floor facing me. I was in a deck chair and as I read I dropped my pencil. Out of the corner of my eye I thought I could see it, and put down my hand to pick it up: the Mallam gasped, and I looked down to see that I was about to pick up a tiny deadly black snake.

The bathroom, next to the bedroom, was a walled-off area of the verandah with the rafters overhead. In the rafters lived a large snake of the mamba family. When the boys brought in the bath water, boiled up in big kerosene tins, the first thing they did was to see if the snake was in its usual place: if so, all was well, if not it had to be located. After the lights were out and we were going to sleep, the snake would climb on to the top of the wall and chase rats: you could hear the patter of dried mud falling. Sometimes it came down to the floor and went hunting. It never did any harm to us.

I learned a lot about Native Adminsitration, for this was the first time I was concerned with a large-sized one. Bauchi then had a revenue of about £25,000 a year: the Kabba N.A.s had no more than £3,000 or £4,000. Bauchi was able to spread itself in many directions. I have already mentioned the roads Walsh built – they were paid for out of N.A. funds. The N.A. had an excellent workshop, capable of repairing their own motor vehicles and maintaining and constructing their own buildings. They had two first-class schools, apart from primary ones. One was a Middle School (where the future Prime Minister of the Federation, Abubakar Tafawa Balewa, was then a pupil). The other was a Crafts School where high skills were taught. Both were under British supervision but their staffs were entirely local.

The Emir was an intelligent man and active in his Emirate; his council were mostly good too. In the Province were five other N.A.s which, though smaller, were good and efficient — from the British point of view. Whether they were equally so from local points of view was another matter and one on which I never had a firm opinion. Most of us always hoped that they were and had it constantly at the back of our minds.

Bauchi town, although surrounded by a wall with pillared openings where the gates had been, was not an old town, like Kano or Katsina, and was considered rather bogus by the true Hausas in their great walled cities with standing gates and guard houses. It had been founded by a Fulani called Yakubu in the Fulani wars (c. 1810), and on old maps you will see the name Jakoba instead of Bauchi. The wide streets and squares in the town were kept in good trim by gangs of prisoners. There were fine trees, closely protected by the ruler: no one dared fell one and all were encouraged to plant more.

I had by now passed the first Hausa language examination which was necessary, together with a knowledge of the laws and of government General Orders, for 'confirmation' in my appointment. I now thought I would try the Higher Standard Examination in Hausa – this was really difficult and meant to be so. In the written paper I was hopelessly sunk trying to translate a word '*kuluba*' which I unfortunately confused with '*koluba*' (bottle) in one of the common fables about animals beloved by examiners. The first word meant a smooth-skinned, steamlined lizard. 'What the bottle said to the spider', which I wrote, seemed to make little sense, and I was rightly conscious of impending rejection. In the oral exam they unkindly asked questions in Hausa about various parts that made up saddlery and about the maintenance of the horse. In that most horsy country I never owned one, although I would borrow one from time to time: when rehearsing ceremonial one had to be on the same level as mounted men. The examiners knew all this and were right to set such questions. I should have known these technical terms, and now took care to learn them. Another catch lay in the names for various species of groundnut.

Later I went to Kaduna for another oral exam and was tested by Gordon Lethem, a great linguist. One of the tests – the oral exam lasted for three hours – was a direct translation of a piece of English read by one of the examiners. You had to translate straight off, knowing nothing about it in advance – just as if it were a speech that had to be translated as it was being delivered. This one started abruptly: 'The garden of this mansion with its terraces and fountains and fine trees was more like a Persian paradiso than the familiar surroundings of the home of an English country gentleman.' It went on to get into some confusion over a spiral staircase. It is astonishing what you can do when you have to, for I translated it correctly.

It was the custom to have a Nigerian on the 'board' – at my examination just mentioned, it was an ex-Waziri of Sokoto. He spoke little English, but he listened hard and said at the end: 'It is clear to me that this man has never lived in a Hausa-speaking country.' Of course he was correct, although he knew nothing about me, and we had never met before.

Lethem asked me to lunch afterwards. There were just the two of us, and in his booming voice he said, 'I trust you care for onions,' and before I could answer a boy put before me an onion about five inches across, unsupported by other vegetable. The L.G. attacked his with gusto and sliced it up. He poured vinega: and oil over it and I followed suit and ate it all. There followed only bread and cheese. I was used to onions but not quite on that scale. 'Eat an onion like that', he boomed, 'and you will never get sick in this country.' He was right, and we always had a fresh salad of anything we could get hold of – sometimes indeed it was only an onion.

As I had passed the exam, I was now an accredited examiner and could put others through the hoop. I must have examined some hundreds of people.* Among my fellow-examiners was a phenomenal linguist who knew many languages and had reduced several to dictionary or grammar form, and his learners to tears. His attack on Hausa was disastrous in many ways, because from a comparatively simple language he produced something which only a linguistic acrobat could tackle. This unduly alarmed many people. There are difficulties, but it was not such a difficult language as Yoruba or Ibo, which are really 'tonal'. On the other hand, in Hausa a simple-looking word like '*kada*' can, depending on the accent and way of saying it, mean no less than seven different things including 'crocodile', 'judgment' and 'don't'.

I was sitting with this chap one day when it was his turn to tell the Nigerian farmer whom we had in to converse with the candidate what his duties were. The peasant looked at him in growing alarm (the examiner was of course speaking his own kind of Hausa and the peasant knew no other tongue but his own), and finally turned to me and said, '*Ban ji Turanci ba*' (I don't speak English).

A foreigner can get along in simple Hausa and everyone will understand, but there is a much more complicated version with genders and plurals and odd verb-formations – the language of the educated, containing a lot of Arabic. The Hausa is usually kinder than the Frenchman or the Italian and will answer in the simple form, but I once took a man to see the Emir of Kano at a formal council meeting. We were talking rather colloquially, when I invited this stranger to speak. He did so in a rather hifalutin form of Hausa. The effect was electric: the council suddenly pulled themselves together and started talking in a special and complicated way. I had to listen closely to follow it and the stranger was soon out of his depth. The Emir came to tea that Sunday and when I asked him if they had switched their method of parlance on purpose, he admitted that they had felt the stranger was showing off, and that they should put him gently in his place.

---

*I ended my service as the senior examiner in Hausa – quite unpaid.

V. Plateau Province

The country

When I was transferred to Jos in 1926 to replace the man in the Mines Section there, it was a new town. The original headquarters of the Jos Division were at Naraguta, a picturesque place at the foot of a high peak, with enough open flat space for the inevitable race course. Further down the Bauchi road was the Naraguta mine, the first opened in Nigeria. As early as 1906, tin was being washed from the Delimi River, which runs through Jos. It was still being washed in 1926. A line of traders' stores was (and still is) called 'the Beach'. Like other roads in Jos town, it was lined with jacarandas.

A light railway came puffing up the hills from the plains of Zaria and then on a further 10 miles from Jos to Bukuru, its inglorious terminus. No one could call the train (the only one on the line) fast, but there were no accidents. It is not surprising that the official running time was seventy hours for the 760½ miles from Lagos to Bukuru. The train left Zaria at 7 a.m. and panted into Bukuru about 8 p.m. – as there was no road, it was the only means of getting from Zaria to Jos. It was of 2ft. 6in. gauge (the main line was 3ft. 6in.) and the rolling stock was in proportion, looking tiny compared with the main line stock in Zaria yards. There was a first-class 'coach–sitting room' with eight swivel armchairs, screwed to the floor. The second and third classes were extremely crowded.

By the time we came to live in Jos, the final Jos–Bukuru section had been pulled up and main line tracks laid, so that Jos became the terminus of the new line from Kafanchan – the summit on this section being 4,324 feet above sea level.

In the general revision of the Provinces in the North in 1926, a new Province called Plateau was created to embrace half a million 'pagan' people, who had till then been administered rather haphazardly as part of largely Muslim Divisions. This meant the creation of a new headquarters at Jos and, with the coming of the main railway line, it was clear that a largish town would soon develop there.

For once Government used imagination and the layout was well planned from the start. Money was voted for twenty or more excellent new houses for the white staff – there were smaller ones for African staff. A fine twenty-bed hospital for senior staff, then largely European, and an African hospital – good but not big enough – were going up as centres for the health of the surrounding Provinces. The Medical Department still seemed obsessed with the primeval idea that the government Medical Officer ministered only to the

Government's African staff and not to the general public. Perhaps this was sensible in the early days of short money and shortage of doctors, but it became less tenable as the years went on. The Residency was on the same road as the hospital. Jos was studded with steep rocky outcrops rising out of thick vegetation, perhaps fifty feet or so high; they were most picturesque and the town was planned round them with skill. A broad valley containing a ravine ran through the station and went on northwards round the back of the native town.

My wife and I were given a little house across the road from the Residency, where we planted trees and tried some gardening. My office was in the excellent new Provincial Office a mile away. The office was busy and there was no getting away on tour as in Bauchi, but it was far from dull. We did a lot of 'lands' work as well as mines; the technique was similar. We could run out into the minesfield for a morning or so on duty, but rarely slept away. There were some fascinating characters on the minesfield and it surprised me to find that the leading men, the mine managers were comparatively young.

Most of the tin mining was technically 'surface'. This could be in 'scrapes' a few feet deep or great trenches cut out by draglines, with depths of 80 or 90 feet. There was practically no underground mining – although much tin was known to be below the basalt sheet, the technical difficulties in reaching it economically were great. The tin concentrate followed the lines of old and lost rivers, though it could also be 'washed' in the waters of surface streams. A lot of money was put into heavy machinery by some companies, while others with different ground got along nicely without. It was possible to make a good living simply by sitting on your verandah, paying for cigarette tins full of concentrate as they were brought in. You hoped that it all came in from your own ground.

This surface digging made a great mess: the deep mining produced huge heaps of scarlet earth which ruined the land round it. At first the miners could do what they liked, but later legislation required that the topsoil must be set aside, and that after a trench had been mined the earth must be replaced and then the topsoil, which would then be planted with some form of vegetation. Eucalyptus was good for this purpose since it grew quickly but the local people, infuriated by the mining and weary of waiting for the restoration, would come by night and tear these saplings out. Even when the saplings flourished, we reckoned that it would take almost twenty years before the ground could become good farmland again.

The pagan farmers were of course paid compensation for the disturbance, but it was not much and hardly any of it was saved. Quite large sums were distributed among families and then very often consumed in local beer; whole villages would be dead drunk for a week or so and then left with no more money. Compensation worked in other ways. Once a party of village women walked across a wooden bridge which broke under their weight; and one was killed. There was great excitement and a large sum in compensation was willingly paid. A few days later, on another bridge of the same company, a crowd of women was observed. When the observer drew nearer he saw that they were mostly old women who were being pushed on to the bridge from one end and being stopped from going off at the other end by men armed with spears. Fortunately this was a stronger bridge and did not break under the weight. So this attempt was given up.

If anyone wanted to mine for tin, he applied for a licence to give him exclusive power to prospect the area shown on the plan. Sometimes this could measure several miles each way. While he held it, no one else could prospect in that area or mine unless the right to do so had been granted before the date of the licence. Miners were supposed to make up their minds what they wanted to 'work' (i.e. to mine) and then peg a small workable area or areas as Mining Leases containing their chosen portion. On this a low rent was charged and the title ran for twenty-one years, at the end of which it could be automatically renewed for another twenty-one years. By 1954 early leases had come to an end and should have been worked out, but in practice they were still often being worked and the miner had to put up a very thorough scheme of exploitation to justify renewal.

In the 1920s fortunes were made by skilful 'pegging' in areas on the probable line of development of some company. Land so held would be sold to the company for large sums. So far so good, but in some cases officials of a big company, knowing its plans, would do this and make huge gains off their own firms. I knew some smallish firms to be cleared out by this process. In some cases they were revived, usually under another name, and the process would be repeated. One such had the impertinence to call the new firm 'Kuma', which is Hausa for 'again'.

This general scheme of leases was part of Lugard's original plan to stop strangers owning land outright. In the same way they could only hold building land in the North on Rights of Occupancy for a limited period, as a rule not more than sixty years. When either of these periods ended, any buildings or plant left on the ground automatically lapsed in the Government's favour. While all unexpropriated land in the North was Crown land, any that was occupied by a village community, including its farmland and trees and fallow, was at the disposal of the village Headman and his elders, and was not normally given to strangers.

Possibly as a result of this system, there was scarcely a permanent building on the minesfield; all houses and offices were of mud and thatch. For safety, the tin stores were mostly of corrugated iron. The miners lived in great comfort and indeed some of them in luxury. Their gardens were superb, and at the annual Plateau flower show they had splendid roses, dahlias as big as meat plates, and every kind of fruit and vegetable. The old 'camps' were deep among shady trees and with green lawns, carefully watered and trimmed.

The same could not be said of the labourers' lines. While the labourers themselves were treated well, they were not spoilt. Food was brought into their small markets at reasonable prices and there were aid posts and help for expectant mothers, and as good a water supply as could be got. But there were seldom trees: the lines were just rows of small huts, clean, tidy and regular, but not 'family'. They could have done more too with schooling, not only of the young. Some of the men stayed on for years with their companies.

Some 1,500 white people, men and women, were associated with the mines scattered over a large area, mostly on the High Plateau. There were private miners as well as the big companies. Some of them lived very isolated lives and when they came into Jos on shopping sprees they brought with them something of the old Wild West of legend. Many of them kept horses and riding was popular. The race meetings were great events, but possibly even more popular among the Africans, and people came from all over the country to attend them. The club dances on race nights were social events, and all the men wore dinner jackets. Gambling often attracted more people than the dancing: I remember seeing three or four of the most prominent men on the minesfield seated at a huge green table with piles of bank notes in front of them: they were always lucky, it seemed, but of course there were some who were not. Fortunately I discovered early in life that I could seldom gamble successfully, and so did not compete. This was well understood: they were an easy-going lot and, as they did what they liked, they thought that others should do the same.

In 1929 my salary had reached £720, and it differed from previous salaries in that it carried a 'duty pay', when in the country, of £72 p.a. – a privilege that depended on the passing of an 'efficiency' bar. We now felt that we could start a family without facing destitution. By that stage the Government could not get rid of me without criminal activities or insanity on my part. We discovered my wife's condition while we were on leave in England, and I went to Nigeria ahead of her and informed the Resident, H.H. Middleton, whom we had known in Bauchi, of the expected event – under oath of secrecy which he kept faithfully. Although against orders, my wife was determined to come out for about six months and then go home to have the baby. The Resident was scrupulously fair and said that he could not change my posting because of a reason he was unable to disclose, and as I was posted to Akwanga, to Akwanga we would go. I was faced with the same situation myself years later, when I had to make similar decisions regarding my juniors.

Wamba

The Plateau Province had five administrative Divisions, all inhabited by 'pagan' people, two – Jos and Pankshin – on the High Plateau, and three in the plains at the southern foot of the great escarpment. Of these Jema'a and Akwanga – the latter came to be called 'Southern' – were the westerly ones, with Shendam on the south; the two latter were not contiguous as a piece of Benue Province interposed itself. The climate was very different here from Jos and they were much more cut off from headquarters. Akwanga and Wamba in Southern Division were just above the 1,000-foot line, but although so far below the Plateau, the temperature was not by any means unbearably hot. Southern Division was about 40 by 50 miles with 100,000 people.

We found Akwanga a depressing place although, strangely, it inspired many white officers with a definite yearning. At one time, not long before we went there in 1930, there had been a company of the Regiment stationed there with a doctor and a policeman, as well as the D.O. and his assistant. So they must have had jolly times, as they claimed, though when questioned, they could never remember what made it jolly. The soldiers were supposed to patrol the 'unsettled district' of the Mada hills, There were very few such places even before 1925 and this was nearly the last of them. They were 'unsettled' because the local inhabitants did not like the idea of anyone else telling them how to run their lives – a common sentiment in Europe, dignified by a number of noble names, but white men in Nigeria seemed to resent people turning away from the 'benefits' of civilisation. I cannot help feeling that these people resented the Africans whom the white men brought with them more than the white men themselves.

When we arrived, Akwanga only had a mud-and-thatch office and D.O.'s house with a rest house in a great cleared space, dotted with fine trees. A derelict tennis court and the plinths of former houses were all that remained of the 'jolly' station. A concrete strong-room stood in solitary splendour. I took over from P.F. Masterton-Smith, who was building a road up the Mada hills, which I continued and completed in due course. It was not a good road – too steep in places.

However, I had been sent to this area to transfer the divisional headquarters away from Akwanga, so we did not waste much time complaining about the place.

We were somewhat limited in the choice of a site for the new station since obviously it could not be far from the P.W.D. road, and for general convenience it had to be near the little town of Wamba, where the chief of a fairly substantial tribe lived. Half a mile west of the town was a low hill standing alone, from which a fine view presented itself: being 15 miles nearer than Akwanga to the escarpment, the lofty cliffs were that much more impressive. On this small eminence my wife and I decided to set up the D.O.'s house and Divisional Office. £500 had been allocated by Government for the Government buildings and about £800 from the Native Treasury, a larger sum because there had to be a prison with a high wall around it. Apart from the view, the place was right because of its distance from the town – these towns could be very noisy on moonlit nights when everyone seemed to be out dancing. Just at the foot of the little hill was a perennial spring, which supplied water for the house and a vegetable garden, and for nearby pagan homes.

My wife went home to England about three months before the baby was due. She had been very active in walking about the Division and had no trouble. I had the whole of the dry season before me for my building operations and for the new road which I was determined to make to the North. I designed, laid out and built the new 'government station' and the N.A. buildings. I had never built houses before, except for a mistaken effort at Agbaja. Here the new house for the District Officer needed to be comfortable and large enough, and to be something that would last, in spite of being technically 'temporary'. Besides an office, a reasonable clerk's house, police lines and a mile of road were also required. For all this, as we have seen, I had £500. We had 3s 6d left at the end of it all. We were greatly helped by the fact that at just about this time Hope's steel 'casement' windows made their appearance in the canteens of the North: they could be handled by even the most simple-minded builders and were cheap: a window 5 feet wide cost about £2 complete and small ones less than £1. Hitherto we had had to make do with wooden shutters or windows that soon got consumed by ants. Fortunately there were people who had experience of building on the mining camps.

The guest house was charming with a high thatched roof and a semi-circular sitting space, following the plan in the Ikoyi bush houses. This later became my standard plan. The office was of three good rooms, with a verandah on one side, again thatched, with a cement floor. The strong room cost us a disproportionate sum, even though we did not have to pay for the excellent steel door. Due to some inscrutable rule of Government accounting, I could buy a kitchen 'range' out of the funds, but had to pay for a bath myself.

The N.A. buildings went on at the same time and were a little more complicated. Here the most difficult feature was the prison entrance. I was fortunate to have obtained two standard steel-barred cell gates. I found that if they were turned inwards I could get a double-gated effect but of course the two inside faces had to fit precisely to let the bolts slide across. It took me a whole day personally hanging them in the exact position and then wedging and strutting them so that they would not shift while the concrete set round the hinges. They were heavy and awkward to handle.

Meanwhile the road north towards Jos was progressing. In Nigeria we would put concrete crossing places in the beds of small streams, called 'Irish bridges.' These allowed the passage of motors in low water or when dry: in flood you did not attempt the crossing. Indicators alongside showed the depth of the water. This road was never particularly approved and it was some years before the P.W.D. produced their masterplan, including it – really my plan drawn large and clear. It was essential to have a road through to link up with the Plateau system as soon as possible. In direct mileage it was only about 45 miles, but the country was rough and big streams cut across the line.

The train journey to Jos was slow; there were no through carriages and you always had to wait at Gudi and change at Kafanchan, and maybe wait there a day as well. When I was alone I found a quick way to Jos but it took some planning. You drove along a little track for a few miles north east of Wamba and then got out and started to walk north. After a while the ground began to rise and before long you were following a narrow path through the little valleys and by the great granite slopes, their faces shining with running water, collecting into small cascades and then into greater streams. The path was steep but not too steep and after about three quarters of an hour the air became cooler and you reached for a pullover. Here the grass was short and, behold, the empty spaces of the Plateau lay before you with herds of great cattle and little villages nestling under the grey rocks. Another hour or so and you could see a lorry, standing out like a battleship in that expanse, sent from Jos to pick you up: a triumph of 'logistics'. You were in Jos by lunchtime. As you returned, the air grew heavier as you went down and by the time you were in the plains you wondered why you had not stayed another night as they had pressed you to do.

Some people travelled in great discomfort on the railways as they took too much baggage with them into their first-class carriage. They took strange things too. On one journey to Jos, I was having dinner with an elder statesman called G.G. Feasey whom I had known on my first tour in Lokoja. Afterwards he suggested that I should go to his cabin for a night-cap. He was travelling alone. He slid back the heavy door: one side was covered with baggage, leaving a seat for himself, and the other seat was completely occupied by an enormous lion, its head fortunately towards the window. Feasey said, 'Give Fred a shove and he'll move up.' With some trepidation I did so, and Fred pulled in his massive hindquarters and gave me room to sit down. I must admit that there was no difficulty but Fred was rather hot. 'No thieves come near us,' said his master.

We were never short of incidents in Wamba. In the low hills to the south a village head was attacked one night and was brought into me the next day with his throat cut. The local dispenser, untrained but with considerable experience, was not taken aback in the least. He sewed up the nasty wound with an old needle and in due course the man recovered, though he was always a little hoarse. He said that three men from a nearby village had attacked him. They were caught in the end and received prison sentences, which dismayed them as they would have to serve them in Jos among strangers and in a climate different from their own. They pleaded with me for a quick death, but as that could not be arranged, they had to suffer as the law directed.

In evidence at their trial two iron rings about an inch deep with little notches on one side were presented. There was string threaded through holes in the top. 'Aha,' said my staff with glee, 'leopard murderers!' There have been various outbreaks of these from time to time in West Africa. There was a famous and most destructive Leopard Society in Sierra Leone at the turn of the century, and more recently prolonged 'leopard' trouble in the south-eastern creeks of Nigeria. The attackers had worn iron claws attached to their feet and wrists and in some cases had disembowelled their victims with the claws. Our manifestation was certainly harmless so far as violent use of the iron rings was concerned, but what were they for? No one could have walked far on them and the resulting foot-print did not suggest any known animal. My people thought they were a kind of warning: if you saw that mark in the path you kept away. It made quite a sensation in official circles.

About 10 miles from Wamba was a place called Kwarra, which in Hausa means 'palm trees'. It was a show-place and we took our rare guests there. We District Officers all had our favourite places and regarded these views and sights and special native towns and markets with positive pride – more so than the local population. In this case the narrow road entered a pagan village of tiny but exquisitely finished mud huts with the finest of roofs, embowered in palms and great trees and rocks. It took a couple of turns and then suddenly came out into the rest house compound, on a low knoll. Beyond the little house, the ground fell sharply two or three hundred feet then steeply to the Ferin Ruwa river about half a mile away. Beyond, the low rolling hills covered with palm trees swelled upwards until the steepness rose to 3,000 feet above the valley, to the pale green of the thin plateau grass on the summits. To the left the great falls were seen as they were, twelve hundred feet of falling water.

Like the people of the High Plateau, all inhabitants of this Division (save for strangers) were naked, with no false modesty. They were the most moral people in the North and adultery among the married was very rare. There was hardly any venereal disease among them, though there was plenty among other peoples. The women wore various hangings over their private parts: bunches of leaves or even single leaves were common. Some hung six large iron rings in front of themselves if they were virgins, and the married wore nine. The varieties were many, and some wore nothing at all. A single strand of string or leather was very common – this was a token of 'modesty' which no one ventured to touch. The men all wore either woven grass tubes or goats' horns to enclose their organs. The tips of the horns were then attached by strings to their waist-belts. These coverings were not worn for modesty but purely for the protection of valuable property.

Some went in for remarkable facial embellishments. Plugs and ornaments through the ears are, of course, common, but decorative plugs in the sides of the nostrils, in many colours and materials and indeed of various sizes are less so. A further stage was plugging the upper and lower lips: this again was decorative but a precise fit was a matter of practical importance. On one trek we had some women among the carriers, a rather unusual occurrence. During a halt we heard a lot of laughter and derision from a group of the men. I went over and found a pretty girl-carrier in their midst, naked save for some leaves; the men were not interested in that but they were watching her drinking out of a small bowl. It must have started as a bet, as she had taken out her lip plugs, and of course the water was coming through the two holes in her lips. She gave it up in a paroxysm of giggles.

Another group of people (all men) seemed to enjoy wearing porcupine quills through holes in their ears and noses and lips and the criss-cross of black and white quills was enough to strike terror into enemy hearts. All these people were good-natured and friendly to us and to each other, and even to African strangers, who sneered at their simple ways and their nakedness. There were few cases of homicide among them, even after the harvest, when whole villages were drunk on corn wine for days at a time, down to the tiny toddlers. They were surprised that they had no corn in their bins in the months before the next harvest. But they could get all the work they wanted on the mines, although it did not attract them.

These people were not litigious like those in Kabba, but my ordinary routine continued and there was quite a lot to do. Official correspondence kept a steady level, with a rise in pressure at the months' end.

I have said that homicide was rare but it did happen. One day we were looking for a murderer who was finally tracked down in a village called Ayashin, in the northern edge of the Division. It was a strange place, one that never had anything to do with its neighbours or with anyone else. They did not even pay taxes. The neighbours were rather envious, but no one troubled to collect it. The police methodically laid flat the murderer's house, like Nebuchadnezzar – a more civilised process than burning the whole village, as some used to do. The destruction took a long time, as the thin mud walls were very tough. The inhabitants retreated up the mountain side, and a rather one-sided conversation developed between my staff and the villagers, who did not reply very audibly. We wanted them to know that the road was being built near them and they could, if they liked, come and work on it and get paid for it with real money. There was stunned silence on the hillside. Later, when the road had reached this point I drove my little car to the road-head near the village. My messenger said, 'Those are Ayashin people working over there.' When I stopped the car they all rushed into the bush alongside the road and made ready to climb handy trees. They had never seen a car before. When confidence had been established they told me that they were getting real money for the first time in their lives.

Years later I came along the same road and stopped just below the village. A very well-dressed man was standing by the road: he greeted me. I asked if he was an Ayashin man. He said he was, but he worked in Jos. He had come down to see his family, only an hour's drive in a lorry. *Tempora mutantur et nos mutamur in illis.*

While all this was going on in Nigeria, my wife was in London and 13 March 1930 produced, without trouble, a beautiful daughter with the name of Verity Ann. Things being as they were I did not hear of this event for four days, although I was careful not to go away from Wamba. She confided the infant to her mother and a wonderful Nanny (who remained with us for forty years), and came out again to

Wamba just before the rains.

About a month before she came back two unusual things happened. The first was a great locust assault from the north-east. A swarm of locusts is a black cloud, thin but long, in the distance. You watch its course and wonder where it will land – it wheels like a vast flock of starlings. We were saved to some extent as the farms were newly planted so that from the air the young shoots did not look as good as the new leaves of the trees alongside. Nevertheless the swarms did immense damage. They are able to strip a tree the size of an apple tree in an hour. The noise they make in the process is audible from quite a distance and their droppings create a sweet smell in the air.

This scourge was not unexpected and in our files we had instructions on what action to take with life-histories of the locusts and the best methods of dealing with them. The country must rise as one man and must be organised to head off the swarms, dig the trenches, fill them in and see that they remain filled in. It is almost impossible to cope with locusts on the wing. We found that they were seldom tempted by the poison (arsenic) bait lavishly spread for them, often in the wrong place. But as hoppers, they are very vulnerable. The eggs are laid in the ground and the tiny hoppers emerge, hundreds from each laying. Then they grow fast and in two or three days are an inch long and capable of marching. This they do in vast formations, moving on a broad front sometimes hundreds of yards wide. They grow to sexual maturity in a frighteningly short time and the cycle begins again. They copulate on the wing: the female (naturally) does the work, the male lying on her in blissful penetration. What a life.

Intelligent people are posted as scouts watching likely places for a hatch. On their reports groups of men and women are sent from the villages to the spot, often deep in the bush. There they form into lines and dig trenches, ideally about eighteen inches deep, across the line of the hoppers' advance. Driven into the trenches the hoppers soon almost fill them. Then the earth is hastily shovelled over them and they are left. Unfortunately locusts are good to eat – like shrimps, we were told – and unscrupulous persons were actually found tending and keeping them for the table! Others opened the trenches in their greed and large numbers would escape.

In the end we destroyed in our area alone thousands of acres of hoppers. The great battle was over. It had taken about three weeks and the entire country had been at a standstill. Office-bound officials found themselves in the most unlikely places directing small battles. We even had a 'locust train' drafted into duty on the railway.

Touring

The second incident was a tragic one. People who have lived in the backward parts of Africa will speak of the 'bush telegraph'. At the time I am mentioning, a friend of ours, Charles Barlow, D.O. of Shendam was out in the foothills of the Plateau attending to a village that was unenthusiastic about collecting and paying its tax. Although this was the 'next' Division to us, a piece of Benue Province came between us. The two Divisional headquarters were about 80 miles apart, and there was no road between them. The tangled mass of foothills and the big rivers along the southern escarpment of the Plateau made travel difficult and the people were not friendly to each other. While Barlow was moving with a small police escort to this particular village, two days away from his headquarters at Shendam, his party was greeted with a shower of stones. He was hit on the forehead and died instantly. The devoted police got his body away with difficulty and sent the news to Jos – 170 miles from Shendam. I heard the news of his death early the next day in Wamba, but I do not know how this was done. Certainly no one, not even a relay of runners, could have carried the message in that time. Just possible, such a message could have been shouted from village to village, but I doubt whether they are so conveniently arranged as to make that feasible. A further obstacle was that there were several different languages spoken in the intervening area. Anyway, the message came through and was accurate. The official telegram from Jos did not reach me till a couple of days later.

I got myself mixed up in another affair, and might have been the victim. While I was building Wamba I received the news that a certain village I had never visited, only about 12 miles away to the south, had refused to re-thatch the local rest house which had been burnt. The villagers made frivolous excuses about a lack of palm-leaf stems and the like. This was serious because, as we have already seen, it was one of the recognised functions of a village head of a certain standing to keep his rest house in a good state even if it was seldom visited. The Village Head was a paid official with responsibilities of which this was one; further he was repaid anything he had to spend on materials and often made a profit. The villagers in many cases did the work themselves; it was the dry season and they had little to do. A refusal to repair was therefore not to be ignored.

I went off personally with my loads and boys to visit the place. We had to cross a substantial river in unseaworthy canoes, an added hazard. When I arrived, a nasty feeling was evident. The Village Head reluctantly appeared but did not greet me correctly – the

Chief's man was normally polite. The rest house was certainly burnt out and my people said he had done it himself. Not far away was a single largish hut, possibly a court house, and there I established myself. Unfortunately it was surrounded by hundreds, probably thousands, of bundles of thatching grass, each a headload. My boys moved as much as they could but the residue was still dangerously near us.

I made the (almost) fatal mistake of not bringing any of my own police with me: normally this was routine, but somehow I had not thought it necessary. I sent a N.A. policeman to the village head with a message about the grass and he did not reappear. The same happened to the second. The afternoon was getting on and I sent the remaining man back to Wamba telling the clerk to send a police detachment at once.

During dinner – we always had three-course dinners wherever we might be and in whatever conditions – a messenger appeared out of the dark. He said that things in the village were unfriendly and indeed there was an unusual air of hostility. Further, the Chief had announced in public that he was coming in the night to cut all our throats and then set fire to the thatching grass so that it would all look accidental. I had with me a sporting rifle, a shotgun and a revolver. We made a good fire and the boys sat with the weapons to share the watch with me.

Just before dawn we heard the purposeful rustle of sandled feet and in a few moments six armed policemen and a corporal halted in the firelight. They had done an excellent march in unknown country in the dark including the river crossing. I could not have been more pleased to see them. We all had a few hours sleep and then went into the village, where we released the two N.A. police and arrested the Village Head, along with his number-two for good measure. He had run himself into a whole variety of criminal charges which, if pressed, would have kept him locked up for a long time. We marched them off later in the day. The elders cheerfully said they would repair the roof if we could let them have the necessary poles – which we did.

The Chief at Wamba was horrified at the whole episode and swore vengeance. But I felt that the village and its Head had already been sufficiently frightened. The trial was deliberately dragged out for a couple of months in the Native Court, then he was fined, not too heavily and sent back home. The man had committed crimes through stupidity and a simple lesson was all that was needed.

While I was away on tour at this time, there occurred the final act of a real human tragedy. This was the time of the Great Slump, and the minesfield reduced its labour force, black and white. Most of the whites went home but a few stayed to see what they could pick up. One of these was an accountant from Base Metals, quite a big company. He came down to Gudi and I found him living there in a poor hut. He had acquired a motor-lorry and was proposing to run it between Nasarawa and Wamba and the mining camp beyond. There was little I could do to help but I put a few jobs in his way. His lorry was not very reliable but to repair it thoroughly he would have had to send it by train to Jos or Enugu, which would have cost him a lot, as well as depriving him of daily income. The Government was being economical at the time.

When I came back from a fortnight's trek I heard to my dismay that he had died of malaria, not an easy thing to die of in those times even in Gudi. I might have saved him by sending him to Jos hospital, but he kept to himself and unless I had seen him by chance I should not have realised how ill he was. In fact he had died of malnutrition. The nearest M.O. was at Lafia and came too late.

I wound up his affairs, a sad task, and read his letters. His widow was desperately badly off in England and pinned great hopes on the sale of the lorry, but it was really only scrap and even though we inflated the price there was little enough to send home. When I told the Company about it, I believe they sent some real help. The saddest and grimmest part of the affair was that among his letters – he had not had the strength or the will to open them – was one from his firm saying that things were improving and that he could have his job back if he wished to take it.

Among the miners sacked at this time was a man unknown but of great cunning. He owed John Holt say £29.15s. He paid them exactly half of his debt and was given a receipt. When he boarded the mail-boat at Lagos the Holts man came on board and said 'Excuse me, sir, but I think you owe us a few pounds, £14.17s.6d. in fact! The miner said he had paid that in Jos and produced the receipt. The Holts man apologised and gave him a drink.

I went up to Kafanchan to meet Dorothy and take her off the boat train. She looked cool and elegant in pale mauve. We travelled to Gudi by a providentially handy train and reached Wamba late in the evening. We could see the single light of a lamp twinkling across the valley from our new house. All was ready: the paint was new, the walls were distempered, and there was running water in the bathroom from a tank on stilts outside.

However when we got there we found another new addition to the family. For some time we had had an assortment of 'steward boys', none of them satisfactory. Finally the cook suggested a young member of his own family who might be trained. All our previous stewards had served with other white men and reflected many of their vices. This one at least would be new, and now here he was. His real name, we discovered years later, was Matthew, but he was always called Yaro, which is simply Hausa for 'boy' or 'youth'. He knew no word of English but was very willing and of shining intelligence. He stayed with us for thirty years.

I had one Hausa boy among my 'Creek' (or Niger Delta) people – they were Ijaws from Patani – partly to give dignity to the proceedings when I entertained and partly to help me with my Hausa. He was, he said, a Katsina man: they speak by far the best Hausa and I was determined to take my Higher Standard. One evening a son was born to him and I 'lent' £2 for a naming ceremony. Forty years later, when in Nigeria to write a book about the Civil War, I asked to be taken to the great new Kainji dam on the Niger River. The highly knowledge-able Secretary of the Niger Dam Authority picked me up in Ikoyi (Lagos) to drive me to the airport for our 280-mile flight in his private plane to the dam site. The first thing he said to me was, 'My father always told me, if I were ever to meet you, to thank you for lending him £2 for my naming ceremony.'

In Wamba we still had no school or any kind of dispensary. On the High Plateau these were supplied by missions; there were some in Shendam, but not on our side of the hills. The area had long been considered unsafe and until not long before we had had the Mada Patrol. There was no forest reserve, although it was seriously needed, for trees were being felled, without heed for the future. Nor did any agricultural or veterinary man come our way. We suffered the same difficulties as in Kabba, the isolation not quite so severe, but real nonetheless – and the fear of sickness or injury. It was a little better here, with the telegraph at Gudi, but every visitor had to come down by train until the road was opened to the North. We still had no refrigerator or radio; our winding gramophone supplied us with music on demand.

We were happy in Wamba. It was such an attractive place and there were so many walks to take. We always walked five miles every evening, a habit we kept until the very end of our service. It certainly preserved our health. It is sad that no tourist can ever catch the charm we found in the place and its people: they are unlikely ever to find the valleys and hill paths that we knew so well.

By this time I had been in Nigeria nearly ten years, with quite a varied experience but had not yet served in any great Emirate, which was essen-tial for advancement in the Service. Apart from Bauchi, I had been posted to primitive areas, and my Bauchi experience was not all that valuable.

We went home for a winter leave, and I saw our beautiful baby for the first time when she was four months old.

Murder

Some splendid rivers crossed the Southern Division, and over the millennia had carved through the edge of the high plateau, leaving in one place a great flat-topped hill, standing alone and impressive in the plain.

This solitary massif was inhabited by people singularly ungracious compared with those in the plains. This is what I thought then, but may be this attitude expressed a deep resentment at interference with their ancient liberties, which included being captured as slaves by the Fulani raiders. Their neighbours did not like them and called them *Mada*. I never found the real meaning of that word or even in which of the several possible languages it originated, but they didn't like it, so it must have been uncomplimentary. They themselves pressed for the name of *Eggon*: 'The Men'.

Many sharp climbs led to the top. The village women thought nothing of a 1,000-foot rock climb every time they went home from their foothill farms; in a severe dry season they would return blithely with a pot of water on their heads. I tried the rock climbs myself. The summit was extensive with trees, thin short grass, reed-lined rocky pools and fine farm lands; with huts tucked under the rocks. On the east side of the massif, the mountain fell steeply into the foothills, and a well-frequented trade-route ran along the foot of the drop. Those who followed it tended to move in groups for reasons which will soon become clear.

One fine clear morning fifty years ago two young Eggon men were sitting on a rock high up the hillside, watching the trade-route far below them. They saw a figure appear on a distant bend in the road. They watched carefully and could see no one with him. 'There's a Hausa', said one, 'and he's alone,' said the other. 'Come', said the first, 'let's kill him.'

They were wearing little and did not show up as they slipped down the rocky hillside. They moved fast and reached the path before the lone traveller. They hid behind a huge rock and some greenery and waited for him. He passed them oblivious of their menace. They crept out and moved up on him from behind in absolute silence. One blow on his head from a heavy stick: a great shriek and then silence.

Some days afterwards a European surveyor called Buckingham came into my office in Wamba. He was a very good-looking man, and always wore pale blue shorts – to match his eyes the ladies said. He was doing some mines surveying in a camp to the north, where there was a certain amount of tin and where mining had been going on for years. He said that one of his labourers, Musa, was missing. There was nothing unusual in a man being missing, they often left their jobs, but Buckingham was holding some savings that the man had accumulated from his pay. Musa was a good worker and doing well, and there was no reason for his continued disappearance. He had been given a short leave to the south to see some relatives who lived across the Divisional Boundary, and had not returned. I said we would do what we could to trace him, but the people he had been going to visit had never seen him, so we had a close check made along the route he must have taken. The result was negative.

Meanwhile, in a village on the edge of the Mada Hills near the scene I have described, the two young men were beginning to get worried. It was a firm belief in those parts that the ghost of anything killed would haunt the killer unless steps were taken to prevent it. There was a simple *juju* remedy to be had on application to the right person and on payment of the right fee, which would afford complete protection – it was usually hunters who wanted it. If all this was necessary for the death of a large animal, what, they wondered, must you do to protect yourself against the haunting of a dead man? The two got more and more anxious: in spite of all their bravado they had never before actually killed a human being. And so they took cautious action.

The Village Head went to the District Head, a wise and experienced man. The Village Head said that two young men had come to him asking for a 'medicine' called *lahubu*. This was a very special medicine, nowadays never asked for, but which had been much in demand in the past. They had been discreet but also frightened. And well they might be, for the medicine was only given to protect a killer from the avenging soul of his human victim. Neither of them knew of the search for the Survey labourer Musa. The District Head sent the information on to me.

I went with him on a long walk to the village of these people, sited in stupendous scenery in the glory of the hills. We searched the houses of the two young men and found nothing. My head messenger, who also was not without experience, said, 'Let us not leave before we have had a look at the grain bins.' In most of the villages of that area, and indeed of many other areas, these were built like great vases in the finest mud. They stood on three stone blocks to keep the white ants out and to hold them above the level of any flood water. They were sealed with mud domes, but in the shoulder was a hole large enough to take a man's head and shoulders, plugged with a loose mud plate.

The grain was poured into them and it would keep fresh and pure for some years. Over all was a small thatched roof that could be lifted off without difficulty.

The messenger took a small calabash and started to scoop out the grain into head-pans. After about a foot had been moved he struck lucky. There was a white Muslim skull-cap, with four pence in coppers in its folds. And on the edge of the cap was printed the name *Musa* in the neat movable type that the Survey use in their original map drawings.

At this point the younger of the two boys broke down and said that he would show us where the body was hidden. The other remained grim and scowling. I had with me a small police escort armed with rifles and bayonets. Now they realised the seriousness of the situation, they formed themselves of their own accord around the two boys and myself. We went down the hillside, not by the route the young men had followed as they ran down to the kill, but by an easier and smoother track, which even so was a quite formidable route. The police were strung out in open order.

When we reached the trade-route in the valley, we moved south for some distance and then the youth stopped. It was here, he said, that they hit the man and he fell. But there had been no blood stains or marks of struggle when the original trackers went that way some days before. The youth smiled and said they had thought of that. He knelt down and started to turn over flat granite stones – like paving stones, flat on both sides – that made the footway. The undersides bore the black marks of dried blood, not much of it but enough. We naturally had no forensic equipment and there was no point in taking samples; both boys agreed that the marks were blood and so did the experts with me. There was no need for the complicated processes of evidence.

Where was the body? We were surrounded by a patch of high trees and the road itself was hedged with thick undergrowth. The youth led us into a side drain – a natural one, for the road was not made up – and in a few moments we were clear of the thick stuff and stood in an area of great rocks, interspersed with high trees. The police tightened their grips on their rifles and checked the loading. It would have been a perfect place for an ambush and flights of poisoned arrows from the villagers, who had had ample time to get there.

However, there was no movement and we followed the youth, now tied to the Corporal with a piece of string. Not far away we climbed up a vast smooth boulder and at the top found that two other boulders joined it. Over the join was a pile of brushwood, looking as though it had fallen there years ago. The messenger dragged it away and uncovered a hole like a manhole. He looked down and said, 'There's a body.' Burning branches were thrown down and revealed a large bottle-shaped chamber, quite wide and maybe twenty feet deep. The flames showed up the figure lying on his side, his head smashed in and his mouth open. There was no point in getting the body out: all was beyond doubt.

We sealed the hole with flat stones and puddled clay and covered it once more with brushwood. And there we left Musa to sleep his last sleep in a tomb as superb as any monarch's, enclosed in the eternal granite. We all felt sad although we had not known him.

The two prisoners were charged and committed for trial by Henry Middleton, the Resident of the Province. He came specially from Jos, a rare visit to the Division and drove up into the Mada Hills where no Resident had ever been. This was in the days of the old Provincial Court and though we were all members of that Court with varying powers, he alone had the ultimate power of life and death. The case presented no difficulty – lawyers were excluded from sittings of the Provincial Court, but they could have availed nothing. Among the witnesses was a Survey draughtsman who remembered setting up the name Musa and pressing the type on the edge of the white skull cap. He had been a popular chap and there was no difficulty in recalling him, he said.

The two young men were sentenced to death and the sentence was to be carried out near the scene of the crime. This was for obvious reasons: it was essential in those days for the people concerned to see that the law had taken its course. There was no ghoulish curiosity on these occasions. In Kano at this time, where executions were by beheading by sword, some Europeans used all means to be present, including bribery of anyone who would accept it. The African population being in a more elementary stage of life, took these things in their stride, with a polite interest and a mild wonder that so much trouble was taken in ending the life of a man, who was obviously qualified for a sudden and painful death.

The finding of the Court went to the Governor for approval in Council, or rather for an expression of the exercise or non-exercise of His Majesty's clemency – a complex way of saying a simple thing. We were not a little surprised to hear that the sentence on the pleasant young man was confirmed and that the law should take its course but, owing to a legal technicality the surly accused was to be released. This kind of result merely confirmed once more in the Nigerian public their firm belief that the white men were basically mad. There was, of course, precisely the same amount of guilt between the two of them. So he was released and we awaited the Warrant with the great black seal to deal with the other.

By the time it came we were in the Rains, and the Commissioner of Police, Graham Callow (later a judge of the Nigerian High Court), and myself, the condemned man and a considerable police escort made our way into the heart of the Mada Hills and stayed the night in a rest house. The difficulty was getting a doctor to attend. You cannot execute a man without one present. We had no Medical Officer in the area; the nearest lived to the south at Lafia and had to come on the night train to Gudi. Then he was to be driven to the nearest point on the road, from which he had to walk some miles to the scene. It was a tight schedule and it seemed that something was bound to go wrong. Callow and I and this motley crew started off from the rest house at daylight to walk the twelve miles to the village. After a while it started to rain.

The police were on tenterhooks as it was their duty to get the man there and carry out the execution, and at the same time stave off any attempt at rescue. This was a very real danger. We had no idea whose side the public were on; they were non-committal and tight-lipped, and there were plenty of them, all armed. To make matters worse, the narrow paths in those parts ran between steep dry-stone walls, in many places ten feet high. In other circumstances we would have admired the ingenuity of their construction, but as things were they were merely a menace. The 'path' was just wide enough for feet in single file, the walls curving away to take bodies and loads. Many fields were divided by similar walls at right angles to the path. There could not have been worse territory. The police threw out flank guards on each side but they were out of our sight and if they had been attacked it would have been extremely difficult to concentrate the fire of the main body of police, strung out as they were in single file. All this was passing through Callow's mind, I admit I was worried too. Further, the prisoner himself had to walk with his escort in front and behind him and not on either side.

The rain became heavier as we went along. The 'path' was soon a small stream in most places, with irregular stones and small obstacles invisible below the water. The policemen were strangers and could not speak any of the local languages, and scarcely anyone at all could speak the prisoner's native tongue. It was a nightmare journey. And there was no doctor in sight.

After what seemed an interminable trek we reached the village of the two youths. Fortunately the rain now slackened off and eventually stopped. We decided in everyone's interest, specially the condemned man's, that the job should be done without delay. Callow and his Sergeant were used to these things and set about preparations briskly. I stood with wet feet and feeling definitely queasy. I had seen a great many men killed in action, but this was quite different.

He was hanged off a huge branch of an immense locust-bean tree, about thirty feet above the ground. Behind the tree the ground fell away sharply into the valley of the murder, and beyond was the magnificent vision of the Plateau escarpment. In another direction were bold rolling hills, tree-clad in every shade of green. No one could have asked for a more dramatic place for his ending. I shall not go into the technical details; they were simple and very effective. The police made it as easy as they could for the young chap and handled him as tenderly as a baby. From the time he stood under the branch to the time his neck broke was just twenty-five seconds.

The youth conducted himself with the greatest courage throughout that miserable last morning of his life. He was much more cheerful than we were. There were some hundreds of villagers in a huge circle round us, perched on every vantage-point. They were quiet and motionless. There was a low groaning sound at the last instant and that was all.

Then we waited for the doctor and had a hot breakfast as we waited. By that time my queasy feelings had disappeared and I was very hungry. I was there on the Sheriff side of my job, also as Coroner to hold the inquest. That had to be done before the body could be buried, and for that we needed the doctor. After a while he plodded in, cross and wet and tired. We had to revive him with spirits before he could proceed. He then made a little incision, found that the correct vertebra was fractured and gave evidence accordingly. I formally concluded the inquest. We then handed the body over to the relatives and took the long march back again.

Months later came a sequel. My wife had returned and we were trekking into the Mada Hills in this particular neighbourhood. As we climbed up the same steep path among the great rocks, we came round a sharp corner and found a couple of youths squatting in the shade. One of them gave an unearthly scream and rushed off across the hillside like a driven partridge. 'The murderer', said my messenger, who shouted after him that there was five shillings of his in the office safe awaiting collection. He never appeared to claim it.

VI. Kaduna: Finance and Native Affairs

After our sojourn in Jos and Wamba, I was brought back into the
Kaduna Secretariat – this time in charge, first, of 'Native Affairs', and
then of 'Finance', the legendary Belmar's hunting ground. These
were two 'Sections' of the Office, like the Lands and Mines Section,
under Assistant Secretaries. Our house, across the road from the
Secretariat, and therefore handy, but rather too near the club, had
previously been the medical office and so had an extra room and a
very wide verandah, an improvement on our previous quarters.

There had been changes in Kaduna. The First Battalion of the
W.A.F.F. were occupying their new mess. The railway line had been
completed to Jos through Kafanchan linking up with the East and
Port Harcourt. Work was progressing on the Jos road, and there was
now a good road to Zaria, 52 miles away, mostly flat, with some
attractive rocky hills at the Zaria end. In the Government station
several new roads had been made, with new houses and improvements to older ones.

The road to the King George gardens down by the river was at last
complete and this opened an old but previously inaccessible feature to
Kaduna social life. In all good tropical capitals a 'botanical garden'
was a *sine qua non*: Lagos and Accra did not have them but then their
planning had been unimaginative. When I first went to Kaduna, I
used to take evening walks there. The garden had been laid our and
planted by a Dr Moiser in 1917 with many varieties of trees, for about
500 yards alongside the river bank. There were grass lawns, orchards
of fruit trees, stone steps, arbours, and many fine flowers, including
bougainvillea of all colours. In the midst stood my favourite tree, a
clove. Around it the air was scented, and its crushed leaves smelt
sweetly in the fingers. It was the only one in those parts. The river was
veined with great smooth grey granite slabs, the water rushing noisily
down crevices, or pouring in cascades so smooth and steady that the
water looked like silk. At low water it was possible to cross dryshod
from bank to bank, about 150 feet at that point. In the rains the whole
channel would fill and the granite would be covered by muddy water
racing down from the High Plateau. The charm of the area was not
increased when a big swimming pool was built by the Army many
years later, although it was undoubtedly a very popular amenity. The
original excuse for spending the money – British taxpayers' money,
we were glad to think, for we in Nigeria did not pay British Income
Tax – was to train African troops who were going overseas to Burma
and did not know how to swim.

Dinner parties went on as before. We all of course wore dinner

jackets or shell jackets with dark green cummerbands – scarlet for the
W.A.F.F. officers – and the ladies wore evening dress. They could not
buy clothes locally and had to bring out an adequate supply from
home or have them sent out by post. They looked very nice. All except
the Nursing Sisters were wives – few daughters appeared in government circles until after 1945, though there were some on the High
Plateau. Women officials first made their appearance after the war in
education.

There were visitors from England in spite of the long voyages and
the tedious train journey from the coast. One of them was a Lady
Mary Thynne, whose name would only stir memories now among the
old, but she was then a well-known Society beauty. She came out to
stay with Lady Palmer, Sir Richmond's wife. Another visitor was
Walter Elliott, then Conservative Secretary of State for the Colonies,
who came with a Liberal M.P. Both were charming and extremely
interested in all they saw and heard. So far as I know, they were the
first British politicians to visit Nigeria, certainly the north.

Finance

When Lugard decided so very rightly to entrust power to the great
Emirs and later to the lesser ones; he authorised them to collect taxes
and, from the money so brought in, to pay for their staff and their
'works' and supplies. After a while it was clear that the old 'chest
under the bed' was not the best way to deal with funds – some of them
quite large – that were accumulating. Richmond Palmer, in Lugard's
time a D.O. in Katsina, was instructed to set up a system of Native
Treasuries, using traditional staff to do the work. This went on in
some places for several years with nothing but cash books showing 'in
and out' transactions, while elsewhere primitive vouchers were issued
to record revenue and payment. It was a wonder that money was not
lost; if it had been, no one would have been much the wiser.

The Colonial Audit Department were looking in this direction with
itchy fingers. They would have liked to take it over, and had they done
so at that stage we should have had trouble, for they might have
imposed regulations for which the Native Treasurers were not ready.
By that time over £1,000,000 a year was taken in revenue by the
fifty-odd Native Administrations, and their deposited reserves
reached a similar figure. These did not appear in any statement of
Government Revenue, and by Independence the figures had reached
£10,000,000 each and were still omitted. In 1931 Alexander, the
Lieutenant-Governor, saw that the only way to keep the Colonial

Audit out was to have an audit of his own. I was therefore appointed to open and take charge of an Audit. This special posting, like all my other ones, was apparently based on my total ignorance of the subject, in this case accounting. It was not of my seeking. A.J. Knott and D.A. Percival, two able A.D.O.s, were given to me to do the practical work in the Provinces. This included all matters involving Native Treasuries and their annual budgets. I was to sit at Kaduna, in charge of the Finance Section work and government expenditure on administration in the North.

John Knott, to whom I allocated the western half, turned into a financial genius and ended his career as Financial Secretary to the Northern Government. He carried the Northern Government through all the complications of Regionalisation and the creation of the Ministries. He had an amusing and attractive wife and everyone mourned when they were both killed in an air crash outside Frankfurt on their way home on leave.

I started John Knott off with Sokoto and, as I had never been in that area, I did the first audit of Argungu Native Treasury myself: this was a small Treasury 60 miles west of Sokoto and we found it a good one. I could not afford much time away from Kaduna, for I still had my work to do in the Secretariat. To play fair, however, I did another audit in the eastern half to help Percival and to gain experience myself, in Lafia, north of the Benue. When we checked the cash balance they were 2 shillings short. There was a fearful hullabaloo: the ancient chief, fierce-eyed and vigilant, was furious, and everyone scurried round. The mats were taken up off the floor of the mud-built Treasury and shaken outside in clouds of dust and, behold, in a dark corner 2 shillings were discovered. Whether they were the ones we were looking for or not, I accepted the omen and called off the search. All sank back with cries of relief.

After about six months we had collated enough reports to see the general line of Treasury routines in use. Then we drafted the *Guide to Native Treasury Procedure* and tried it out in practice. Later we squared it off and issued a booklet which, in spite of a few amendments, became the 'bible' of the Native Treasurers for the next thirty years. Even when the professional Audit department took over, as they eventually did, they accepted and adhered to it. It was a striking fact that when all the Treasuries had been checked, few discrepancies had been found and they were small ones. After this time they all had very simple forms to use and Administrative officers going from area to area on transfer found the same practices in each place.

Native Affairs

'Native Affairs' was interesting and at times, bearing in mind that I had not yet served in a big Emirate, hard work; without such experience, you did not get very far in the North. The work covered all correspondence about administration and courts. Appointments of chiefs came through this Section for the Lieutenant-Governor's approval. Also the rare 'depositions' were particularly important, and they had to be legally right.

Again it appeared that guidance was needed for the provincial staffs on a variety of administrative questions. The principles and rules were already published in a large number of circulars of all ages, which were not only hard to find in some small offices but had been changed from time to time: it was therefore difficult to establish with any certainty which was the current version. All these circulars were now checked through by me and, where necessary, rewritten, and then printed and issued to all Provinces. This gave the procedure to be followed in the bush: a companion volume set out the Secretariat lines of action. These booklets avoided waste of time in local research and guaranteed that, if they were followed, the action would be correct.

When my wife was at home in England, I startled Kaduna by taking an unusual 'local leave'. We were then all allowed up to three weeks' 'local leave' in the country: in practice it was rarely taken in full but was a handy and reasonable arrangement. Some people used to go to Lagos or to Jos, others to some place to shoot game. I went south by train to a station just north of Minna. There we – my faithful boys and I with our touring loads – travelled by lorry 30 miles north to the Kaduna river. It was at this place that the young wife of a cadet later to have a distinguished career, was bitten on the buttock by a crocodile. They were bathing in a deep pool by the river: she thought that her husband had gripped her in a basic way. Fortunately the crocodile fled when he rushed it, and after a time in hospital she was none the worse. ·

My boys and I walked by short stages upstream more or less parallel to the river. The country was very beautiful, especially at the great Shiroro gorge, already designated to take a new hydro-electric dam. The area was quiet and peaceful and no white faces had been seen there for a long time. After a week we emerged from this lovely country and returned by train. This enjoyable exploit caused much envy and indeed astonishment among the more staid people of Kaduna.

In Christmas 1931 Dorothy and I rebelled against the round of

Christmas parties and went to bush – I remember one man saying he had consumed no less than twelve Christmas dinners with growing nausea. We did, however, go to a dinner at that time in the old Government House where a splendid, specially imported sirloin of Scotch beef was served with a delicious sweet sauce, gaining the congratulations of the guests. The plaudits turned to dismay when the Christmas pudding came in with the horseradish sauce. Humphrey MacMichael, the Private Secretary, took a long time to live that down.

Anyway we set off a couple of days before Christmas by train to a station short of Kafanchan. At four in the morning – it was bitterly cold with a keen harmattan wind – we left the train and walked a dozen miles into, to us, unknown country, a place called Zungun Katab. There we stayed over the festival and were joined by a lanky, morose senior education officer seeking solitude: he soon melted under Dorothy's well-known charm. The District Head was most efficient; we had from him fresh fish and guinea-fowl and pawpaws and vegetables and great logs for the camp fire. Although this was the most remote of the Zaria Districts, he used to send us little notes hammered out in Hausa on his typewriter. After the festival we walked another dozen miles to a point on the Jos line, the other side of Kafanchan, and so back safely to Kaduna, again to the consternation of our friends.

It was at Kaduna that we saw the first aircraft in Nigeria – it landed on the racecourse. It was small and appeared to be made of corrugated iron. The intrepid owner took people up for 10 shillings a flight. I went up and paid for my cook to do so. The owner survived quite a time on the coast before the plane finally packed up. A private miner had an aircraft which he flew out from England, and about this time the Duchess of Bedford appeared in the Nigerian skies. She landed in Potiskum market, and the clerk, knowing only too well the habits of motor-engines, rushed out with a four-gallon can of petrol.

After this tour, I was posted to Kano. We were not to be stationed in Kaduna again until the late Sardauna made me his Commissioner for Special Duties in 1959.

VII. Kano Province

Kano City

Across the most northerly part of Nigeria stretch the great Emirates of Sokoto, Kano and Bornu, with the smaller but important Emirate of Katsina wedged between the first two. They are as different, each to the other, as the titles of their chiefs – the Sultan of Sokoto, the Emir of Kano and the Shehu of Bornu. Their northern edges are semi-desert (*sahel*) and to say that this country is inhospitable is a pitiable under-statement. Yet it is home, and to be defended, for hundreds of thousands of people. Further south the vegetation changes, the rain-fall becomes reasonable, the soil improves: life becomes easier.

These four territories carried in the 1930s an 'official' population of over 6 millions – but many more in reality – in about 120,000 square miles of country. This was a third of the 1925 total (19 million) for the whole Protectorate and half that of the Northern Provinces. Of this Kano held over 3 million tightly squeezed inhabitants and Bornu a million scattered over 45,000 square miles. These human figures are bewildering and vastly greater than anything to be found in the rest of Africa.

Kano City has had a number of walls and the latest one is 12 miles round, with fifteen gates. Much of it, being of mud, has washed away and some is just a long mound, but there are still sections, notably on the west side, where it is complete. The gates were originally set in re-entrants so that their approaches could be swept by gun-fire from the walls. The great double ditch was once filled with a dense and terrible thicket of thorn bushes, far worse than the British bramble, a serious obstacle to an attacker. Each gate had, until quite recently, a little cluster of huts in which lived its own garrison. The 'Captain of the Gate' was paid by the Emir, and every night at sundown the gates were shut. Their woodwork was covered with iron plates and in war with wet 'fireproof' hides.

Kano City was famous for mud buildings of very high quality and excellent finish. Their exteriors were slightly 'battered' and steeped in a fluid boiled out of the locust beans, which gave a water-proof effect. Without this treatment the walls would need to be patched after every rainy season. The roofs in the City were flat – none was of thatch or corrugated iron. Yet they were slightly domed, a feature visible from inside but not from outside because of the parapets. Water drained into pottery pipes carrying it well clear of the walls. Split stems of a special local palm were set in the walls outside and built out, one on top of the other, in cantilever, and then plastered over and painted.

117

Elegant results were obtained in this way, and provided cool shade in the hottest weather. The ants did not like this palm fibre.

Important buildings like the Emir's Council Chamber had vaults as high as 30 feet above the floor, painted in bright colours mixed with mica, so that they glittered. Images of rifles and swords and writing blocks were painted in black and gold at random. Great carpets covered the floors and fine chairs and settees stood around for visitors. The Emir, true to type, would sit on a low raised dais cross-legged, the pile of fine rugs under him topped with white sheepskin.

The occupation of Kano and its consequences is an often-told tale, but as memories grow dim, it should be told again.

On a raw misty morning in February 1903, Lugard's soldiers saw, through the great locust trees, the line of the city wall stretching away before them on each side. It stood smooth and sheer, forty feet out of the plain, in a perfect state, newly repaired. Men on horses galloped along the top behind the heavy mud merlons.

The Protectorate army was made up of just over 700 foot soldiers, with a small unit of mounted infantry (all Nigerians) and about fifty white officers and N.C.O.s. The plain was filled with clouds of brilliantly dressed Kano horsemen. The odds were against the British, but the cavalry drove off the Kano horsemen: the little guns opened fire on a section of wall near one of the southern gates, making a narrow breach through which the infantry clambered. Had there been any real heart in the defence, a few defenders could have made the breach impassible. Behind the wall open fields, empty of troops or citizens, stretched away to the dwellings. There were no civilian casualties.

The city was entered and the people hardly spared a glance for the dusty sweaty troops. The slave market closed of its own volition for ever. By the next morning the general market was in full swing, and the people were going about their business.

The Emir, the Waziri and a mass of fighting men streamed off to Sokoto. With them went the Madaki of Keffi who had started the whole war by killing the unarmed assistant Resident, Maloney, in his own gateway. Six hundred Nigerian soldiers, with thirty-four officers and N.C.O.s set off from Kano in pursuit. About half-way to Sokoto there is an unpleasant waterless area some 60 miles across, and the greater part of the Protectorate force took a less arduous route to the south of this desert. Forty-five men under Captain Wright and Lieutenant Wells were to reconnoitre another route. Lugard's Annual Report recounts what followed:

They [this detachment] fell in with a party of 200 of the enemy's horsemen whom they defeated capturing a large number of men and horses. From them they learnt that the main body was behind. Capt. Wright . . . decided to advance and oppose his little force . . . to the enemy to delay their advance on Kano till the main body of our troops should have time to anticipate them.

It seemed like certain annihilation, and his men, hampered by carriers on foot and by captured horses, had barely time to form square when they were charged by 1,000 horse and 2,000 foot under the Waziri and several of the more prominent fighting chiefs. Fortunately there was a little scrub around, of which, during the action, a *zariba* was made. Ten times the little square was charged, and yet the men held their ground with perfect steadiness, firing only at 50 yards range to save their ammunition and only by word of command. Each charge was repulsed, though many of the enemy were shot within fifteen feet from the rifles. The Waziri and seven other principal chiefs were killed and the attack was beaten off with only one man wounded and three horses killed on our side. The enemy lost very heavily. . .The enemy retired in good order to a village named Chamberawa where Captain Porter, with another small detachment of Mounted Infantry, came upon them and charged incontinently, taking them by surprise and routing the whole force. The people of the village shut their gates and thrust the Kano men from their walls when they attempted to enter, but received our party with cordiality. These gallant actions finished the opposition of Kano. A notable incident, proving the attitude of the people towards us, was the fact that at one time Lieut. Wells was cut off and would undoubtedly have been killed with the handful of men under him had it not been for the action of [another] small village, whose inhabitants, seeing his danger, came to his assistance, received him within their walls, and shut their gates in the face of the Kano army.

In this particular case, there were no white troops; no white 'other ranks' ever served in Nigeria – only officers and senior N.C.O.s were white. In the Kano action the troops were men of various Nigerian tribes fighting in a country as strange and hostile to them as it would have been to British infantry. Two officers received the Victoria Cross.

This campaign was not merely to capture the Madaki of Keffi, but to stop the internal slave trade, which was in the hands of the great Emirs. Unless they were convinced that the white man was in earnest, the evil trade and the great raids would have gone on, with millions living in fear. Lugard's first objective in Northern Nigeria, to stop the slave trade and bring in the King's Peace, was what he achieved by this single brilliant cmpaign.

Lugard himself did a pretty piece of marching at that time; 170 miles on horseback from Zungeru to Zaria between the 2nd and 11th of February, following on to Kano (another 150 miles) a few days later. He arrived in time to welcome the huge Kano army returning to sue for peace.

The Kano people now sat back to watch what these white men would do. Fortunately, affairs were in the hands of a man who, above all, could be trusted to act correctly, for Lugard was absolutely fair in his dealings and capable of pushing over kingdoms and then immediately putting them on their feet again.

For a millennium before Lugard's men arrived, the city had been a great trading entrepôt, a centre of commerce from the Niger Basin to the Mediterranean. Millions of camels had passed that way, bringing their merchandise and departing with the produce of the Niger, the fine goatskins, spices and woven cloth, and slaves. For two hundred years a caravan of 20,000 camels left annually for the Oasis of Bilma in the southern Sahara to bring back the precious salt prepared there, which is essential to both man and beast.

The original Kano settlement had been where the great market is now and round the low ironstone hills: walls had been built and extended and extended again until they were on their present scale. In the earliest days blacksmiths, the wonder-workers of the early tribes, smelted the iron from the hill and made the vital tools and weapons, stronger than the weapons Achilles' men fought with at Troy. Giants lived there before them, who thought nothing of going hunting and returning with an elephant slung over their shoulders on a stick.

The city had endured many sieges and had fought battles with everyone round about in every direction, but it had kept its trade, as had its lesser sister Katsina 100 miles away. The old Hausa dynasty had fallen before the Fulani in the great Fulani wars of the early nineteenth century. Katsina was intellectually the more powerful of the two centres, while Kano was the commercial genius of the southern Sahara.

Lugard put in a Dr. Cargill as first Resident of Kano. He used the title 'Resident' from his Indian experience, to stress that their appointments were to be advisory to the Emirs: the iron fist was to be in a thickish glove. Quite a number of the former Emirs were deposed before the right people were found in the right families. On the whole, the Emirs did their best to rule according to the new ideas. In fact the new ideas were really those of the Koran, so there was little that needed to be changed.

Cargill set himself to build up a Government on the foundations of the Hausa-Fulani tradition. The Kano nobles were not unused to ruling; they had several million people whom they ruled with intelligence and a steady hand. They had a genius for administration and it was gradually developed. How it was done in the early days is scarcely recorded: the local people had no education beyond a profound knowledge of the Arabic of the Koran, modified by that of the itinerant traders, while the Europeans had little knowledge of Hausa. Cargill established his headquarters on the east of the city in a big mud house belonging to the Emir, surrounded by fine trees.

The health people condemned Cargill's area and the Administration was moved further north to rising ground to Bompai, where a better fort could be built: here over the years a residential area was developed. The trading community however, settled in nearer the wall, where the inevitable race course was built.

I was twice posted to Kano Province. The first time, in 1933, I found myself in the Divisional Office as an assistant to J.H. Carrow, the best known of the District Officers of that place. A huge man with large gestures, he was an expert on Kano Emirate, in the way that people sometimes became who had been for long in the same place. There was a great advantage in keeping a man in the same place but often it did him little good and, if prolonged, quite a bit of harm: he might begin to think that there was no other place worthy of consideration. This was the first (and last) place in my whole service in which I was not in charge either of the Division or the Province. It was good for me as a transitional stage in my life. I was to do what I was told and was concerned only with the matters put before me. I was made responsible for Kano City, the whole area within the walls, not the Government station outside, which came under the Station Magistrate.

My counterpart in the N.A. was a Fulani noble with the coveted title of *Galadima*. The Hausas and some other tribes had a system of title-holders under the Emirs. Of these historic titles, some were hereditary but most were appointed by the Emir from the notables or from his own staff. The *Madawaki* (usually called *Ma-daki*), the Master of the Horse, was in charge of the Districts, a large and complicated job, which came under the D.O.'s own hand. Both these men, first-class administrators by any standard though comparatively uneducated in the European sense, were, with eight others, members of the Emir's Council. The City administration included all those departments that come under a town council.

The city was threaded by narrow alleys opening into grazing grounds, big and small, and the areas around borrow-pits of which there were hundreds of all sizes and depths. The mud taken from them made the houses standing nearby. They were usually full of water and floated water lilies, blue or white: there were Muscovy ducks, Egyptian geese, and goats and sheep. The Emir told me he had learned to swim in one of the big pits near the Kofar Mata, where the lines of evil-smelling dye-pits are found. One of the historic wards was actually called *Kududufawa* (people of the borrow-pits) for in it the few houses were all squeezed against the pits.

There were 145 historic wards of all sizes in the City, each with a ward-head, a scribe and hangers-on. When the *Galadima*, the Councillor responsible, had a meeting of the ward-heads, he was addressing a mass meeting of well over 500 people. It was impossible to administer with such a body, so the Emir and I evolved a grouping of wards into four units. After much discussion he decided to call them *Fuskas*, (correct plural: *fuskoki*), literally 'faces' or more freely 'directions' – e.g. the 'south direction', etc. On these were based a whole subordinate set of services: taxation, police, sanitation and minor works, all coming under the co-ordinated authority of the *Fuska* chief. It worked surprisingly well.

The Emir's police came under the *Galadima*. They were mostly old soldiers with little education and of course local Kano men. Their discipline was high, as was their sense of duty; they were useful in any crisis, and indeed on ordinary duties. There were about 500 of them and their duties were entirely inside the City. Their uniform was a long dark blue tunic over white trousers in the heavy local cloth, and on their heads they wore red fezzes, bound in blue with blue back-flaps. They were armed with long batons, carried visibly at all times. The Chief of Police, an excellent man, wore a uniform of dark striped silk, skirted like a ballet dancer.

Their organisation, which was sketchy, was one of my first tasks. Obviously they could not have worked under the historic ward system, but they could easily fit into the *Fuska* system. So the *Galadima*, the Chief of Police and I sat round a table with the big detailed maps and we drew all the beats in red ink, so that in future the city would be covered day and night. Each *Fuska* unit was under a sergeant and connected by telephone with headquarters. All this was very novel. So far as I know those beats remained effective for at least twenty years.

Strangely, the most awkward unit was the Blind Ward. This was also an historic ward, next to that of the primeval blacksmiths (the hill behind them was full of iron ore). The police utterly refused to go into the Blind Ward except in twos and if possible threes. They were terrified of these toughs who, although blind, knew the nooks and crannies of the ward instinctively and in the past had caused grievous harm to strange policemen.

These were, of course, the Native Authority Police, not the Nigeria Police, who had responsibility in the Government Station outside the walls and were never allowed inside the City. The Emir was very firm about this; all warrants were executed by his men and those arrested were handed over to the Nigerian Police. Similarly the Emir would never have any troops in the City, not even the excellent W.A.F.F. band. This was perhaps not too much of a deprivation for the public who did not appreciate European music, but it was a pity for ceremonial occasions – the Shenu of Bornu had created his own police band for this purpose.

Rubbish collection and sanitation were allocated to the *Fuskas*, and so was taxation: the head of the *Fuska* was responsible for calculating and allocating the tax among the local population. In practice the tax was a matter of shillings per head and could easily be raised. The tax-payer would say to his family 'I am going to the market with this goat to buy six shillings.'

The great market in Kano City was attended by at least 10,000 people every day and perhaps twice as many at harvest time. There were endless rows of covered stalls, each group devoted to a trade in the oriental manner. Leatherwork was one of the leading lines in the market and many rows of stalls were devoted to the sale of every kind of leather product, specially those connected with the horse – saddlery, bridles, stirrup leathers, whips and straps and so on. Corn was sold in huge quantities and so too were innumerable spices. There was hand-made ironwork for all purposes. Silversmiths plied their trade, and of course thousands of bolts of the fine cloth, for which Kano was famous, were on display.

The stalls were rented from the N.A. and there was a complex organisation of police and cleaners and inspectors, many of whom were no doubt much richer than they appeared to be. There was even a market *Alkali* (Islamic judge) with low but effective powers, who could hear cases as they arose and administer instant justice. All this was directly under the Emir; *we* said very little.

Not far from the market was the *Kofar Mata*, the 'women's gate', and immediately outside it was the great spring which, before the new waterworks was installed, gave the City its water supply, it was a picturesque sight, with plenty of green grass and reeds and all manner of livestock. Also close to the spring was the small fortified suburb of Fagge; surrounded by high mud walls in which there was only one gate. A bunch of pretty reckless thugs lived there – as the toughest citizens of Kano, they had been the right people to defend the vital water hole. When the police were looking for specially wanted criminals, the doors of the Fagge gateway would be closed as the police went in. The main haul was outside, for the crooks dropped off the wall like ripe plums.

Kano City was the first place in the North to have electricity and a water supply on a large scale. Government stations like those at Kano and Zaria had some street lighting, and houses in the Government area had a few light points, but there was none in the native towns, where consequently there was a rule under the Townships Ordnance that anyone abroad in the hours of darkness had to carry a lit lamp – this was usually a kerosene hurricane lamp. If a light was not carried the passer-by was presumed to be on some criminal mision, and conversely a criminal seeking technical invisibility would carry a lamp.

Water and electricity

About 1927 the great Emir of Kano, Abdullahi Bayero, ruler and saint, was looking at his Native Authority estimates. He found that the balance at the end of the previous year was more than that of the year before, which had been more than in the year before that. When the 'emergency reserve' had been subtracted, there was still more than £300,000 unallocated. So the Emir asked the Resident, H.O. Lindsell, what it was going to be used for. There was no plan, he was told, it was just for a rainy day. He had heard that before; there had been a lot of rain and it had not been used. He said he wanted a complete water supply for the whole city, not merely the Government area. He was told it would be very expensive and that it could not be installed without electricity to drive the pumps. Then the Emir said, 'Let us also have electricity and let that also be for the whole city. Every house shall have at least one lamp on a pole in the centre of each compound.'

The Public Works department, their headquarters 700 miles away in Lagos, were in a state of injured pride at this invasion of its territory. They played their usual winning card: staff were not available, and even if they were, plenty of other places were higher than Kano on their priority list – enough to keep them busy for years.

By this time the Emir was beginning to enjoy himself. He now played his last card. 'Let us', he said, 'go to a British contractor and ask him to help us.' This the Administration did. They found people to estimate for the plant and put wells in the Challawa River 10 miles away with generators to pump the water. The P.W.D. had apparently never thought of this. They spent some time trying to prove that it would not work, and threatened that if we were silly enough to put it in and it worked, they would not help us to maintain it. To this the Emir replied 'Let us employ our own maintenance staff.' To which the purists said that they would be expensive European engineers, who would want passages and housing, and problems would abound.

They would not 'know' the country and we did not know what we were letting ourselves in for. Nevertheless the Emir persisted.

The scheme was formally opened in 1929, under bunting and festoons of coloured lights. That night the people of Kano, normally uncommunicative, went mad with excitement and joy. The maintenance staff was duly appointed and all went smoothly until eventually the P.W.D. took it over. Meanwhile it had amply paid for itself.

I do not mean by the above that I disliked the P.W.D.* I did not, and had many friends among their officers. But like everyone else they were human, sometimes conspicuously so: for example, no one could conceal the fact that the new Provincial Office in Kano had been built with no stairs to the first floor — it was, of course, bad luck, and an awkward change of plan became necessary. The D.O. had a big office upstairs in this building with another for the A.D.O.s sometimes three of them dealing respectively with City, Finance and Districts. The Provincial Clerks were downstairs. Across the road stood the high mud walls of the Emir's country house of *Nasarawa*.

One morning Carrow came into my office and said that a crisis had arisen. He loved crises and obediently they rose about him. The chief clerk of the Gas Light and Coke (local slang for the Electricity and Water Office in the Township, based on the name, then current, of similar offices in England) had decamped, so would I take over and clear it up. I went down to this office. The (white) Manager, an amiable man employed by the N.A. to supervise the non-technical running, was in despair. Not only was there no key to the safe but the account books had gone and he could not find the receipt stubs. He had no idea who had or had not paid their electricity and water bills. The N.A. charged for both on meters. The European accountant was on leave and the Manager had been doing his work but had obviously left most of it to the clerk, a Gold Coast man. After some hesitation we asked all consumers to send in their latest receipts. So far as I can remember we had the meter books and eventually we found part of the cash book. The safe was opened by the Works and was found to be empty.

It took me two months hard work to reconstruct the accounts and to make sure that people had paid properly — some had paid too much — and at the same time to evolve a foolproof system for dealing with future accounts. Much depended on customers insisting on receipts. The bills which, like every other N.A. document, were printed in Hausa and English, had written on them in Hausa 'For God's sake

*Until 1946 there were no large building contractors in the North. The P.W.D. did most of the work.

demand a receipt' (*Don Allah ka tambaya resiti*): the English lacked the religious urge. We created a new branch of the Native Treasury for collecting these charges under a Kano man who became a very successful Native Treasurer.

I have mentioned taxation. One of the foundations of fair taxation is a fair count of the population. At that time the city was shown as having officially about 64,000 people, but Carrow was sure that this number was too low, as were the Emir and his Council. The only thing was to count it. After I had finished with the Gas Light and Coke I started on this. It took me six weeks working all day to count the whole city. After a while I delegated some areas to Kano men, but had to take spot checks to satisfy myself that all was well.

We invented a new system of counting people. We were prohibited under Muslim custom from going into the houses and counting everyone we found, as that would have been a gross affront to the ladies of the household – some houses had thirty or forty people of both sexes and all ages. We had no women workers so there was no one to send in. Roughly our plan was to summon everyone out of the house (fortunately it was in the dry season). We then sat down outside with the existing tax lists showing those counted in the previous year. We checked those present against the lists and enquired about those whose names did not appear. Then we turned to the women who had come out and asked them who their husbands and children were among those present. They were of course all married, so if a husband was not listed, his name would be added. Then we checked on the children and got new names if their parents were not present or listed. We teased the young women about the number of children they said they had, and they often coyly admitted to more. Finally, and the meanest stroke of all, we asked the neighbours, who were watching it all with great interest, whether they knew of any missing from the household. This at first annoyed the householder but he soon realised that he would get his own back when it was their turn to be questioned. It all became a game, rather a grim one, but very real. All who were counted were given a printed slip which they were enjoined to keep safely, and later, as we proceeded with the count, we and the police challenged everyone we met or who passed us in the alleys. If they could not produce a chit they had to identify themselves by their addresses, which came in handy if their ward had not been counted so far.

I should say that before we started we had put big white numbers on every house and later these were replaced by embossed tin plates on the doors. Thus for the first time every house in the City acquired an 'address', and these addresses were meticulously entered on the great maps of the city. The final result of this tiring labour was a figure of nearly 120,000 for the total within the walls. The people did not care for the women and children being counted so carefully as they felt sure that they would be taxed. In fact only the prostitutes were taxed, and they cheerfully paid quite large sums. When the new tax demands were issued it was abundantly clear to all that no women or children were taxed.

At that time the N.A. offices were by the Emir's south gate, two long mud buildings, flat-roofed, insignificant, grubby and unimpressive. Carrow persuaded the Emir to authorise the building of a new and splendid office building across the square from his great rebuilt gateway. 'The main gate of this palace should be lofty enough to take a man on a camel' said the Emir. 'And who in the world is likely to come out of your house on a camel, Emir?' asked Carrow laughingly. 'I am' said the Emir, and that was that. All that this cost in 1935 or so was £25,000 and the result was that respect for the N.A., specially among Europeans, went up hundreds per cent.

Not far away was the School of Muslim Law to which young men came from all over the North to learn the law from the experts on the Koran and to study the practice in the Native Courts. Then there was the Survey School, whose best effort was the city map on several different scales. We should have been lost without it. Their printing department not only printed maps in several colours on the litho machines but also the bulk of the forms for the Native Administrations of the North. And the entire Emirate, some 10,000 square miles, was covered with an accurate map showing every farm holding in every village, and constantly under revision. One white man supervised it all.

In the same neighbourhood was the N.A. Works, in a building whose semi-Moorish style belied its up-to-date efficiency; here was organised and carried out not only all the Works activities of the Emirate but also those of the many Government buildings and institutions. The Provincial Engineer and his staff, black and white, were busy people.

There are areas of farmland inside the walls – the city proper occupies only the north-eastern corner. The area outside the city is densely occupied and farmed. The roads radiate from it and go out to the District Headquarters, themselves quite large towns. We used to calculate that there were over a million people within 15 miles of the city. It was obviously an under-estimate. This vast population round Kano City was willingly and cheerfully in the hands of the Emir of Kano, whose forefathers had held power since about 1820 and the Fulani wars: he was a Fulani himself.

In those days the Emir received the princely salary of £6,000 a year, as did his so-called equals, the Sultan of Sokoto and the Shehu of Bornu – they were not strictly equals since the other two were, under Islam, Commanders of the Faithful of the west and east respectively. He further received a 'duty' allowance of about £1,500 a year: the British Resident of the Province got £2,400 plus an allowance of £280, but nothing for entertainment. In order to defeat various unworthy remarks, we had a little enquiry on this supposedly high salary to see, with the Emir's active help, where the money went.

First of all, there was the place he lived in, which was about as big as the grounds of Buckingham Palace, covered in mud buildings intersected by tortuous passages and little courtyards. The standard of mudwork was very fine but even so plenty of maintenance work was required. The perimeter walls, 15 feet high, presented quite a problem in themselves. We found that he had to maintain 100 horses for riding purposes and half a dozen camels, with another twenty 'riderless' horses for ceremonial. This was a custom dating from the Askias of Songhai (a powerful kingdom on the Niger in the sixteenth century), where all processions included riderless horses to indicate that the owners were so rich that they had more horses than they had riders to mount them. It was a very costly show-off.

Then there were the male members of his staff, his own household police, the scribes, the craftsmen and so on, and their immediate relatives and dependants. Worst of all there were more than a hundred old women – all they could do was eat, the Emir said – willed to him by various deceased men who had had little or no personal connections with the ruler. Under Islamic law it was possible for anyone, so far as we could see, to bequeath his widow to the state, i.e. to the Emir. There was no earthly means of getting rid of them: only Heaven could intervene and carry them off, and that took time. For an Emir to refuse this pious duty would be to lose a great deal of face; we thought of setting up some kind of institution for these people, but the same argument would have applied and besides, there was not enough money for that. So the Emir went on supporting them and being made the target of innumerable complaints from their voracity.

The mathematical result of all this was the Emir personally had about £500 a year (out of £6,000) that he could spend on himself and his immediate family. Fortunately he had large farms and did not do badly. Above all, he must not lay himself open to charges of stinginess.

The Emir's great concern in later years was the building of the mosque at his north gate, an important landmark of the City at one time. There was a huge mud tower by the old mosque near the site, about 80 feet high and 30 wide. Beams stuck out from its mass to carry scaffolding. We British thought that this was a great object of veneration, but we were wrong. It was revealed to us with great delicacy that early in the British occupation some white men had done something (unspecified but embarrassing) to or on the tower – maybe a survey party had climbed it seeking a vantage point for taking angles. Whatever it was, the act removed any sanctity it might have enjoyed and its demolition was watched unmoved by the citizens.

The P.W.D. sent me (I was Resident at the time) a beautiful scale model of the new mosque, designed by their architects in the most appropriate style. My wife and I asked the Emir up to tea, and I had not told him I had the model. He sat in the centre of the settee as was his wont and we put it on the floor before him and unveiled it. Never have I see such a light in a man's eyes, as though a vision of paradise lay on the Residency floor with angels guarding its corners. His life's dream was taking shape; his days were accomplished and he had given his fellow-men the beauty of holiness.

The Division

When I first went to Kano Division I was alone and was given a mud house of rather inferior type, called 'the Catacombs'. It was dark but clean, and not only cool but also water-tight with its flat-roof; a mud stairway leading to it permitted one to sleep on it. The 'garden' showed the regulation salvias and periwinkles, with large trees. Grass was difficult and needed an infinity of watering and tending. The station in general round about me had fine flowering trees, specially the flamboyant and some ragged jacarandas and the wide-spreading fig trees (*chediya*) – not an eating variety. Lantanas made good hedges, easy to trim.

By the railway station was the Club with tennis courts and a poor, sandy golf course, with a terrible 'rough' of very coarse grass. It had snooker tables and a fair library, as well as the usual bar and dance floor. Somehow dances in this club were not as good as in Kaduna or Jos. Across the road from it was a small church, St. George's, built in concrete and maintained by the Europeans in the neighbourhood. Though these were 'European' churches, Africans were welcomed. In practice few came, as they preferred their own churches where the congregations were crowded and the proceedings less restrained.

Not far away was a fine 'European' hospital. The native hospital, with 200 beds, was in the heart of the city, where the Emir could keep a fatherly eye on it. The children's wards especially attracted him. This hospital had two operating theatres, the only hospital in West Africa then to enjoy such luxury. A number of large mud houses were built for government staff round the Residency which we preferred to the P.W.D.'s concrete buildings. They were cooler and more impressive.

Food was easy, with plenty of vegetables grown in the lush little valley north of the walls. Cape gooseberries made delicious tarts. Chickens and guinea fowl were easy to obtain and so as a rule were fish from the Wudil river, duck and even turkeys. Dinner parties among us were common. Almost all the government departments were represented in Kano and many had more than one European official: commerce, too, was there in strength. The Regiment had moved to Kaduna, but in Kano there were a number of white officers of the Nigeria Police. And there were many foreigners too – French, Greeks and Lebanese. There were always a lot of visitors in later years, Kano being a show-place.

The stores were good and had a variety of supplies, but we still brought out our provisions from Fortnum and Mason, in Piccadilly, London. After the war the canteens had improved so astonishingly that we no longer brought food out. If one lived by the railway, as we did in Kano, it was possible to send once a week to the restaurant car and buy butter, bacon and kippers. You could also get lumps of ice, to keep the drinks cool, in ice chests, which were chronically infested by cockroaches. The legs of meat-safes stood in tins full of water to keep out the pervasive 'sugar ants', and this water in turn had to be covered with kerosene to stop mosquitoes breeding.

When you went new to a Government station, your house would be invaded in a week or so by a swarm of sanitary inspectors. If they found mosquito larvae you would be fined; if they did not, they had a supply with them in a dirty old tin which they poured furtively into suitable places and then discovered them with whoops of joy. There was only one way to deal with the inspectors and that was on their arrival, with a pound in one's hand. I, of course, knew nothing of such transactions, but an entry suitably disguised would appear in the market book. Naturally we all fought our own war against the larvae, which were nearly as ingenious as the inspectors. They would breed in the tiny thimbles of water in the bases of the canna leaves, for example, and other broad-leafed plants.

A quarter of a mile from Sr. George's church was a mission, the S.I.M. (Sudan Interior Mission), famous for its ophthalmic work – the man in charge was first-class. But the other ordained missionaries never came near our church, or attempted to help when we were short of clergy. They had a leper settlement outside the city which was a most depressing place: it was like a poor mines labour lines – bleak,

treeless and pitiless. Some Muslims believed that leprosy was con-
tracted by men having sexual intercourse with menstruating women –
something they don't approve of – which, so I was told, accounted for
their having little sympathy for lepers. I was used to the fine
settlement at Mulai, by Maiduguri, where the lepers lived in villages
round old trees in a huge compound and enjoyed more or less family
lives, leprosy not being immediately contagious, that is to say it takes
a time to transmit and indeed 'clean' wives are known to have lived
with their leper husbands without contracting the disease. At Mulai
the lepers had their own farms and, though they could be helped if
necessary, they lived on what money they could make. They are said
to be quarrelsome and argumentative – more so than normal people,
that is – but I never found any evidence of this.

I only heard of one case of a white man getting leprosy – he was one
of my brother-officers. He was invalided out of the Service but lived
on for a long time in England. I even thought at one time in
Maiduguri, having produced an insensitive spot, that I had it myself,
but it was towards the end of my thirty-month tour of duty in the war
(the normal tour was twelve months) and they said that worry can
produce some of the symptoms.

People used to ride a lot, and of course polo was the game of the
snobs, black and white. I was never good at games so avoided these
dangerous things. There were plenty of walks round about: many
roads were then grassy paths, wide and smooth and convenient for
cattle, and inside the walls were great areas to explore. I had acquired
a close knowledge of the alleys of Kano and would take nervous guests
into tiny crevasses that I knew would just take my car. Few visitors
could entirely appreciate the absolute peace that reigned in Kano.
Serious crime was minor compared with Europe, and homicide rare.

When Edward, Prince of Wales visited Nigeria in 1925, it became
clear something would have to be done to the City Market. There was
going to be a great durbar of Chiefs from all over the North, and many
other visitors. They would naturally want to move about this famous
trading centre. The obvious thing would have been to widen the alleys
but there were strong arguments against this, so it was decided to cut
more or less straight roads into the centre. The surveyors got on to the
flat roofs and put in pegs to mark the proposed lines. All was quiet
until the word 'compensation' was whispered. Hell broke loose and
grim fights took place every night to secure the coveted pegs. In the
end the pegs were pulled out and the roads were constructed, as it
were, at ground level, working on a compass-bearing and demolish-
ing the houses immediately in front of the workers.

One firm decision that paid off well was that no road should go into the actual market. A ring road was built round it by means of which vehicles could come close but could not interfere with or imperil the lives of those trading in the market. It was agreed that bumps should be built into the roads to stop speeding; these saved many lives, for the roads were awash with children and old women, sheep, goats and ducks, not to mention other movables, and immovables like sleeping donkeys.

In 1933 the Bank of British West Africa put up an ostentatious building for themselves by the railway, to wipe the eye of Barclays whose establishment was much more modest. (It was demolished and replaced in 1974). One day a labourer came out of the Bank with a bag containing a hundred shillings on his head. A car drove past, and a hand came out of the back of it and swept the bag into the car. Just around the corner the car drove on the wrong side of a barrier and was stopped by a policeman, who noticed the bag on the back seat and became suspicious. Justice was swiftly done.

When my wife came out we were given a much better mud house, with some fine rooms and an 'upstairs', containing a bedroom and bathroom, with fitted bath and running water. Later that tour I took over the Kano division from Carrow, when he went on leave, and we moved into the best of the houses. It was here that we bought our first refrigerator – the invention that made the greatest difference to life in the tropics after quinine – and our first radio. When the Shehu of Bornu was shown the new 'fridge and the flame which had to be kept permanently alight to activate the refrigerating agents, he laughed and said, 'you white men, what will you be up to next? Getting cold out of heat – God's inscrutable will be done'. The radio too was a great thing. It suffered from atmospheric troubles but a good reception could be obtained on long wave. We were at last in direct touch with England, which meant among other things that the newspapers arriving a fortnight later had lost much of their appeal: it was still some time before they came out to us by air. The Lagos papers, meanwhile, had changed greatly for the better and were readable, though often the reading gave some officers apoplexy: the editors did not seem always to approve of the actions and intentions of the Colonial Government.

Science was again to reveal its wonders soon after electric street lamps were installed. One night a man went off the road to relieve himself and chose a place near one of the newfangled standard lights. Unfortunately this was not as other lights, and when his jet struck a guy wire, he received a shock which killed him outright. He had not touched the wire or the light pole. At the inquest there was a complicated argument between the Coroner and the M.O. who had done the autopsy. The M.O. stated that this case was 'a history of electro-cution'. The Coroner replied that anything of this kind was instan-taneous and could not be described as 'history', a word which connoted a continuity of events of at least some duration. The M.O. was a pompous man and argued laboriously; however, the facts were established. The technical staff were alarmed when evidence showed that everyone in the neighbourhood knew that things were not normal with this particular pole, and the children had invented a game of running up to it and touching it lightly: it was 'the pole that bites'. Somehow none of them was electrocuted.

At Jos a booster pump in the water supply, new and working perfectly, stopped pumping. When it was stripped down, it was found to be jammed with mango seeds, large and fibrous and about two inches long. The Provincial Engineer reported this to me in the office and one of my messengers who was taking some files away turned and said the word '*jepji*'. The Engineer, who spoke no Hausa, asked what he meant. The *jepji* was a kind of large outdoor rat. The messenger said that these rats collected mango seeds at this time of year and hid them in convenient places. He said, 'Look into the piles of pipes in the yard and you will see for yourself.' This was done, and there were the seeds. Some new pipes had been installed into the system when the pumps were changed and no one had thought of looking through them first.

One of the difficulties was that the local population regarded the white man and his works as quite inexplicable, if not actually imbecile, so that if anything went wrong it was taken for granted and not reported. Electricity and motor engines were not expected to work, in fact it was quite remarkable when they did. Water could not always be expected to come out of the taps: did not the rivers them-selves sometimes dry up? People did not complain of failures but they appreciated successes.

The job of D.O. Kano was a very pleasant one. There was plenty to do but nothing very complicated arose. There were not the problems of Kabba or Jos, or even Bornu. The Native Administration was first-class and ran itself. No one would really think that there were all those millions of people being administered: the peace was well and simply kept. Our people went on tour, as I did myself, and we walked about the place and talked to all and sundry in Hausa direct: it would have been easy enough to spot any signs of trouble. Their farms were good and they worked hard. Kano was the only place I have known where the manure of the donkeys, cattle and other animals was systematically taken from the towns and villages and spread on the farms. These, because of Islamic inheritance laws, were small. In law, all land was vested in the village, as Lugard had so wisely laid down long ago; no one could own large tracts, indeed no one 'owned' land at all, and it could not lawfully be sold. It was the 'tenure' that was inherited – and subdivided, even into isolated strips.

I never toured as much in Kano as I should have liked. As A.D.O. I was concerned with the City, and as D.O. there was not much time. But others were on tour for long periods. Many Districts could be reached by car or kit-car (it was a temptation to make hit-and-run visits) especially in the dry season: the obstacles in Kano Division were the great wide rivers, some 300 yards across, of dry sand with small streams, swelling to a vast flood in the rains. I never owned a horse in Nigeria, although I did keep one for a fellow D.O., S.A.S. Leslie, when he went on leave, and rode it sometimes. It did not care for donkeys, which created problems since there must have been at least a million donkeys in the Emirate. We would progress with a small group of men riding ahead of me on horseback driving donkeys off the road into the bush. This confirmed the local peasants in their belief that the white man was raving mad.

I was transferred to Lagos with little warning, and handed over to an Irishman, Fred Noad. I was vexed because I had just planted some green peas and would not see them come up. Otherwise the transfer could be regarded as a distinct advance in the Service.

VIII. Lagos, 1934

Executive Council

When I next served in the Lagos Secretariat it was in 1934, twelve years after my departure for Koton Karifi. I do not know why I was transferred from Kano; the posting came unexpectedly. The Secretariat had not changed; the furniture was just as austere: a plain table with two drawers, sometimes covered with green baize, an armchair and two upright 'kitchen'-type chairs in mahogany, enormously heavy to lift. The Chief Secretary and Deputy had carpets (we still had bare boards stained black) and a couple of so-called 'lounge chairs'.

The Lagos Club had disappeared from its advantageous position by the Treasury – the 'gin-tank' they had called it, with every justification – and a new hospital stood in its place. Some of the houses round the race course had been replaced, and the Southern Secretariat had been burnt down. It was re-established at Enugu in the East, and then half of it went on to Ibadan, when the group was divided into East and West. The new offices were pleasant and suitable, yet they lacked the gracious charm of the Lagos Secretariat. Ikoyi had many good new houses in its western half, nearest to Lagos; the best ones were there by the lagoon but they were subject to thieves travelling by that most silent means of transport, the small canoe. The rest of the island was much as when I had walked about alone in its strange wildness.

In 1926 a Housing Committee had been set up by Sir Graeme Thomson, then Governor, with (wonder of wonders) a woman on it. After a good deal of painstaking discussion and travel about the country, a set of plans was produced for several grades of houses for Europeans, with – and this was the intelligent development – a different set of flat-roofed houses for the North. These plans were taken as standard, and even the Residencies (except at Jos) were only an enlargement of the original theme. During the slump a panic set of economy houses was designed but otherwise this standard, with modifications held its sway almost till the end.

In general there was little scandal, but stories did crop up. For example, a bachelor became enamoured of a beautiful wife: he was Government, she was trade. The difference was more subtle than a pure matter of snobbery. Government stopped work for the day at 2 p.m., having worked through from 8 a.m., but business people went back to their offices at 2 p.m. after a lunch interval. The coast was therefore clear for the afternoon in the case I have mentioned, and he

135

took full advantage of this happy arrangement. All went well until he went on tour for a fortnight. On the first afternoon back he drove to the house and rushed up the stairs. As he burst into the bedroom he found a strange lady having her siesta. His loved one had moved house while he had been away and had failed to tell him. The woman in the bed naturally knew the other one and the story lost nothing in the telling.

In practice the general standard of sexual morals between white people was high, in spite of the attractiveness of many individuals. The houses were very 'open' inside and outside and the house-boys moved silently – maybe these facts acted as deterrents to affairs. Also, cars standing in open compounds at unusual hours could not escape notice. Many white men had black mistresses.

Our second baby was born in 1935, during this tour, a daughter Veronica Jane.* My wife did not come out with me, but joined me in Lagos a few months later, leaving Veronica Jane with her sister and our Nannie in London.

I was by now a District Officer and had risen to No. 58 in the Service and was entitled to the white uniform. I found that I had more to do than in 1921 for I was not only in charge of 'Native Affairs' but I also became Clerk of Councils. There were two Councils. The smaller, with weekly meetings on Thursdays, was the Executive Council; the larger was the Legislative Council. The former body met at Government House in a corner of the ballroom that had been built for the Prince of Wales' visit. Executive Council, colloquially 'Exco', was made up of about ten officials, excluding the Governor who always presided. Four members rarely attended, as they lived outside Lagos, namely the three Lieutenant-Governors and the Commandant of the Regiment. This was the 'cabinet' of the Government and all matters of importance went to it, including those that had by law to be considered. All death sentences were discussed (including those passed by the higher Native Courts). The Council advised the Governor on the 'exercise of the Royal Prerogative' (of mercy), and it is no breach of the secrecy which bound these proceedings to say that these latter, very rightly, took much more time and consideration than any other items that came before the Council. The Governor was not bound to take the Council's advice – for they

---

*She married and had two children, a girl and a boy, and was drowned when their new catamaran capsized off Ramsgate in 1970: she dived several times with the highest courage to find the little boy who was trapped in the cabin; and failed to surface. Had she been an indifferent swimmer she would have been alive today. The little girl Oriel was saved with her father.

could only advise, unlike the U.K. Cabinet – but he had to explain to the Secretary of State as soon as possiblewhy he rejected it.

The Governor was now Sir Donald Cameron, who had returned to Nigeria having served in Tanganyika for five years as Governor. After the departure of Clifford we had had five years of Sir Graeme Thomson, the only Governor I did not know: strangely, I never even saw him. After a distinguished career at home he came to us via the Gold Coast, still apparently knowing little of the Colonies or their habits and customs, and their aims and ambitions. He made little impression on Nigeria. It was also unfortunate that his Chief Secretary, Sir Frank Baddeley, was also a stranger to Africa, and is better remembered for his great feud with the North than for any progressive steps.

Cameron had George Hemmant as his Chief Secretary: charming, efficient, highly intelligent and receptive. He smoked ceaselessly without taking the cigarette out of his lips. The ash would get longer and longer, drooping just a little, then rather more, and all beholders would watch with bated breath for the inevitable fall on to his tie and shirt. It was too much for one of us, who at the crucial moment darted forward with a brass ashtray, nearly cutting the Chief Secretary's throat and still failing to catch the ash. He was an excellent foil to his master, who could be tiresome as well as right. He had theories about Native Administration which he had introduced in Tanganyika; and back in Nigeria he found they did not agree with current practice. However, he was now in a position to bring in changes that he had long contemplated. The first of these was the reorganisation of the judicial system. The country then had a Supreme Court, conducted on British lines down to tiny and quite inappropriate detail – the bewigged, scarlet-clad judges might have come straight from any English Assize Court – and the law was the same, save for varieties brought in by local ordinances.

Parallel to it were the Provincial Courts and the Native Courts, where there were no robes, no complicated proceedings and, most important, no lawyers. It would have gone ill indeed to have put trained lawyers in a court where the judges were not trained men, but rather worked on general principles and knowledge. This, not unnaturally, enraged the professional lawyers, who coveted so vast and potentially fruitful a field lying so close at hand yet so firmly fenced off.

Cameron replaced the Provincial Court by a new professional High Court, which was given powers in the Protectorate. Fortunately there were officers with legal training in the Administration and some other services and these now had a wonderful chance to better themselves.

Some did very well and even reached the giddy heights of the Bench: others remained magistrates. So there were now professional magistrates in the larger centres and the rest of us were called magistrates (of two classes) when filling certain defined posts. Thus we did exactly the same things as before but with a different title and filling in different forms. The criminals found themselves up before the same old faces – everyone was delighted. The new Native Courts were far more numerous, possibly 700 or 800. From obscure little courts with powers to impose no worse than three months' imprisonment to courts with full powers, they presented a vast range from fairness and average ability to downright incompetence and prejudice. But whatever their effectiveness in our eyes, one always had to remember that to their officials and members, and to the public, who came in contact with them, they were the epitome of justice and the very mirror of local dignity.

The former laws permitted a genial vagueness and a sense of genteel autocracy that was rapidly becoming out of keeping with the progress being made in Nigeria. There was also a necessity to have these important bodies so strongly entrenched that they could not be challenged by keen-witted practitioners. Their powers were now closely defined and set out in the warrants establishing them. All the courts were listed in the Schedules to the Ordinance and set out under their correct grades. This presented a considerable task for the Attorney-General and myself, for we had to get it all right without fear of error or confusion. It came with my responsibility for 'Native Affairs'. At the same time Cameron brought in a new Native Authority Ordinance which put those bodies on a proper legal footing and established their powers and rights clearly and beyond doubt. There were then hundreds of small authorities as well as the great chieftaincies.

Cameron often asked for legislation to be drafted and, to give him his due, he would sometimes send down a minute for the Attorney-General setting out in some detail the content of the bill he wanted. He did this one day with a bill about some sanitary control. I sent it along to the Attorney-General for action without giving it much thought: we could count on Cameron having his facts right, better than we knew them ourselves, and he knew the kind of bill he wanted. In due course a little three-clause bill came back from the Attorney-General – this one was Herbert Cox, one of the ablest and certainly the most patient we had; it looked good and very straightforward. Then there was an alarm signal in my mind. I had seen the wording before somewhere. So I turned up the likely volume of the Nigerian Laws, and sure enough I came across an Ordinance which gave just the same provisions as were required in the new one. I could find no difference, and nor could the Attorney-General, so we told Cameron and our bacon was saved. I could imagine only too well the fun that the lawyer-members of the Legislative Council would have made of the Government bringing in a bill that duplicated an existing statute.

Cameron's main work – which he had not sought – at that time was the struggle with the Slump. Government Revenue fell from about £4 million a year to under £2 million, and somehow expenditure had to be balanced. This was probably a serious mistake: it would have been wiser to run the country on deficit accounting. We also made the mistake of not buying stocks of needful supplies when the prices dropped to absurdly low levels: steel joists, for example, which we could have used in quantity later. But the Colonial Office would not have countenanced any policy so *outré* and 'unsound'. As it was, numbers of good men were dismissed, to their great loss and the even greater loss of the Government.

No one knew the country's departments so well as Cameron and he went through them with the finest of combs. Agriculture and the Geological Survey were about to be 'axed' altogether, Cameron having little regard for their achievements. They got wind of this and by brilliant improvisation, born of despair, each one saved itself. Agriculture announced that for years they had been working on proposals for 'Mixed Farming' – which came as a surprise to many people. They proposed that selected farmers should be given (or subsidised to the extent of) two bullocks, or cows which would, at seed planting, draw a simplified form of plough, and for the rest of the year produce progeny or milk. It would take some organisation, of course, but would not cost much and would be of great value if spread over the North. Cameron was interested and the Department was saved.

The Geological Survey lived a strange life. For part of the year they were in Nigeria in what they termed the 'field' and for the rest they laboured in England over their results. The latter were not impressive. However, they came up very suddenly with the theory that they were the right people to sink deep wells – again in the North – as their scientific knowledge was essential to ensure success. This was not immediately apparent to cynics like us; but luckily Cameron accepted the idea and the Department remained. In fact, they did sink those wells which became known as 'Geological Wells' – a title that remained long after they had been taken over by the Public Works.

As the Administrative service was the key to the whole administration it was difficult to cut us very much, though we renounced a tenth of our salaries and allowances. We also saved by reducing drastically the recruiting of new cadets. It was very galling for us to be attacked as the 'Untouchable Service' by the departments, when we knew that every morning we had been fighting fierce battles to retain the very people who were attacking us. It was indeed a bad time: people were scared to go into their offices in the morning for fear they would find the fatal letter awaiting them.

Among others threatened was the Police Band. The Police themselves could not be cut very much, but all their trimmings were removed. The Band was an obvious target. It was a very good one, made up of African musicians under a white Bandmaster, and it played at all functions in Lagos and sometimes went on tour to the larger centres. Cameron used it often at Government House parties, and the people of the town liked it, even though they were not enthusiastic about the police in general. It cost quite a small sum, about £2,400 a year – but every little helped in the effort to save expenditure. So the end of the band came in sight and the Inspector-General invited the Governor and leading people to their last Retreat. The police parade ground, on the way to Ikoyi, was an attractive place, with green turf and a background of palm trees on the Macgregor Canal. The men played well that night and performed the usual ritual for the finale, playing – yes – *Abide With Me*. It was played with great emotion. The crashing chords gradually died down into the last verse. The music faded softly into a gentle whisper and ended almost with a sigh. I was sitting just behind the Governor and I watched his bowed head and tears trickling down his hard cheeks. He was not the only one so publicly moved: all of us were, and the bandsmen were crying like children. Then Cameron pulled himself up and turned to the Inspector-General beside him. In a great stillness, I heard his harsh voice say 'We cannot sack those men. Look through your figures again and see if you can't scrape up £2,000, we must cut elsewhere and keep them.' And so that evening, as the sun set, the Police Band was saved.

Legislative Council

The other council of which I became Clerk was the Legislative Council, known as 'Legco'. (Crown Colonies had them as miniature forerunners of parliaments.) Its forty-seven members met with great solemnity three times a year: two of the sessions were short, but the third, the Budget Session in the spring, lasted some days. This was very formal, with a guard of honour of the Regiment on the grass. All officials including, oddly, the Attorney-General wore white uniform and the unofficial members (M.L.C.s) heavy broadcloth under shiny top hats. The Governor, in full uniform for the first day, presided over these meetings and we followed our version of Westminster procedure.

The Chamber was between the two towers of the Secretariat. It was panelled in mahogany, and the floor was black with a high polish that shone like glass as long as no one walked on it. There was a small gallery with a limited number of seats, the object of endless female intrigue for weeks before the meeting. By tradition the Governor's wife sat in the centre above her husband, flanked by the wives of the Chief Secretary and the Chief Justice. When skirts were long this presented no problem but, as they became shorter, the Works intervened with a 'modesty' veil hung behind the safety rails.

The Governor sat at a desk on a little dais and the Clerk sat below him. By that time we had progressed to the extent of having a lady reporter, Miss Arabella Reading, whose main duty was to take down proceedings, type them out and see them through the press. When she was not doing this, she reluctantly helped senior officers with their work. We had no one who could take any dictation, and every word had to be written out in longhand: matter to be typed had to be sent to a pool of African typists, who varied strikingly in their understanding of what they were doing. The Clerk shared with her and the Governor the duty of having to keep awake through the droning speeches of those sticky afternoons.

Although the proceedings were largely formal and at that time did not affect the North, they formed a valuable platform for expounding Government policy and explaining difficulties that arose from time to time. There was always a Government majority; this was essential, as there was no way in which an alternative Government could take over should the actual one be defeated. A further complication was that the Governor himself presided and he could scarcely be considered an impartial chairman. This custom continued until quite a late date in constitutional development, when it became necessary to have an independent Speaker. That left the Governor to pace up and down the carpet in his office in anxiety as to the outcome of the debates.

In the House at that time twenty-eight members were officials, including ten Residents who were seldom allowed to open their mouths. Eighteen unofficials (five of them white) batted for the other side. These unofficials represented not only places by direct election or selection but also interests such as commerce, shipping and mining. The African members spoke at inordinate length but had little real knowledge of the country outside their own areas. Some of the white members also talked a lot. Bills were passed into law with solemnity and speed, and sometimes with lack of understanding of their effects on the local people. However, most of them were technical and only affected a limited section of people, so that the rest of Nigeria's millions went on their way in happy ignorance. The bill, as passed, was printed on fine parchment, the scarlet seal of the Colony was attached, and the Governor signed the Royal Assent. In each case the Secretary of State would formally report that he had 'not advised His Majesty to exercise his right of disallowance'. Only once was this power used, as far as I remember, and that was when the Government saw too late that a mistake had been made and wished to recall and annul the bill. These formal copies were bound in annual volumes and locked away with the despatches in the strongrooms. Ordinary printed copies came out in the weekly *Nigeria Gazette*, printed along the verandah by the Government Printer, adding to the clutter of paper in every administrative office in the country.

The Government Printer was a hard-working man who produced the 1,500-odd different forms then in use by the various Government Departments. When paper became scarce during the Second World War I went through every form with the Head of Department – how surprised they were to see some of them! By excision and reduction in size we reduced the consumption of paper for this purpose by half, and Departments were saved much sterile and time-wasting labour filling them in; some forms were never seen by anyone higher than a clerk once they were completed.

At one time the Government Printer was gravely harrassed by an irascible Comptroller of Customs who, in a moment of exasperation, scribbled in red ink across a proof, 'Why the hell can't you get anything right?' The Printer's revenge was swift. He sent back a pile of correctly printed forms with those words printed in big red capitals across the sheets. The Comptroller was aghast, till he realised that only the top half-dozen sheets were so defaced.

Among other things, examination papers were printed there, being set up in type and proof-read by his senior and reliable staff. On one occasion there was a startlingly high percentage of successes on a certain difficult paper. Everyone was puzzled, until it was found that the formes of lead type were stacked in the Printer's own office before being broken up. An ingenious fellow went in wearing a new white duck suit and sat on the type. It was easy enough to read the questions on his bottom and sell them at a reasonable figure to candidates.

The two half-yearly Honours Lists were a special problem for the Printer. The final approved list would reach the Governor from the Secretary of State a few days before publication. One copy was taken to the Printer by hand. By convention absolute secrecy shrouded the whole operation: the recipients kept their mouths shut and many never even told their wives. The Printer set up the type himself under the 'Gazette Extraordinary' heading and locked the forme away in his safe. On the appointed morning very early he and his Deputy put it on the machine and printed off the first copies for Lagos distribution; as soon as these were sent out, the ordinary printers printed for general distribution. A List was telegraphed to Provinces and then followed a spate of congratulatory telegrams to the lucky people. In India, I understand, there was a set of standard telegraph 'forms' for various events in life, some of which dealt with Honours. One of these is said to have read, 'Congratulations on your hardly-earned honour'.

Recommendations for Honours were made by Residents and Heads of Departments, who usually typed out the papers themselves. The honorands naturally included African staff and distinguished chiefs and non-official Africans.

The *Gazette* may sound rather a dull subject but to us it was not only a legal bible, but also a staff news-sheet. The first pages contained lists of new appointments and arrivals, those going on leave and returning from leave, sick leave and an obituary. Then there were monthly provincial lists showing who was where, and of course promotions, read variously – like the Honours– with pleasure, indignation or dismay,

In such a large country, with an inevitably scattered Service, there were quite large numbers of people in Government whom one knew only by name – which did not stop us following their careers with interest. The Northern and Southern officers rarely mixed due to the geography. East and West were much nearer to each other and there was a small degree of interchange. On the mail boats we did, of course, meet. Nigeria wore green cummerbunds with dinner or white shell jackets (the North had originally worn grey), the Gold Coast wore old gold, and the W.A.F.F. scarlet. When air travel came, these pleasant associations ceased.

In those days people were beginning to sail little boats in the harbour and an otherwise derelict Englishman turned his skilful hands to building them. The adventurous would go across to Tarquah Bay on Sundays to picnic and bathe: this was a sandy beach that had formed itself between the west mole and the training bank, the latter an ingenious piece of marine engineering which directed the current of the Ogun river. Later this use of the bay developed further: at first, people started to build palm-leaf huts with cement floors, and primitive furniture appeared in them – they got temporary building rights from the Commissioner of Lands. Then gradually the spaces between huts were filled in with more huts, till they became a continuous row. Some were good enough to spend a comfortable week-end in, with water laid on and refrigerators installed. The final cachet was added when the Governor built a good hut, invitations to which were greatly prized.

By 1934 there were many improvements to our life in Lagos. The shops (still called 'canteens') were better and the standard of food was quite high: market food – that is all fresh food, vegetables, chickens, eggs, fish and fruit – was comparatively cheap. There was a lot of entertaining and one could have accepted an invitation every night had one been so inclined. There were many wives, and also single ladies working as hospital Sisters or school-teachers. It was Dorothy's first stay in Lagos, although she had often passed through. She enjoyed the friends she made so easily, and the excellent tennis there was on the sixteen grass courts of the Lagos Tennis Club behind Government House – there was a door through the wall into its garden, as Governors sometimes played. The early golf course had been on the race course, like everything else to do with sport. The new Ikoyi course was where our bush houses had stood. The greens were hard sand and the bunkers were soft sand, and in between there was a rough grass cut short: feathery palms and the odd mango or tamarind lined the course and part of it came down to the lagoon. Altogether it provided a pleasant way of spending an afternoon.

The new Ikoyi Club was then being built and when complete was a vast improvement on anything there had been before. In the centre stood a round ballroom with a sprung floor, unique in West Africa. There used to be dances on Saturday nights, alternating with the Railway Club at Ebute Metta and Apapa. The Railway dances were peculiar in that the 'floor' was a tarpaulin tightly spread over a tennis court and heavily waxed – local beeswax being easy to obtain. The result was an excellent floor, not tiring for the feet. At that time the dances were attended by white people only – the Lebanese had their own clubs – but of course we were a varied community of several nationalities. There was a good deal of controversy as time went on about black membership. The thing became absurd as there were so many black lawyers and doctors and before long judges of the High Court, better educated and better mannered than many of the accepted members. In the end the Committee changed the rules and some Africans joined at once, but once having achieved that goal they seldom came.

Lagos native town was getting bigger every day. It reached round to Apapa across the harbour where the wharves, which were being built when I first arrived in 1921, were in full operation. It had also spread along the road towards Ikeja, then a small town on its own (14 miles inland) and a District Headquarters, with the reservoirs behind it. From these Lagos got its water supply, in those days excellent and reliable, but as the town grew in post-war years the supply did not expand with it and the source became dubious. The reservoirs used to be a charming place where the favoured few (e.g. the Chief Justice) could go for evening picnics.

During my last leave I had spent seven weeks in London studying 'Office Organisation', but had learned nothing of significance to us. The Treasury then had a small unit called 'O and M' (Organisation and Methods) who arranged my visit to Ministries. I spent some days in most of them and their experts explained how they organised their input and output of paper. They varied, the most cautious being the Treasury itself, where almost every paper was summarised on cards at various stages, so that they could reconstruct any file should it be lost – not that any had been. They would not let me see the Colonial Office system; they said that its standards were deplorable and not to be copied. The Admiralty were the most charming at all levels and the Post Office and the Law Courts a strange mixture of the primitive and the advanced. It was a surprise to be told in the Law Courts that they had taken special care of money on legal deposit, ever since their losses over the South Sea Bubble. Their clients included the 1,000 certified lunatics and their properties, and their deposits stood (in 1934) at over £55,000,000. All this was before computers, but the addressographs and multiliths were just coming in and we bought one each for Lagos as a great gamble; they certainly paid off.

No plans had been made for me to see commercial houses. The Treasury said, of course, that I could see anything I liked but in their opinion there was nothing to learn from that source. So I went to Unilever and the Euston offices of the L.M.S. Railway. The Treasury were right; their methods suited them but we could not possibly have brought them into Nigeria without disaster. They were working in a very limited field with people who spent many years doing the same or similar actions in the office; hence personal knowledge was priceless. There was nothing like the huge sweep of Government correspondence even in Nigeria. Still I was surprised to find that the Railway favoured the nails-on-the-wall system of filing.

In each place I asked what they did about personal Confidential Reports, the bane of the Colonial Governments. In some they were very elaborate, in others simple, in yet others non-existent. Where they existed they were as a rule shown to the subject of the report: they were not shown in the Colonial Service unless (*a*) they were adverse and (*b*) the trouble was one that lay within the subject's own powers of amendment: so in practice they were not normally shown to anyone. We felt that the British method meant that the report had to be watered down in one way or the other. Some felt that the reports could become in practice reports on the reporting officer, rather than on the reportee.

Every Resident was expected to write a brief report on every senior officer who had served in his Province at any time in the year, which gave the Residents a sharp pull over the public behaviour of such people. If I wrote reports which I felt might be biased, I would insert at the foot, 'I do not personally like this Officer.' I thought this fairer than the Chief Commissioner whose sole comment on quite a good man read, 'This officer does not play bridge.'

When I was Clerk of Councils I was put on to the overhaul of the card index. Alan Burns had started this but in the passing years 'subjects' had evolved and strange ones had appeared, all full of odd ramifications. The old plan, though excellent, was bursting at the seams and something new was required. I went through some 70,000 files and produced a system of 'subjects' for indexing that not only included all existing matters but left openings for the future. The list was printed and everyone with a little intelligence was able to find the section of the numbering in which a particular subject should fall – libraries use a similar system for numbering their books. The difficulty was where a subject could fall into a number of categories; against this eventuality I wrote an elaborate card index of some hundreds of cards setting out all reasonable variations and permutations. It was interesting, and one learnt plenty about the country from the Lagos angle.

I must stress those words 'the Lagos angle'. The fundamental truth was that Lagos was not Nigeria;. it was an island and induced an insular mind. People working there could consider Lagos and 'Colony' problems from the point of view of the people directly concerned in Lagos, but it was difficult to deal with Nigerian problems in the same way. There was an old saying that a thick fog hung over the far end of Carter Bridge and the mainland beyond it. Though widely recognised, it was almost impossible for the Lagos officials to see through that fog. Even when they went on tour, as many of the seniors did, they came back with *their* view of the matter and not that of the people who had to carry it out, or on whom it would be carried out.

I must mention an interesting change in our routine at that time. The King George V postage stamps had always conformed to the dull Crown Agents' 'standard' colonial pattern. A change was agreed, and this time it was to be a pictorial issue, the first in Africa or in almost any British territory. I was in charge of 'Posts and Telegraphs' on the Secretariat schedule and so the matter came to me. We decided to have an open competition for the designs. Unfortunately at that time local African art of suitable quality was not available; ten years later, first-class drawings could have been obtained. Some photographs and a few drawings and sketches by Lagos Europeans were submitted. A lady produced the basic design for the 4*d* – a fishing village. A few were excellent but some, such as the tin-mining stamp, were incomprehensible to any but experts. I supplied the photo for the 2*d* – a huge tree – but the Crown Agents cut a piece out of the middle and added little figures at the base, who had no business to be there. The issue came out in 1937, by which time the old King had died. Without any Nigerian approval, an unattractive set was issued for King George VI: the pictorials were not repeated. Indeed there were no new pictorials until 1953, when the design was by a French artist, Maurice Fiévet.

Work in the Secretariat was always under pressure, and a lot had to be taken home to be dealt with over the week-ends. We always worked a half-day on Saturday throughout Nigeria. It was rather more relaxed and conversational than other days, but you could be sure of a 'Saturday crisis' from time to time. At 12 o'clock there was little standing on dignity in the rush home or to the club. People would come in for a drink before lunch, which was rarely before 3 p.m., Sunday lunches tending to be even later.

In Lagos it was the custom to go to church on Sunday evening. There was seldom a morning service, though there was always one at 8 a.m., usually quite well-attended. Canon Wright – the Colonial Chaplain, as he was misleadingly called – was very popular and better supported than many others would have been. He was the mainstay of an institution at Apapa (across the harbour) called the *Wharf Inn*, a kind of seamen's home, to which the well-disposed white youth of Lagos would go on a rota to act as hosts to whoever might be there.

Hemmant retired as Chief Secretary, a severe loss to the service and his friends: his place was taken by another able and pleasant man, John Maybin. We also had a new Governor, Sir Bernard Bourdillon.

On the morning of his arrival we all went down to the Customs wharf, the men in white uniforms and the ladies superb in their best; Bobby Foulger, the Commissioner of Police, held his drawn sword. The wharf was alive with bunting in a brisk wind. The Regiment mounted one of its immaculate guards of honour and the band played on a flank. The invited guests sat uncomfortably in their finery on hard chairs, carefully arranged in the order in which they had to be presented. The guns (brought specially from Zaria) fired their slow salute from across the water. The A.D.C. Hugo Petit appeared first, setting the standard of the show with his full-dress Lancer uniform. Then the tall figure of Sir Bernard came down the companion way in his blue uniform and plumes, with his dazzling wife. They shook hands with all those entitled and each one was singled out with the same marvellous smiles. One and all felt that they had made an impression. They drove off to Government House to give the others time to get to their seats in the Council Chamber where Sir Bernard came to be sworn in before Legislative Council by the Chief Justice.

Nigeria at last had a real Governor, in the Indian tradition, who knew what was wanted and what he had to do and how to do it, with precision and distinction; and he was backed by a superb wife. He had started life in the Indian Civil Service; then went to Mesopotamia as a Colonel in the Indian army and became the first Civil Secretary in Baghdad. After a term as Governor of Uganda, he came to us. So he had experienced the best of both worlds. A competent Arabist, he was immediately at home in the far North. He had a gift of listening to people and weighing them and their opinions; always ready to accept new points of view, but once he had made up his mind he stuck to it. It was Bourdillon who really started the flow of new constitutions. Naturally there were those who did not like him, perhaps because he did not suffer fools gladly.

My wife and I got on well with both the Bourdillons, and the friendship continued until his early death in 1948 and into her widowhood at Oxford. Their life was clouded by the death of their eldest son when the King David Hotel in Jerusalem (used as a branch of the Palestine Secretariat) was blown up.

IX.   Bornu Province

The country

Lake Chad is at the centre of a vast shallow depression called the
Chad Basin, some 800 miles across. This has no connection with the
sea and is therefore an area of inland drainage – although little water
seems to reach the Lake. The Lake itself is about 800 feet above the
sea. Kano at 1,500 feet is in the basin and most of the rivers there flow
towards Chad. The western half of Bauchi Province, at about 2,000
feet, drains into Chad, while the other part runs to the sea, via the
Gongola and Benue and eventually the Niger. The Sahara, which on
average is quite high above sea level, is not far from the northern
shores of the Lake. The frontier between Nigeria and the French
divided the Lake from north to south.

The ancient kingdom of Kanem, of which Bornu is the south-
western segment, was sovereign for centuries over the greater part of
the Chad Basin. On the eastern or (formerly) French side, it has
disappeared as a kingdom, but Bornu still remains. To the Administration Bornu was always known as the Holy Kingdom. It followed
its own way; it did not care for strangers; it was extremely Muslim in
outlook, yet there were a number of small pagan villages on its
southern fringe. Its people were outstandingly intelligent, in a
country of intelligent people. Its climate, even to the African, was
shocking: its rainfall was negligible and yet few starved. Its cattle and
livestock were beyond count, and their herdsmen spent the time
evading the tax-gatherer. The country spoke its own exclusive
language, but was also proficient in Arabic. It was on the great trade
routes southwards from Tripoli to the Niger and eastward to the Nile
and had close links with surprisingly distant places.

Its women were uniquely respected and strode out in trousers; and
their children were taught the Koran, both boys and girls, from an
early age. Its Queen Mother was on the pay-list of the Native Administration; its Chiefs mounted thousands of men on good horses. There
were court poets, court musicians and court jesters – all officially paid
– who lived on their ample wits.

In recent times its educated men spoke the best English of all the
Nigerians: their accent and pronunciation were faultless. Their habits
of life differed essentially from those of the Hausas. Their buildings
were different; their town-planning was rigid and strange compared
with the muddles of the others, and their clothes and hair-styles were
their own. Their commerce and trade also differed from their
neighbours'.

149

In the first days of the Administration a great character called
Hewby was Resident of Bornu for three or four years. He created the
modern administration, knowing little of its principles himself, for he
was the Niger Company agent on the Benue before he came over to
join the new Protectorate in 1900. He is still remembered, especially
for the splendid trees he planted in Maiduguri, then his new capital
town for Bornu. Lugard could never get on with him, for both were
powerful personalities. The two men once met at Nafada on the
Gongola, the frontier post of the Holy Kingdom, then the so-called
'quick way' to Bornu. Hewby appeared with an escort of Bornu
lancers and Lugar spoke the immortal words, 'I may be High Commissioner of Northern Nigeria, but I see, Mr Hewby, that you are
King of Bornu.' Hewby went his own way and got on with his work,
and that has been the guiding principle of Bornu administration ever
since. After him came greater names, such as de Putron, Palmer, and
Patterson: Gordon Lethem, closely associated with Bornu in the
popular mind, was never Resident of the Province, although he was
District Officer of Bornu for some years.

I have always regarded it as the highest honour I ever enjoyed to
have been in charge of that Province twice, to have spent a longer time
within its bounds than any of those famous men, to have survived its
ferocious climate, to have struggled with its diverse problems with
some success and to have been accepted as friend by high and low.
Lugard was right. The Governor of Nigeria enjoyed his own glory and
had his great responsibilities, but the Residency of Bornu was something essentially unique and out of this world.

Bornu's greatest difficulty was 'spatial'. Its huge size made administration difficult and travelling often a nightmare. Probably the old-
fashioned horseback progress was the best, but it was not for me; I
could not afford to be away from headquarters for long, so motor
transport it had to be and that had its own grave problems.
Maiduguri was nearly 1,000 miles from Lagos; our nearest supply
point was Jos, 365 miles away. Kano was 320 miles by track – the road
was not developed until later. We were, however, one of the first stops
to be established on the air route from Khartoum. While that was a
help in many ways, it did not bring heavy goods. We had to look to Jos
and the railway there for men and materials.

Every 12 miles or so there was a gate across the road manned by
Native Authority police. These were closed in heavy rain and kept
closed in spite of all prayers and entreaties (and possibly bribes) until
twelve hours after the rain had stopped. The ground dried quickly
and so gave a reasonable chance for the road to recover. The only
difficulty was when it was raining at one gate and bone-dry at the

next. The dust from the road permeated everything, and all travellers would appear bright red at the end of their journeys. When the late Sardauna was Premier, he had a splendid Rolls-Royce, which was fitted with air-conditioning so effective that it sucked in great quantities of the finest red dust. (The dust was carefully collected, to the distress of the makers).

For many miles this road was dead straight. A tiny deviation occurred in one such stretch, and within the kink there flourished for many years a fine lime tree, 'owned' by the head road-overseer: and therefore heavily 'protected'. Then there came a new and strange overseer, a man of rigid and undeviating principle, and the next time I went along the road I was shocked to see that the tree had gone and the kink had been straightened out. Over the whole distance from Jos to Maiduguri equivalent to London to Berwick I suppose, there were only two 'canteens'. Before Independence, when we knew them, these dismal tin sheds of the United Africa Company had changed little since the early days. Their contents must have been much the same too, lengths of soft iron, exercise books, nauseating soft drinks, quantities of sardines and some inedible biscuits. Before the 1939 war there were rest houses, unfurnished and primitive but water-proof, about every 10 or 12 miles, originally for the official on foot or horse. Later they were useful to the broken-down mechanical voyager.

Bourdillon earned eternal gratitude of travellers with his policy of building Catering Rest Houses. Why, he asked, should officials (and indeed others) travel about 'like tortoises' – i.e. with their furniture and belongings on their backs, when they were not changing station or going to tour in the deep bush? So money was provided. Until this great idea came into effect, rest houses, though 'furnished', did not provide linen or meals or staff, even in places like Bauchi or Maiduguri. The traveller had to bring his own with him, including stores and kitchen equipment, and his cook would buy local food in the market.

Kanem and Rabeh

The ancient kingdom of Bornu was ruled by 'Mais'. Their capital was on the great Yobe river which rises near Zaria and runs through Kano Province, then parallel to and finally along the northern frontier. At Gashua the river is so wide as to be crossed by a great six-span bridge; 150 miles further downstream it is just a depression in the landscape. On this river to this day stand the ruined walls in fine burnt brick, covering many acres, of the Mais Queen Mother's palace.

The extent of the Bornu influence, if not actual 'empire', is shown by the continuing existence, scattered across a vast extent of Hausaland, of isolated communities of Kanuris, descendants from the settlements maintained long ago by Bornu.

Just across the road from the Emir's wall in Kano is a large mud house called the *Gidan Shetima*. *Shetima* is a distinguished Kanuri title only awarded to the eminent. It was a curious coincidence that when the British took Kano in 1903 this house became the 'town residency', as an alternative to the proper house in Nasarawa 3 miles away. It must have been a Fulani with a keen sense of history who so allocated it at that time, and the dominant Power continued therein. It later became a superior rest house and later still a library and museum.

For centuries there was intermittent fighting between the Hausa and the Kanuri, and in the great Fulani wars at the beginning of the nineteenth century the pressure on the Kanuri was very great. They finally appealed for help to their parent-state, Kanem, and the Kanemi people twice came across the Lake and defeated the Fulani. The second time the eminent Shehu al Amin el Kanemi, one of the great rulers of Africa, came to help but stayed to rule. In 1814 he took over the tottering Kanuri power and established the present line of rulers, who still add the words, '*El Kanemi*' to their own names on accession.

The kingdom had a chequered and dramatic career; the last incident took place in the years after 1893, when a man called Rabeh came from the Sudan, bringing with him a rapacious army of some 3,000 trained men, wearing the Khalifa's 'uniform' of patched gowns. Across hundreds of miles of semi-desert they came, unsupported, with their arms and dwindling ammunition. They defeated the first Bornu army they met south of Chad, a huge army, greatly their superior in men and horse but not in arms or discipline. Then Rabeh fell back on Dikwa to rest and reorganise, protected by the swamps of the Yedseram.

A new Shehu arose, a man of courage and determination who, with bloody hands, seized the throne of Bornu from his weak uncle. He met Rabeh and broke his lines, but his men turned to plunder. Even then all might have gone well. The Shehu's restive horse flung back its head at a moment when the rider was leaning forward; the heavy silver head-pieces on the horse's neck struck the ruler in the face, and he fell, his face covered with blood. The army, thinking he had been fatally wounded, gave a shout of despair and broke their ranks. They rallied later but to no avail.

My Shehu, Umar, was the son of the Shehu thus defeated by Rabeh. Rabeh, the polished professional soldier, said to his captive in

Arabic, 'You and your men have fought a gallant fight this day'. The Shehu said, 'Had I won, my slaves would have killed you long before this'. Rabeh said, 'So brave a man shall not hang', and gave a sign: a soldier behind the Shehu pulled his head back and another beside him cut his throat. Umar, then a youth of eighteen, was standing there and saw it all. Rabeh let him and all the dead man's family go free. He remained master of Bornu and more for seven years, and was finally cornered by a French column in 1900 and (they say) killed in personal combat with the French commander, Commandant Lamy, after whom Fort Lamy was named. Throughout his rule Rabeh lived in his early headquarters in Dikwa (it became German, as part of Kamerun, until 1914) and there built a very solid mud house. Later, his house became the house of the British D.O.s, and many of them heard one of Rabeh's wives stumbling screaming down a narrow staircase with her throat partly cut. Sir John Patterson told me he had heard it when D.O. Dikwa.

When things settled down after the Great War, the British retained Dikwa under Mandate as a separate unit of administration with its own Shehu, a man of the same house and lineage as the Shehu of the main kingdom of Bornu. It was only 50 miles from Maiduguri, yet hard of access: in the rains the swamps I have mentioned got in the way, and in the dry season deep sand made travelling a misery – as in huge areas of Bornu.

Administration

When I took over the Bornu Division, with an area more than half that of England, its putative population was over one million people scattered very thinly. To run the complex organisation of this immense area I had one Administration Officer at Nguru at the end of the railway from Kano, 250 miles away from my own office. In Maiduguri I had another Administrative Officer with me and, if I was lucky, I might have a third. There was enough for one A.D.O. to supervise in the detailed affairs of the town of Yerwa, where the Shehu lived two miles away from my office. This included checking the Native Treasury – their revenue was about £100,000 a year – and supervising the prison, with 700 or 800 prisoners, and of course the Shehu's police. All this meant long hours for all of us. The native officials were first-class, but nevertheless it was our duty to supervise and advise.

We arrived in the Province by lorry – the normal way of coming, for you brought your boys and your loads with you. The lorries did not go much faster than 25 miles an hour, and the front seat, called 'first-class' on the transport warrant, was acutely uncomfortable; long distances were impossible seated this way. In those days breakdowns were frequent and commercial lorries were grossly overloaded, until Arab Transport received the contract. Then things improved, and others had to improve to meet their competition.

In the course of years the contribution to the development of the north-east made by the Arab family was noteworthy. Their transport system expanded into a considerable empire, entirely due to their inflexible punctuality and reliability. Many years later I was standing in their garage yard in Jos, and saw a long-distance lorry come in covered with dust from the Bornu road. Immediately a mechanic came out, unscrewed the sump and drained off the oil. This was the invariable practice every time one of their vehicles came in: the engine was washed out and new oil put in. Then it was carefully overhauled and certified ready for the next job. I am sure that not many similar firms did this. The Arab family deservedly gained respect and pro-minence, and Ibrahim Arab sometimes entertained on quite a scale. The family were of course Muslims and drank no spirits, but that did not interfere with their generosity to others.

The first house you met at Maiduguri (before the advent of an airport) was the Bank, on a tiny 'trading lay-out' that had obviously been designed by someone who did not care for traders and wanted them as far as away from the rest of the station as possible. There were some canteens on the north-west of the town, but the idea was that they too should move close to the Bank. Needless to say they did not move and expanded where they were. The Government station was strung out along a ridge called Mafoni, some 20 feet above the plain, which was said to run the whole way round Lake Chad and to have formed its shore in the distant past when it contained more water. On the side of the straight road were the low insignificant buildings that were the Divisional and Provincial offices. The D.O.'s flat-roofed office opened on to a wide verandah, as did clerks' offices further along. The messengers sat on the verandah and slept or gossiped in Kanuri (unlike the Hausas they did not 'salute' Europeans on their knees but by stiff and formal bows). Senior officers had excellent brick houses, built by de Putron some ten years earlier. The Post Office was nearby, its siting typical of the period. The European Government area was given the privilege buying its stamps and sending its telegrams at the end of the road, while the needs of the trading area and the large African town were completely ignored: later, I had a new post office built that was central for everyone.

There were about fifteen European officers in the station. Apart from the Administration we had education, doctors, agriculture and forestry, an engineer or two, with a yard superintendent and a mechanical foreman. One of the key jobs was maintaining the feeble electric plant. This had been brought in by de Putron for the N.A. to give the Shehu and the small hospital electric light: it was agreed at that time that each European quarter should have a few light points but no power points. The current was supplied only from 6 p.m. to 11 p.m. each day. In the course of years more and more light points were put in, until the position arose that when you went out to a party in the evening you switched off all your lights so that your host could use all of his. Failures were common and exasperating. The oddest aspect of the installation was that it was produced by an engine burning charcoal – in a country where good timber was at a high premium. And so it remained until the war.

The plant was in the Works Yard beside the *dandal* (Kanuri for a wide ceremonial approach to the Chief's 'house') in Yerwa. Every Kanuri town or village had its *dandal*. In Yerwa it was three-quarters of a mile long and about 150 yards wide, and thus formed a most impressive street. As one entered the town through the dummy gate pillars (the town had no wall), the *dandal* stretched away to the solid but uninspiring frontage of the Shehu's house. His actual residence covered the whole width of the street and a great depth behind it. We made attempts to enliven the gate-house but the Shehu liked it as it was. However I persuaded him to have a clock on its upper surface and conspired with the Engineer to get one with a ten-foot open dial, and therefore so large that the hands could be seen clearly on entering the town. There was nothing else like it in the whole of Nigeria and the Shehu was delighted.

Beside the Works Yard stood the Chief Alkali's court, with its corner turrets – the court was unfortunately better than the Alkali. Further up by the Shehu's gate were the N.A. offices, set in compounds of brilliant green grass, which a squad of prisoners watered ceaselessly, through the long dry season: they were not averse to this damp work. In later years a large office block was built on the *dandal*, designed apparently by someone who had never heard of Bornu let alone been there, for it was quite unsuitable with great glass windows and no shade.

Also close to the Works Yard was the rather insignificant entrance to the Middle School compound, its simple brick class-rooms set around a square. Here the new Bornu intelligentsia learned their faultless spoken English – helped by Dungus, their main teacher, being a good mimic. I once heard him say to his class: 'Im-med-i-at-ly, dear boy' (imitating my own mannerism), unaware that I was passing by on the verandah.

We used to talk a lot about education and its advantages and the urgent need to press on with it. The words 'primary education' were on everyone's lips, but what we all forgot was that it is no use teaching people to read unless they can apply their knowledge. They must have stimulating literature, be it books or magazines, fact or fiction; without it the reading skill will wither away. In our day there was little to read beyond the Lagos newspapers, which were not renowned for stimulating or accurate presentation of news. There were no magazines or weeklies. But it was difficult to see what to do. Libraries could not be set up to cover the vast areas involved, and the individual could not afford to buy books – who would give a day's pay for one book?

The D.O.'s work was much the same as in any other place, complicated by the great distances and the persistence of the Kanuri complainants, who never took no for an answer: in this they reminded me of my friends in Kabba. They used to herald their approach to the office by a peculiar ululation – they would even perform thus in the dignified and austere drive of Government Lodge in Kaduna. The complainant thought nothing, in the true litigant manner, of describing the origin of their sufferings, even if it meant going back scores of years. They were very eloquent and obdurate. They would come to me first in the D.O.'s office and, if they got no satisfaction, would set out for the Residency along the road. One most persistent man, with a peculiarly disagreeable manner, had just left my office – I was D.O. – and after a while I went up to see the Resident on some other matter. On the way up to the great house, I met the complainant running down the drive. When I reached the office, Patterson, the Resident, was sitting ashen-faced. He said 'Did you meet anyone as you came up?' I replied that I had. He said, 'Did he say anything?' I said I thought he had said he was going to complain at Kaduna. 'Oh dear!' Patterson exclaimed, 'I have done a terrible thing: I have never done anything like it before, but really he was so horrible — I threw a flower-pot at him!' I had noticed a smashed pot on the threshold. 'Thank God I missed him,' he said fervently; 'what in the world will the Chief Commissioner say?' I said, 'he would never believe that anyone like yourself could do such a thing' – Patterson had a well-deserved reputation for courtesy and consideration to all. Fortunately, nothing more was heard of this complainant. We used to get queries from Kaduna on some of these cases, and we never ceased to wonder at the ingenuity of simple villagers in creating completely wrong impressions from so few basic facts.

I was once with Carrow in the Kano office when a similar thing happened. An arrogant (and apparently well-known) complainant was shouting that he would go at once to Kaduna and there get justice. Carrow looked at his watch and said, 'If you want to do that, I would advise you to hurry. The down-train will leave in twenty-five minutes and you have just got time to catch it: you may have to run.' We heard no more from him.

Then there was an old man who wanted to be a ward-head in his village. This was an unpaid job, and, though it had a certain dignity, it also carried tiresome duties and was not to everybody's taste. He wanted the job very badly. I was with Patterson when he appeared, looking very grubby as usual. The old man sat on the floor and explained the situation and the machinations of almost everyone since he left his village, miles way in the bush. He movingly concluded: 'I have bribed the Village Head, I have bribed the District Head and [awe in his voice] I have bribed the Waziri, even the Shehu himself, and no one will help me: so I come to you.'

Patterson looked at him for a moment and then said, very gently in Kanuri: 'But somehow you have not bribed me.' The man gave a gasp of dismay, covered his face with his hands, and sank to the floor. After a moment he gave a convulsive leap and fled down the drive. We did not interfere in these domestic matters, which could get us into very deep waters.

Some years later, when I was myself Resident Bornu, I went one morning into the D.O.'s office at about 10.30, the traditional time for the complainants. I wanted to discuss a point with Guy Money, the D.O., who was large and genial but quick-tempered when roused. While we talked, I watched with fascination as the messengers drifted in and out, as though they were not really there. Each would unostentatiously take an object off the table, an inkpot, a paperweight, a heavy ruler, and so on. I said nothing. When I got outside the head messenger saw me off and I asked him why they had removed these objects. Sheepishly he said, 'Sometimes Captain Money gets a little cross and throws things during interviews. He does not aim at anyone and he has never hit anyone, but we think it is wiser to clear everything off the table, especially the inkpots.' He repeated the last phrase, and then bowed in the Bornu manner and went off with a slight smile.

As elsewhere the administration worked through the District and Village Heads. The former included Kanuri nobles but, strangely, a few of them had to be of slave status, as their jobs were traditionally done by slaves (men of importance, notwithstanding). The most influential post was that of *Kaigama*, the commander-in-chief of the Bornu armies, who was always of slave status. By our time there were, of course, no actual legal slaves but many still cherished the status.

The District Heads had a heavy job in their often remote districts, many days' journey away from headquarters, and they did it excellently. Some of them had areas as large as English counties but the population was small compared with, say, Kano Districts. In parts of Bornu the population averaged less than one per person per square mile. The Village Heads in the North did not generally have much influence, but this was not so in Bornu. Some of them, although not high in the social scale, could trace their lineage back for a thousand years, or, as I once thoughtlessly said, 'before the Norman Conquest'.

As elsewhere the Bornu Village Head and his elders were responsible for the peace of their village. They arrested delinquents and brought them to justice. They had no judicial powers of their own, but one often suspected that a few corrective wallops in the right place at the right time saved a lot of future trouble. They knew the local bad boys only too well, but it was the strangers whom they watched keenly. These were always worth watching: there were eyes everywhere in a village, even an apparently empty one. Where a serious crime had been committed and the suspected culprit had fled, the village trackers took up his trail, across the most unpromising sandy wastes. At their border they would call in the experts from the next village and hand the 'trail' over to them, and so on. It was not unusual for such a trail to cover 60 or 70 miles before a man was caught up with.

Touring was as essential in Bornu as in other Provinces but more difficult. Young officers were supposed to go out on horseback for a couple of months at a time, which was hard, lonely and uncomfortable work. However they learned a lot and the people had a visible presence of Government that they could see and talk to. These officers were supposed to check tax figures and tax collection, look at the local courts and their records, and of course keep an eye on any works going on in their neighbourhood that involved the spending of N.A. money. It was always a problem to ensure that money was correctly spent and that it actually reached the hands of those entitled to it.

During the de Putron period, every administrative officer had been expected to play polo. New arrivals were put in a walled enclosure on a horse, with a polo stick and a ball and set to learn strokes by the hour. I can imagine nothing more depressing. Geoffrey Colby told me that on arrival he had refused to play and had even refused to learn. He was immediately sent on tour for three months. On his return to the so-called civilisation of Maiduguri, he was permitted three days in station and then sent out again for another three months. At the end of that he still refused to play polo and he was eventually accepted. Colby was a very able man, and ended his career as Governor of Nyasaland.

When the D.O. himself went on tour, things were more comfortable as he could usually visit only the District Headquarters, most of which were on some kind of motorable track, with separate hazards in the rains and the dry season. The country was featureless, with nothing to see except low trees and an occasional river-bed. Vague trade routes abounded and great areas of dried swamp furnished points at which you could go seriously wrong. When travelling in Northern Nigeria, knowledge of 'picnic trees' was valuable – the chief of the Northern Public Works, Sir Hubert Walker, had a map showing all the better trees conveniently near to the road where a car could be driven off under their shade, preferably with room to sit and eat. As the roads improved, many of these trees were deplorably thought to be too near the carriageways and were felled, to the wrath of all sorts and conditions of travellers, and deep ditches were dug by enthusiastic road men, preventing a car reaching the shade. Thompstone planted a group of trees at every tenth milestone on the Maiduguri–Potiskum road to give shelter to the foot-slogger, a kindly thought typical of the man. In some areas you would find the rest house floor covered with fine carpets, often three or four thick. It seemed that Bornu had limitless supplies of these rugs and the Chiefs would give them as presents from time to time, which involved costly return gifts to them.

We lived for the whole of the tour in the same de Putron house and found it comfortable and convenient, though stuffy in the hot weather. Patterson went off to Kano and H.L.M. Butcher, an old Bornu hand, came in. We got on well and the whole atmosphere was friendly. This was just as well, for any ill-feeling in such a place only leads to unpleasantness and consequent inefficiency. It could and did happen sometimes.

The installation

Every Thursday the Resident and the D.O. drove down to the town for the ceremonial Council meeting. In Bornu the Councillors sat round a table, whereas in Hausaland the Emirs would sit on a dais and the Councillors on the floor in the order of their precedence in the Emir's eyes. Bornu people generally tended to sit at tables rather than on the floor.

On our journey to the Shehu, we were always escorted by a car with two leading Councillors to pilot us in through the town gateway and along the *dandal*. There was a strange guard of honour of very old men with a medley of ancient rifles and muskets, wearing patchwork uniforms in faded colours. They shambled into a 'present arms' to words of command that I could not understand. It was years before I realised that these were Turkish army commands, as used in Rabeh's army whose uniform they wore.

The Shehu would sit quite still and silent, apparently taking no notice of what was being said at the Council; then he would suddenly break in, if the subject was something that interested him or his people. It was always very much to the point. Our biggest job was to make the great Bornu officials understand that they, and not we, were responsible for the people of Bornu: we were merely there as a last line to see that the machinery worked and that everyone got as fair a deal as possible. I can still hear Patterson urging with all his earnestness in Kanuri: 'You are Bornu, you are Bornu; we are strangers – we come and go; we are not Bornu, you are Bornu!'

The Council had the last say in all local matters, but the Resident had to see that it did not go against Government policy. Normally this was not difficult, but occasionally a crisis arose. They were very able men, and would have been in any circumstances, but they were mostly uneducated in our sense of the word: they were beyond the elementary level yet not as far as secondary. They had all the authority of Arabic education as well, a great asset. They gave full consideration to problems and reached logical decisions to which they clung tenaciously. Here as elsewhere in the North, the Council members were appointed by the Chief and confirmed by the Resident. They were well paid by the standard of that time, and fitted their exalted positions. The legal experts were the most impressive, but the others were very practical in their ideas. The point was that they knew the country, where they and their forebears had lived and what they could get over to the people and what would meet with difficulty.

Going to Council meetings in Bornu, when I was Resident, was a severe tax on the wits. You had to have planned what could be jettisoned and what had to be pressed at all costs. In a Hausa council the set-up was quite different and they rarely – until latter days – argued with the white officers. This was of course, most dangerous and one had to be sharply alive all the time to hidden perils.

The Shehu's Council, like that of the other great Chiefs, was also a Court of Justice with powers of life and death. All murder cases came before it for hearing. The death sentence required the Govenor's confirmation but the judgment was theirs. Considering how quick-tempered everyone seemed to be in Bornu, and how heavily-armed, especially the sharp wrist-knife that lay along their fore-arms, handy for the quick draw, the number of murders reported was remarkably small – out of the million-odd people, less than one a month. Most were stabbings with pretty good reason.

The most original was the case of a paramour, caught in the act. The injured husband tied him up and flung over him a small thatched granary roof that was lying at hand, to which he then set fire. The most ghastly occurred when a woman was having a bad time with a birth, and a kind friend tried to help by thrusting up her vagina a very dirty knife, inserted in several positions. The shocked M.O. reported it to me, as the woman had been brought to him in the final stages before she died. I told the Shehu and he was mildly interested: that sort of thing, he said, happened quite often. I said that action had to be taken and for the only time in the latter part of my career I insisted on a case being brought, at least of manslaughter. A reluctant Court passed a suitable sentence.

The condemned were hanged in those days in the prison, theoretically in private, but as no one would believe that they were dead, men had to be allowed in from a prisoner's village to bear witness when they got home. Everyone was very gentle with prisoners, their food was excellent and there was little trouble. Once, however, we had a huge Shuwa Arab in the garden gang at the Residency and one morning he took exception to something said to him by another prisoner. He very nearly killed the man and it took half a dozen strong men to hold him down. I had no idea what to do with him, and the obvious penalties seemed out of place. So I drew a circle in the sand by the carriage drive and said that he was to stand in the circle till I gave further orders. Then I drove off to the office a mile away. Some time later Dorothy rang up and said, 'You remember that prisoner you told to stand in the circle: well, he looks terrible, and I think he is going to faint: what do you want done with him?' I had forgotten all about him, and naturally said that he should be moved into the shade to rest with the others. After that he became the most helpful and loyal weeder and sweeper, and kept the other prisoners alert.

The highlight of that period in Bornu for all of us happened in 1937. When I reached Maiduguri the then Shehu was very old. A tiny man, he was pushed into the Council in a rickety canvas chair. His Councillors were visibly scared of him – no bad thing for they were a tough lot. There was an authenticated occasion when he clawed his way up the gown of a huge Councillor and bit him in the face. He had been Shehu for many years, and now a strange sequence of events developed in which I was directly concerned.

It chanced that I went on tour in the east near Dikwa. The D.O. Dikwa was away, and I had told the Resident I would like to have a look at the place on my return journey. I had heard so much about it, and the country was oddly at the right season for travelling. The Resident gave me a message for the Emir, whom I found to be a huge man, slow of speech and gait, but quick of mind. My message was that a flight of British fighters was coming to Maiduguri the following week from Khartoum, the first ever to come to us. The Resident and the Shehu would welcome a visit by the Emir to Maiduguri to see the planes at close quarters. The Emir promptly accepted.

It must be said that in the huge genealogical table of the Shehus were 143 high-ranking *Abbas*, equivalent to Princes of the Blood. These were entitled, without notice, to drop in for any meal in the Shehu's house – imagine having enough food for all of them (and their followers) on hand at all times. It would have been shameful indeed to be caught lacking. Among the *Abbas* the Emir of Dikwa was nearly heir-apparent, although no such thing could be thought of in the circumstances of Bornu. The old Shehu had not been feeling well for some days, but there was no special alarm, in spite of his age and frailty. None of the *Abbas* was in any state to seize power – there was an enormous quantity of varied fire-arms in Bornu and plenty of people to use them, but they were scattered. Some co-ordination would be needed to produce a successful coup.

Round the east of the town runs a broad river, the Alo, bone-dry (apart from waterholes) for eight months, and running deep for the remainder. As the Emir of Dikwa crossed the river-bed that fateful morning, the old Shehu died.

Rioting started at once. The market closed and the people kept to their houses. The hospital was cleared for casualties; the R.W.A.F.F. Company stood by their vehicles; the leading *Abbas* closed their great doors and checked over their arms. The Resident sent down a Vickers machine-gun to cover the great *dandal* outside the Shehu's gate. There was sporadic firing in the streets but, when I drove through the town as District Officer, all was quiet – in a rather sinister way. The Resident, John Patterson, spoke excellent Kanuri. The king-makers (two or three Councillors and the Chief *Alkali*) knew what they had to do and that they had to do it quickly; before anyone knew it, the Emir of Dikwa was proclaimed Shehu. He never went home again, and thus started his long rule of over thirty years.

Those who did not know Bornu, including some in high positions, seemed to regard the new Shehu as some kind of cattle thief, if not worse. There was no justification for such a belief, but it deprived the Shehu of the recognition he should have received. His real handicap was that he could speak neither Hausa nor English. The Hausa language had been anathema under the old Shehu – the Hausas were not popular in Bornu at that time.

Some years after his appointment I was talking to the Shehu privately, with an interpreter, and said that I was surprised so many British officers thought he was various kinds of bad man. He laughed and said, 'How many people were there in Maiduguri town when you first came?' I said 'About sixty thousand'. 'And now?' he asked, 'how many?' I replied, 'Well over a hundred thousand.' He said, 'If I were the bad chief they say I am, would all those extra people have come to live in my capital under my protection? People don't come of their own free will to live under bad rulers.' Although this was not entirely logical, it was certainly difficult to refute.

On state occasions an interpreter sat at his feet hidden by his great gown. At a Government House dinner in Kaduna, his sepulchral voice issued from beneath the table. At that party the Shehu caused great confusion – it was his first large 'European' dinner – for when offered the fish on a great dish, he helped himself to the lot, saying he was fond of fish.

And so, in 1937 Umar ibn Kiari Alamin al Kanemi was installed Shehu of Bornu and *Amir-ul-Islam* of the East (this meant 'Commander of the Faithful' far into the Sudan; the Sultan of Sokoto is Amir of the West.) The Governor, Sir Bernard Bourdillon, came up from Lagos to preside in blue uniform with silver lace and flying cock's plumes. Twenty-five thousand men and five thousand horses came from all over the Shehu's territory; some of the great stranger rulers came too. There was a vast circle round the low dais. The Shehu was sworn as the King's man, the ancient oaths to his own kingdom were administered and he was lifted on to a great shield of pure white skin, below which the learned scribes had written suitable texts from the Koran in the firm sand with their forefingers. Then the leading men came up in their grades to render allegiance. This was the tense moment, for at least one of his predecessors had been shot and killed at this stage in the proceedings; now all went well.

The great circle advanced, with many hundreds of drummers and pipers, some in splendid robes and others in copies of Rabeh's patchwork uniforms, representing hard times in the desert. Over their heads flew huge scarlet banners, gold-embroidered with Koranic texts, their spear-headed staffs sticking up through the ostrich feathers. Swirling clouds of dust covered everyone and the men were dripping with sweat. Everywhere drums were beating, deep-toned and shrill, making a solid wall of sound broken by shouting and ululations. The pipes wailed and the horns throbbed. The mounted formations wheeled outwards into long columns to line the ceremonial return into the town. All this required some tough rehearsal for a couple of days, supervised by two chamberlains of the Shehu's court, with their forked wands of office, riding nimble ponies in a confusion more apparent than real: they knew exactly what was required and saw that it was done. It was all my responsibility, and my function required that I, too, mounted a horse.

A sequel occurred months later when an old man came to Maiduguri on a white donkey from the East. An Arab, grave and distinguished and, without his travelling garb, well-dressed. He had travelled all the way from Darfur in the Sudan, 1,000 miles and more, to bring fealty and greetings of the Muslims there who regarded the Shehu, as King of Kanem, as their own religious leader.

The next day the Governor carried out the usual round of inspection of official buildings and offices, bright with an unusual sparkle of cleanliness and order that must have struck an intelligent observer like the Governor as probably unspontaneous. Even the humblest were unrecognisable in their best robes.

The following morning we set out by car for Lake Chad (the gubernatorial party had come up by road). Bourdillon had himself said that arrangements should be made for a visit to the Lake, something no Governor had ever achieved before. The Lake itself, about 15,000 square miles of water with ever-varying margins, is the most eerie place I know. The country round it is completely flat for many miles, and in the dry season the east wind blows the surface into Nigeria and you find tongues of Chad twenty miles from the apparent Lake shore; in the rains the Lake is blown over into the old French colony. At its deepest the water is only 8 feet deep, and one can pole oneself across.

There are vast areas of papyrus along the shore and in islands. On an earlier visit to the Lake I had seen antelope in the distance and set out to stalk them. I said to myself – one gets dazed with its sheer loveliness – I will get up that hill gently and find them on the other side! But it was not a hill at all, only a thicket of tall papyrus reeds. I found myself wading through quite deep water among those reeds and tripping over their roots: the inevitable happened and my rifle went barrel-foremost into the mud. When I got through the reeds, the antelope were there quietly grazing, but I could only have fired at some danger to myself. When the Governor's party came, no game was visible, exasperation was thereby spared.

As far as Mongunu and Kukawa, the ancient capital and district headquarters, where we built a complete camp for the Governor, there was a passable track, but the last 15 miles were across difficult sand. We had no way of consolidating this, and no money to do it, so we laid miles of brushwood and at one point about 3 miles of specially woven grass matting. We prayed that there would be no bush fire to burn up the track before the great day, and strict orders were issued that no one on any excuse was to use that track: every white man in Maiduguri was itching to take this chance of going to the Lake, usually cut off by sand.

The party reached the Lake without incident and dead on schedule. We went on the Lake on two beautiful papyrus rafts specially made for the occasion, identical to the 'hunting' boats to be seen in ancient Egyptian tomb paintings, but of a kind still used on the Lake. Big enough to carry cattle, they have clay platforms on which fires can be burned. It was beautifully calm and some of us swam in the fresh cool water. We went back to the main camp at Kukawa content.

The trip to Chad was a great success and the Lagos party enjoyed themselves. There was of course a lot of work behind the scenes: furniture had to be taken to the camp and our whole kitchen department was carried there too. Seven of us sat down to an excellent dinner that night, with fresh fish from the Lake and the best Government House cutlery and china. There was an air of peace and comfort: no telephones, no papers, just a strange world to look at. Governors did not get enough of this; when they needed relaxation on official trips, everything was usually so 'laid on' that they might as well have been at Government House. The days were hot by the lake, but the nights were very cold. We all woke up next day different people, much refreshed in mind.

During the whole of this unusually important visit, Butcher, the Resident of the Province, stayed in bed and it was left to my wife and myself to do the honours. I don't think that there was much the matter with him; it was just nerves. An able man, he was so timid that he could seldom bring himself to open the official mail from the Kaduna Secretariat when it arrived once a week. He would ask any of his staff who happened to come into his office to open and glance at the letters. Gazing aimlessly out of the window, he would say after a while: 'Is it all right? Is there anything nasty?' I used to assure him that there could not be; he was very 'blue-eyed', as the phrase was – in other words he could do no wrong in the eyes of higher authority.

We went on leave shortly after this and Bourdillon, who had been very friendly to us both, transferred me to Lagos for my next tour.

X. Lagos, 1939

By 1939 I had eighteen years' service behind me and arrived to act as a senior Assistant Secretary in the Lagos Secretariat. I was fortunate in having two of the ablest men in the service as my assistants, H.R.E. Browne (known as 'Phiz' after his great-grandfather, the illustrator of Dickens' novels) and T. Farley-Smith (known as 'Farley'). My job was in consequence not so onerous as it had been in lower posts, for here other people did the initial work, which saved much time.

I brought in a new system. Instead of all papers going first to the juniors, they came to me when filed. I had a look at them and sent them down for action. Sometimes I put a note to say what should be done, sometimes I left it to them, and sometimes told them to come and discuss it after they had been through the precedents. Sometimes, where it was just a matter of the Chief Secretary having to see the paper, I would minute it up without delay. This all sounds a bit fussy but in practice it speeded action and made for smooth working. It was, I always felt from my own experience, a waste of time for the junior to work at an elaborate draft, only to see most of it changed on its way up.

The residential area of Ikoyi was filling up gradually. There were new buildings in the town of Lagos and many more across the water in Ebute Metta and Apapa – the swamps between these areas were being drained and since then have been built over. When the original rails to Apapa Wharf were being laid over these swamps it is said that a shunting engine was left unattended at the end of a new section. Next morning men found just the smoke stack and top of the cabin above the ooze. It was allowed to sink and then the track was laid decently over it. When all this was complete and the wharves were functioning, the fortnightly mail-boat moored against the wharf near a series of railway tracks. Those first-class passengers not staying in Lagos would travel up-country by train. But the custom was that they could be taken off the boat by friends or friends' friends and given lunch and a place for the wives to rest. The husbands went off to see their baggage through Customs.

The boat train left at 9 p.m. When the whistles blew and the long train set off into the night, to many it was a journey into the unknown. It was impossible to see it go without emotion. The red tail-lights disappeared round a curve, and the Lagosian hosts went back to their homes.

The reverse journey was quite different. The boat train arrived from the North early in the morning and felt its way on to the wharf. Passengers would look out of the train windows up the towering side of the ship – a moment of deep gratification. Some would go on board in pyjamas and dressing gown to have a bath – for many possibly the first real one they had had for months. There were no Customs formalities on homeward journeys and their baggage was hoisted aboard and taken to their cabins. They would have a wonderful breakfast – again, to some strangely nostaligic and unreal – and then sit about reading papers until the Lagos people came on to see their friends. Great parties were held in cabins and in the lounges – at ship's prices. At noon precisely the cables were cast off and the ship drew away; husbands and friends were left behind and went off to their cars or got into launches. When a distinguished official was leaving on retirement, a W.A.F.F. bugler sounded the 'Hausa farewell', a particularly haunting and original call, from the Lagos side of the harbour where the course of the deep water channel brought the departing ship close inshore.

The boat left on alternate Saturdays. It was usually easy to leave the office early to go on board. In the Secretariat the main strain was on the immediately preceding Thursdays and Fridays. Despatches had to be sent up for the Governor's signature by Friday noon. Being communications between the Sovereign's representative and a Secretary of State, the despatches had to be immaculate in every respect and no alteration was permitted: the typing had to be absolutely clean and perfectly laid out. At least six pairs of eyes scrutinised every word before these crisp white sheets reached the august presence. Even then, errors crept in. Our attention was drawn to one in a reply from the Secretary of State. The first paragraph conveyed approval of the request made in the despatch in question. The Minister went on in his second paragraph: 'Though second to none in my liking for a convivial occasion or celebration, and like many others appreciating the advantages of alcohol in reasonable quantities both for pleasure and for stimulation, I feel perhaps that I should take some exception to the manner in which Your Excellency has been kind enough officially to address me.' We searched anxiously through our despatch copy and could not see what he was alluding to. Then someone spotted that the despatch had been addressed to the 'Tight Honourable' instead of the 'Right Honourable the Secretary of State for the Colonies'.

There was a steady stream of cables between Lagos and London in a private code used for economy reasons. It had large numbers of phrases to match every incident of official life, all expressed in five-letter groups for transmission. Those skilled in its use could say much in a short message. During a wartime economy drive, old files were torn up for use as drafting paper on the unused surfaces. Great confusion was caused in the Colonial Office when a girl at our end ciphered the wrong side of a sheet – a long discursive minute on something which had passed on its way many years before. It took some effort to straighten that one out.

There was an awkward period between the Munich Agreement in September 1938 and the declaration of war a year later. The moment war-clouds appeared on the horizon, a whole series of Government precautions came into effect, quite additional to military activities. Emergency legislation lay in the office safes ready for passing, with dates blank. Blank telegrams in sheaves awaited despatch. Many regulations had to be made and published; Emergency Gazettes stood in type; there was policy to be decided, and reserve equipment had to be laid in, and stores of all kinds ordered. Legislative Council had to hold a special session.

Nigeria did not seem likely to be invaded, as we had the then friendly French all around us. We had no protection for the harbours, for it was thought that the Royal Navy would deal with that. There were no particular reserves of food or, also very important, of paper, so newsprint became very short. Our airfields were rudimentary and the new airmail service depended on the route through Khartoum and the Nile Valley. The W.A.F.F. were highly efficient as infantry but they had no transport of their own and only six field-guns. I never knew what sort of reserves of ammunition and stores they had, but they were probably low. Steps were taken to correct these deficiencies.

I found myself in charge of the 'war-effort' section of the Secretariat, an alarmingly wide field of activity. One of our troubles was manpower. In the 1914–18 war heavy losses from drownings and sickness had gravely depleted the Government staff, and too many people had been released for the services. There was no staff to go round all the duties. In 1939 we had no idea what the future might hold in this respect, provided that we had enough drugs, sickness seemed less of a menace than a quarter of a century before.

Every man of military age wanted to be released, but this was manifestly impossible. Naturally no instructions were received on this from London, so we evolved a fairly simple formula. Anyone who by his own *personal* effort could make a contribution to the war was released, if he wanted to go and if he was asked for. This covered anyone who could fly an aircraft or who had some Naval experience, and a few soldiers. No others were released. Engineers, technicians, doctors and the like were wanted just as much in Nigeria and we were likely soon to be short of them.

The matter was confused because a number of young officers had joined the special reserve of the W.A.F.F. and these were called up without much notice. We soon found that some of them were being employed by the Army with little regard to their potentialities. After a long fight we got some of them back again. There were naturally hard feelings on the part of the people who were not released and some acrimonious correspondence developed. But it died down as people realised Nigeria's position. After all, though not in uniform, all of us in the Colonial Service were just as much the King's servants in Nigeria as those in uniform, and doing vital work on what later turned out to be a great line of communication. The peace had to be kept among all the varied and often mutually hostile peoples that made up Nigeria. It was a striking fact that through the long years of the war, when development stopped and the local population were obviously getting very little for their money, there was no rising or civil strife.

On the very eve of war, the whole Secretariat decided that all that could be done had been done, and on that Saturday night (September 2) many of us went to the pictures in an open-air cinema converted from an old tennis court. The screen was of concrete and lizards ran across it in the brilliant light chasing bugs. The picture was Disney's *Snow White and the Seven Dwarfs* – her first appearance in Nigeria. I sat next to the German Consul: a new residence was just being completed for him on a splendid site overlooking the open lagoon, and no money had been spared. I knew him well and asked him when it would be finished. He said, 'Some time next week', and as soon as possible there would be a house-warming and he hoped I would be there. I made a polite reply in the knowledge that unless something very remarkable happened, he would be arrested and interned the very next day. It was said that in his files was found a dormant commission from Hitler appointing him Governor of Nigeria!

In spite of the war, people were coming and going by ship from England, but gradually movements were restricted. Wives going home on leave found that they could not get back again to Nigeria. Some people did not see their young families for several years.

The Royal Navy set up a shore establishment. Merchant ships were camouflaged and mounted 6-inch guns aft, and the W.A.F.F. took on recruits in great numbers. The Army found itself in difficulties, because the whole strategy had been to develop some military action against the Italians in East Africa, and it was not till France was about to fall in 1940 that Italy came into the war. Then the Nigeria Regiment went off to Kenya and took part in a long and difficult campaign against the Italians in Abyssinia.

Bourdillon stayed on as Governor beyond his normal five-year term. He was to have gone to Khartoum – his great ambition – but that was not to be. He finally completed an eight-year tour as

Governor of Nigeria, and though beset by wartime problems, he spent time thinking of future constitutions and outlining political possibilities. Maybin left us to become Governor of Rhodesia and sadly died of appendicitis. A very good man. Alexander Grantham succeeded him as Chief Secretary.

XI. Bornu, 1940

At war

My second service in Bornu was during the war, beginning late in 1940. I had just returned by slow convoy from England which was then experiencing the start of the Blitz. For most of the two and a half years of that long wartime tour (the normal tour was between twelve and eighteen months) I was alone and acting in charge of the Province – the Resident, Vere Walwyn, left two days after my arrival in Maiduguri to be Secretary Northern Provinces in Kaduna. This was mentally and physically a great strain. I was Senior District Officer, a step below the correct rank for the job. There were few white staff and supplies were difficult. We had two companies of the Regiment, who had so far not fired their first musketry course. We had no anti-aircraft device of any kind to defend the airfield. To make things worse, the entire external frontier, hundreds of miles long, abutted on to French territory ruled since June by the collaborationist government of Marshal Pétain – the 'Vichy' government. We therefore were not only threatened from that quarter but were also completely cut off from the Anglo-Egyptian Sudan to the east beyond Chad Territory. We had a major airport 5 miles from Maiduguri – an inviting target for an enemy.

The normal boundary between the two French Governors-General ran across Chad. to the south, the area (Equatorial) under Brazzaville was controlled by the anti-British Boisson; the territory to the north, (Occidentale) was under Dakar, then not quite so anti-British. The Governor-General there had his troubles, for he brooded over the great battle-cruiser *Richelieu*, the pride and joy of the French fleet, which had got away from Europe just in time. However by the time I had reached Bornu there had been dramatic changes in French territory.

Our pre-war relationship with Fort Lamy (headquarters of Tchad Territory) had never been close or even tolerably good. This was a pity, because closer ties would have been useful at this time. The French had no one with whom they could discuss their difficulties unofficially in Maiduguri, so everything had to be very official, and the French tended to be extremely formal in trans-frontier affairs. The Governor of Chad was then a black man, Félix Eboué, from Cayenne (French Guiana). His was one of the remotest of governorships in any administration, and his staff was not high-powered when it came to offering advice (compared, say, with the Brazzaville staff or ours in Kaduna). Amid the disasters of June 1940, with the collapse of the

French Army and Hitler's division of France, Hitler's triumph seemed complete, and he heard constantly that Britain would make peace. This was the line followed by the secret information he received from his Governor-General.

Eboué looked out at the muddy Logone river and pondered. The official line did not correspond with his own thoughts. He listened to the radio broadcasts of de Gaulle and the Free French from London. Giles, one of our officers who spoke good French, went over from Nigeria to offer him advice, but Eboué could do little in the face of Boisson's negative attitude. Should he declare for de Gaulle? Eboué felt that someone should do so. He could not discuss it with his fellow-Governors. Should he make the move himself? If so, how was it to be done? Pro-Gaullist officers arrived in Fort Lamy towards the end of August and had discussions with him. His younger officers were strongly in favour of continuing the war. Possibly the final turning-point came with the instruction that Italian officers should be permitted access to the French Colonial frontier forts abutting Tripolitania – the Vichy government had signed an armistice with Italy. This was a grave blow to French pride and Eboué refused to give the necessary orders.

At this point Boisson went to Dakar on transfer as a kind of overlord, and Husson, who took over from him at Brazzaville, was more amenable. Of course, de Gaulle's name was at that time unknown to the ordinary Frenchman and indeed many French Colonial officials had not heard his broadcasts from London or, if they had, paid them little attention. For Eboué a considerable difficulty was that Nigeria could not supply him with the arms and equipment necessary for his purpose, having little enough for their own needs. Britain had agreed to supply him, but this would take time. Economic arrangements were made with Nigeria for the disposal of Chad crops and produce.

Eboué met the officials of his administration, mostly white Frenchmen, in the Cercle Tchadienne (Fort Lamy's colonial club) on 26 August 1940. As a result of his eloquence, negotiations and canvassing, and that of the Gaullists there, they all signed a statement proclaiming their adherence to de Gaulle and their determination to continue the war. In the next two days the Cameroons followed suit under General Leclerc's vigorous initiative, and in Brazzaville Husson was deposed.

Thus the Gaullist movement, till then very much a paper tiger, suddenly acquired a vast supporting territory in Equatorial Africa. There was hardly a word about these events in the British press, yet they were decisive. Thus Eboué, the unknown man from Cayenne, set out on his way to burial, only four years later, in the Paris Panthéon, with the great of France. It was Leclerc himself, then commanding in Chad as a Colonel, who told me these details, and more.

When Boisson was being transferred to Dakar, his aircraft came down unexpectedly at Fort Lamy to refuel. At all costs he should not be allowed to come into the government station and spoil the situation. Eboué sent his A.D.C. to the airport, 2 miles away. He met Boisson and reported the deplorable news that an epidemic had broken out in the town and that a *cordon sanitaire* was being established between the town and the airport. The Governor therefore begged His Excellency to accept his apologies and excuse his inability to attend him in person; the Governor-General was further urged, with the fullest courtesies and most distinguished consideration, to go on his way before the airport itself was officially closed. Boisson took off and action proceeded on the ground.

Those days have always seemed to me the 'end of the beginning', in Churchill's famous phrase. The air route was now clear from Nigeria to the Nile valley, which meant that service people and material landed on the Gold Coast or in Nigeria could be flown direct not only to Egypt, which was crucial to the campaign there, but also to India and the Far East. Two routes were eventually established. Ours was the quick one but considered more risky; the other ran further south, through the Belgian Congo to Kenya. I was told by Air Marshal Sholto Douglas, when he was staying with us, that if a stick of bombs had hit the Maiduguri airfield accurately just before the battle of El Alamein, Egypt would have been lost to the enemy and the war would have been infinitely harder to win.

The poor airfield at Fort Lamy was now hastily strengthened – the runways were made of burnt brick laid herringbone fashion. Those at Kano and Maiduguri were extended 2,000 (later 8,000), yards and petrol was accumulated for refuelling. At one time we had 6 million gallons near our airfield at Maiduguri. It was scattered round the area under trees and camouflage, and was invisible from the air – we went up to find out for ourselves. The oil all came up from Port Harcourt to Jos by rail, then to Maiduguri by road (900 miles). To Fort Lamy was a further 150 miles of poor road. Nigeria produced no oil then.

Leclerc built up a force, in addition to the Foreign Legion battalion at Fort Lamy, based 300 miles away in the mountain region called Faya: this was a secret force in a secret headquarters – a secret so closely guarded that it was known to no less than 100,000 people. But it somehow escaped the notice of the Germans. Here Leclerc trained the troops eventually to Division strength, and from here he suddenly appeared on Montgomery's left flank in Libya. All his supplies came up from the Nigerian coast by rail through Jos and thence by lorry, a round trip by road of 1,500 miles. The roads were so bad that many lorries perished after a single journey. The African hauliers made substantial fortunes, mostly untaxed because it was all so secret.

To return to my own adventures. I went into the huge 'mud Residency' as soon as it could be made habitable. When I examined the many nooks and crannies of this house, I found a vast accumulation of 'stink bugs'. They were in every corner, especially on the staircases, and along cornices. Two messengers cheerfully took charge of the job of cleaning them out and, with a dozen prisoners, shovelled them into containers which were taken away in lorries. After four days of hard work, over two and a half tons of bugs were removed. When the place had been fumigated, I moved in.

I was not there for long. The new District Officer's house nearby – the first 'permanent' house to be built in Bornu – was by then complete, so I moved in there to give my Residency to the officers of a squadron of the Free French air force which appeared with six Blenheims and transport aircraft and made their base with us for some months. The *Force Tropique* was its official name, and it was very secret. They were an aristocratic lot, mostly Spahis and using assumed names: they were also intelligent, strongly for de Gaulle and for France. This had embarrassing consequences at the time of their arrival, when, as a small courtesy, we flew a tricolor with a Cross of Lorraine sewn onto the white band. Their Colonel said: '*Monsieur l'Administrateur-en-Chef* [meaning me], *nous sommes Français, nous suivons le Général de Gaulle, nous n'avons pas trahi la France*', and so on, for some time. It was smoothed over by our unstitching the fatal Cross of Lorraine and putting it on a tiny Tricolour *guidon* under the main unblemished flag of France. For a while I was afraid that my unaided efforts had somehow lost us the war.

They were splendid officers, and their sergeants and 'other ranks' were almost as good. We got on well with them. In their mess they made our local food taste quite different. One day they said they wanted to test two of their officers as navigators and would I come with them in a Blenheim to act as umpire. The course was westwards to Damaturu, then another 80 miles south to Biu and finally direct back to Maiduguri. Their maps were specially drawn for them and merely had the corner points and one or two rivers. I had our standard survey map, and my job was to identify the two distant corners and see that they passed over them correctly.

It was a good flight and they reached the points indicated. At Biu we came down to a few hundred feet and circled the town, flying low

over the streets. I had been able to send a message to the Chief so that
the people would not be alarmed – it was the first time that anyone
down there had seen an aircraft. The people were delighted, and
waved; later, of their own accord, they collected some hundreds of
pounds for the 'Spitfire fund' – the official theory of which was that
£5,000 would buy a new Spitfire fighter. Bornu in all raised enough for
three. We liked these Frenchmen and were sad when they flew off.

Then the R.A.F. appeared and wanted quarters for their officers, so
I handed the Residency to them as their mess, with its ample room for
officers and visitors. I could never understand why in such an
important staging post they only had a Flying Officer in charge. A few
months later an advance party of an American group appeared. The
United States was not in the war then, so their status was uncertain;
this was the 'lease-lend' period of the war. The Americans asked for a
huge site by the airport, some 5 miles out from the city, as their camp.
I refused and it took some time to quell the wave of polite indignation
I had inadvertently stirred up. I explained that there were a number
of good reasons why they should not be at the airport, and offered
them instead two large vacant plots inside the Government Station.
These they inspected, and accepted with alacrity.

I did not explain my reluctance to have foreign nationals in a large
area which I could not control. I wanted them under my eye, and did
not wish an army of occupation to take shape, out of touch with my
own officials. In the event my scheme worked well and a close liaison
developed between the British Administration and the U.S. Air
Corps when they came. They sat on our Service committees; we went
to each other's parties; they attended the Native Administration
functions and were greatly impressed – none of which could have
happened if they had been at the airport.

The great local event was the *Salla*, the feast at the end of the fast of
Ramadam. Everyone wore his or her best and all went to greet the
Shehu, tens of thousands of them with their horses and their children,
and (only in Bornu) women wearing trousers and striding out like
men. The horsemen rose in endless waves and galloped the length of
the *dandal*, reining in their excited steeds just short of the Shehu's
gate-house. The Shehu himself sat on a balcony and acknowledged
the people's greetings.

The Americans were horrified to find that we had no running water
in our houses. They were going to instal a system for themselves and
begged us to accept at least a standpipe in each Government compound; we gladly accepted and in return promised a suitable water
tank on a thirty-foot steel framework. One was available and was
brought up in sections by road from Port Harcourt. By a miracle, or so

it seemed to me, the correct measurements of the base were sent in advance, so that when the steel arrived, the concrete bases, with holding down bolts, were in position and had set. The frames were put up and the water-tank was bolted together in the incredible time of four days. Water was soon running into it from pumps in the river Alo. So water flowed and there was joy in the hearts of the house-boys.

The river Alo rises in the mountains to the south and in the rains fills Lake Alo, a large sheet of water bordered with papyrus and full of wild duck and fish, about 10 miles south of the town. One of the great rulers of Bornu, Idris Aloma (meaning 'connected with Alo') is buried in the middle of the lake. When it fills up early in the rains – there is always some water in it – the water spills over into the lower course of the river and starts running along its dry bed. About 100 yards across at Maiduguri, it is quite dry, except for water holes scooped in it and a few scummy pools under its cliffs and grassy banks. Once the river starts to run, reports of its progress are sent to the Shehu at frequent intervals. It takes about a week to travel the 10 miles. At last the tongue of the advancing water is within reach of the town. The people stream out on the dry bed with little calabashes and try to guess where the tip of the leading trickle will find itself. A great crowd watches and cheers and advises from the banks. This is the epic struggle between hunger and plenty, between thirst and satiety and, therefore between darkness and light, and good and evil. So not only does it have a physical meaning but it has a spiritual one too: not only the quenching of a thirst but the satisfaction of a frustrated spirit.

It is not easy, however, to find the right place to scoop your little groove and sink the calabash to its receptive brim. You can try but the water may pass you by, or it may slow down and the leading tongue may be elsewhere. Someone else will get it and rush off with the sacred water to his or her home: it will bring good luck in the year in the farms and will cure mother's nasty pain. There is no limit to the number of times you collect, but it must be from the stream which is leading at that moment. The oddest part of it all is that a hundred yards upstream of these thin streams of water trickling in the sand, the flow is from bank to bank and the children are splashing and diving in it. The river goes round Yerwa on to the north towards Chad, but it never reaches the lake. It fans out into vast swamps.

While we still depended for electricity on the little engine in the Works Yard, the Americans flew out an installation large enough to supply the whole of Maiduguri, although they said it was only suffi-cient for their own camp requirements! They flew in almost every-thing they used: the complete camp came in frames, including a perfect hospital with some thirty beds and everything any doctor could want. Their three doctors made our staff look rather feeble. However we were one up, for we had a Nursing Sister (Alison Macdonald, whom I married to Dick Peel, one of my A.D.O.s): they said they would never risk bringing one out. Ours took the risk but we were compelled, at her request, to mount a double police guard and wrap the pillars of her sleeping porch with barbed wire, to discourage the attentions of the U.S. sergeants. The American contingent were in fact a great help to us and they deeply appreciated anything that we did or them. Their presence brought great prosperity to the Nigerian ladies in the town – some bought lorries with their gains and were soon deep in the transport business. During all this we were building a new Provincial Office by the bank, a charming red-brick building with two projecting wings. For the first time in the history of the Province, the Resident and the D.O. had comfortable offices in the same building as their staff and clerks, and a high standard of cleanliness; the era of the permanent stink bug had at last gone.

An advantage of being Resident of a Province was that one could visit the Divisions without an elaborate excuse (as was usually required of a D.O.). Apart from Nguru, which was strictly in the Bornu division, there was Potiskum, on the way to Jos and Kano, flat but pleasant with a very good chief. Ten miles or so to the south in a fine valley is Fika, the Chief's former home town under its splendid date palms. In season the place was yellow with fine succulent fruit as fresh dates should be. North of Potiskum comes the independent territory of Bedde, set in appalling swamps. Then 80 miles to the south the lovely territory of Biu stood 2,000 feet above sea level; much higher than Maiduguri: it was a relief to go there and enjoy its fine air. One rest house was popular with honeymoon couples. Its design was very simple, just two rooms and a wide verandah, but as you came out on the other side, the ground dropped away 1,500 feet to the Hawal river, beyond which the hills rose steep and rugged – you could see across them far away to the high mountains of Adamawa. It was a view you could look at by the hour without wearying; and of course all was utterly quiet.

To the east of us was Dikwa. This was in territory mandated to Britain by the League of Nations, where it was incumbent on us to establish our presence. The old town was held to be unsuitable as a headquarters – we wanted somewhere that could be expanded. The choice fell on a place called Bama, about 30 miles up the Yedseram, another river that dries up. There we built a sensational town, the first place in Nigeria to have a proper modern 'town plan' with everything in the right place. It even had roundabouts at the main intersections, again the first in Nigeria. The D.O., W.S.E. Warren, put into it everything he had. Oddly he was, in normal circumstances, rather an idle type who seemed to do as little as possible, and used his abilities, which were considerable, to find ways of evading work, but something took hold of him here and he produced, largely by his own efforts, a charming and distinguished town. Even the hidebound Emir saw the advantages and moved his entire household to the new site. The fine new N.A. office in brick – everything was in brick – had one of my elegant clock towers. Warren planted trees in profusion and within a few years it was a little paradise in a rather grim landscape.

In Maiduguri itself, we set up a Defence Force and an air raid service. Air raids seemed more than likely, but mercifully they did not happen. An airborne attack was also not unlikely and for that we could only make tentative plans. So we had first aid classes and rescue squads, and motor transport, demolition and rescue squads. Rehearsals were unconvincing, because no one in the African town had the least idea what the reality might be like. We felt that we should demonstrate an actual explosion to the various units before they met with a hostile one. The Engineer laid a good charge under some mud buildings which we wanted demolished. The fuse was lit, and everyone retired behind various bits of cover. We held our breaths and said our prayers. Then there was a little 'boom' and a small cloud of dusty smoke drifted across the Dandal. It was unimpressive, but the children who had been watching loved it. They rushed about shouting 'Boom, Phufff', then falling down flat with shrieks of delighted laughter. Whenever they saw the Engineer afterwards they would shout 'Boom, Phuff' and fall on the ground.

We had a serious armed unit, like a home guard, who wore armbands and badges. Sporting rifles of many different makes, far more deadly than the official weapons when in the hands of expert marksmen, were available. Then came a moment of great excitement when a huge case arrived, containing two splendid Italian machine-guns captured in East Africa – in pieces. Naturally no instruction book or drill manual came with them. We set about reconstructing them, without really knowing the principle on which they worked, but succeeded in the end. Then we had to invent a drill for getting into action, loading and picking up, but because the guns were very heavy, it would have been impossible to change position with them quickly – no wonder the Italians suffered so many defeats, we thought. With them came cases of very high-velocity ammunition. All we knew about it was that the trajectory was very flat, so the aim had to be dead accurate; this again was not conducive to effective machine-gun fire.

The great day came when we had perfected our drill and there was no further excuse for not doing some firing. As Commander (self-appointed) it was obviously my duty to fire the first rounds in case the blew up. One of the guns was set up on the range and I aimed at a standard target at 200 yards. Everyone tensed and I fired a burst. It was a perfect group in the bull. Unsportingly, I changed the aim and invited the next man to do better. After that no one even hit the target. I was about to make myself a Lieutenant-Colonel – after all our organisation had by then reached a total of about 2,000, black and white – when the war shifted away from North Africa and the danger passed.

Every Tuesday evening I would go to the Middle School to talk to the boys about the war news. I drew on the blackboard and showed them the maps. The boys took a great interest, and asked intelligent questions. At that time I gave the Middle School a silver cup for the best essay on a non-school subject plus a general knowledge paper. I wanted the boys to use their wits and their good reference library and throw off the strait-jacket of the curriculum. I also gave a cup for soccer in the town. After the Middle School I would go along the *Dandal* to the Shehu's gate and there sit down in a circle of townspeople and tell them too about the war news. Great was their interest. I gave the news in Hausa and a 'shouter' yelled it in Kanuri. Oddly the crowd varied with what sort of news it was: if we were doing well there might be two or three thousand people, if not so well it would dwindle to hundreds. I explained this procedure to Lord Swinton (then the Colonial Minister detached to West Africa, and based in Accra) and he asked how I dealt with bad news. I said I always told the truth, at which he seemed astonished, especially when I said how when the news was bad the crowd became noticeably more sympathetic. He said it was unusual for any public figure to tell the truth about disasters. I asked what you did when things got really bad after you had kept the people on a high wave: he said there was no answer to that.

There was a recruiting office in the barracks and many hundreds of tough fighting men from among the Shuwa Arabs and tribes in French territory joined up. In the end Nigeria raised as volunteers over 150,000 men. The Gold Coast and Nigeria between them manned the 81st and 82nd Divisions which served with success in the Arakan and Burma. Their engagements there being echoed in the strange-sounding names of military installations all over Nigeria, such as Kalapanzin barracks in Kaduna.

Meanwhile we were growing food and collecting special articles for export, such as kapok and chicle gum (for chewing gum) which grew only in the north, and in the south rubber and the oil products of normal commerce.

Food for Europeans became difficult and we improvised. There was a good brown sugar, sold in saucer-shapes in the markets, made from boiled-down sugar cane which was grown all over the southern parts of the great Emirates. Then we found that a lot of wheat was grown there too – a surprise to the experts – from which we got good flour: wheaten cakes baked very hard could be ground roughly for 'grapenuts'. Wild honey was excellent for plenty of things, and local milk made good cheese. We were able to smoke and preserve our own bacon and ham. Fresh food presented no difficulty and vegetables were plentiful. Thus we had some compensations. We had the news on the radio and a surprising amount of letters got through, though with great delays in transit. There were no new cars, of course, and tyres would have been difficult if an enterprising Greek in Lagos had not started a retreading factory. This was Zarpas, who also owned Lagos passenger transport.

The administration had to go on, and in spite of having a reduced staff, we managed. We left much to the N.A. staff and found that on the whole our previous 'nanny' attitude had been unjustified.

Security

The N.A. Works Department, under several Engineers, did an astonishing amount of building. Some of it was for the war effort – barracks, extra housing and offices, two new hospitals, roads and bridges. Most of the material, except for the cement, could be got locally and as much as possible was salvaged and re-used. Existing roads and buildings, and the airfield at Maiduguru and Potiskum, had to be maintained. The Engineers were Andrea, Armstrong and – best remembered – Effion Jones.

I built semi-permanent rest houses at District HQ in the bush to replace the mud buildings and make touring more comfortable. Their designs were based on the houses where I had lived in Lagos on my first tour, with semi-circular ends, all thatched and brick-floored. Roads were improved to carry war traffic, tar could be obtained with difficulty, and to put down tar strips cost £1,500 a mile.

Time was wasted drawing plans of French stations north of the frontier, based on agents' reports: it was extraordinary to me that our Survey Department had no copies of them, and that they were not to be found in any reference book. We could hardly go to the de Gaulle people and ask their advice, and so admit to our astonishing incompetence. The plans I got from the French after the war had little relation to those we concocted. Fortunately it did not matter in the long run.

At about this time, the area north of Nigeria became Vichy territory and therefore naturally hostile to us. The frontier, about 400 miles long, ran mostly through thinly populated country, marked only by bare iron telegraph poles at intervals, and in its eastern stretch by the sandy bed of the Komodugu Yobe. It had no roads across – only tracks – and not even a customs post. So I was rather surprised to receive a telegram from the Chief Secretary in Lagos saying, 'Please close all Northern frontiers immediately.' I did a few simple sums, and wired, 'To close frontiers with Vichy will require two infantry divisions, and even then full closure can not be guaranteed.' Asked why, I explained. There was a long pause and I wired for instructions. They replied, 'Kindly do your best.'

As a result of the telegram from the Chief Secretary mounted units were set up on the frontiers under Bornu men of distinction and we gave them a pretty free hand: we prayed that nothing too bad would happen. The only real frontier crisis was not caused by them. a *garde champêtre* came over the frontier heavily armed and entered a village. We do not know what he was doing or what his orders were, if he had any, but the villagers were too much for him. They offered him five shillings to go away, and as he put out his hand the men grabbed it and pulled him off his horse, tying him up in a few moments. They brought him, in great discomfort, to me, a journey of 100 miles across the desert; we kept him sweating for a day or two and then let him go back. Under international law we retained his arms, and the excellent villagers were rewarded.

With the Free French in Fort Lamy we had quite close relations. I paid a number of official visits there when P.O. Lapie, a lawyer-politician and a member of the Chamber of Deputies, was Governor. Many of the Free French were under sentence of death at home: their property had been confiscated and they had no news of their relations and friends, yet they were mostly more cheerful than we were. When we lost Singapore, a French major said, '*Ça ne fait rien, vous avez beaucoup de territoires à perdre.*' We arranged for French families to go to Hill Station in Jos for a month at a time for a change.

Leclerc, a remarkable man, highly intelligent, was commanding in Fort Lamy, where intellect was not an outstanding feature. He gave me lunch once in his mud house, when he told me about Eboué – just him and me.

After some months with us the *Force Tropique* flew off on a mission in support of a raid by Leclerc into Tripolitania. They never came back once their training was completed. The raid was on a pay day and the

French found the Italian C.O. at a table covered with money. This they enjoyed immensely.

One evening the O.C. R.A.F. rang up and asked me to meet him between our two houses. There he told me that something had happened in Fort Lamy as they had had no signal from their small detachment there since 1400 hours. We wondered what it could have been. Lapie had been in Jos and was staying with us in Maiduguri that very night. As I walked back to the house I had to make up my mind whether or not to tell him that we thought that something had happened, maybe an air raid, at his own headquarters (there was no telephone or telegraph between the two towns). If I did, he would naturally gulp his dinner and rush through the night over 150 miles of very bad road, and possibly run into serious, if not fatal, trouble. I knew he would be leaving early the following morning, so I left it.

Next morning we got a note by lorry saying that there *had* been an air raid on the airstrip there at 1400 hours – a dead hour. Little damage had been done to the surface but two million gallons of aircraft fuel had been destroyed – in the event an exaggeration. They had plenty there, but in fact only one dump had gone up. As a result of this raid, a British A.A. battery was sent to us all the way from Yorkshire three months later.

My wife and I set off at once up the west shore of Lake Chad to find whether the enemy plane (or planes) had crossed Nigerian territory or come direct from the Vichy oases to the north. We had an interesting and, for once, successful run, but gleaned nothing about strange aircraft, which meant that they must have come from the north down the Lake.

Meanwhile my D.O. and the D.O. Dikwa (Tupper Carey and Warren) had collected real facts which they gave me on our return that evening. An aircraft had been sighted by four intelligent and reliable African men who had, individually, taken note of the times: these fitted exactly. The plane had come southwards down the Lake, had found the mouth of the Yedseram river running into it from Bama. It had gone some 50 miles up the river and seen nothing of importance. They had swung of eastward and then north to cross the Logone river. They had followed this downstream towards the Lake and then sighted Fort Lamy. Hence their 'perfidious approach' (the French version) from the south-east. Fortunately the damage was slight and we had no more visitations.

Security gave us much trouble. A captain came to me and said that the higher command wanted every man working on the airport – and there were about 1,500 from all over Nigeria – to be properly 'screened' and vouched for to the third generation. I asked him why and he said, to prevent the enemy learning about aircraft movements. This surprised me; had he said he was against sabotage, it might have been more reasonable.

I said, 'A man sits in the bush, half a mile (or even more) from the perimeter; he puts a small stone into his pocket for each fighter taking off and a large pebble for every bomber. At the end of a week he walks off northwards for a hundred miles or so – nothing to a Bornu man – and meets a friend. They pass the time of day and quite casually the bags of pebbles change hands. The friend goes off to the nearest French military post. There the pebbles are counted and a cypher message is sent off. Very simple and no one has any suspicion that it is happening, indeed it may well be happening at this very moment.' The officer was dumbfounded and said they would probably be content with the issue of passes to reliable people. These were used – any child could have copied them.

The official map of Nigeria showed several main roads running northwards across the northern districts of the Province into French territory. At that time these were just much-used tracks passable with difficulty. I received a telegram from Kaduna asking me how much explosive I needed to blow up the bridges on the roads leading to the frontier – I sent the short answer 'Nil'.

Some time later, two sapper subalterns appeared with a copy of my telegram. They pointed out the roads on my wall map. I said I knew all about them and there was nothing to blow up. They were politely sceptical. Would I mind if they went and looked for themselves? I said, 'just help yourselves, but don't shoot any game without a licence.' They came back ten days later, very brown and fit, and said that I was quite right. I thought that I had heard the end of it. But no. Two captains came on the same mission, with the same result. They went away, apologetic. Then, believe it or not, there came two majors all the way from some military headquarters hundreds of miles away. They produced a like result, and finally a lieutenant-colonel (they weren't able to pair him). He was of sterner stuff. While he realised that there was indeed nothing to blow up, he noticed that there was a six-span bridge at Gashua on a road parallel to the frontier (and 40 miles inside it). It would satisfy his General if we arranged for its demolition. It all seemed crazy to me and I said so, but, rather than cause a further waste of manpower, I agreed. In due course little chambers were cut in the piers of the bridge for the charges, and a suitable amount of explosive arrived and was taken on charge by the Engineer.

Years later I was again Resident of Bornu. One evening my wife and I were sitting on the lawn of the new Residency, overlooking the city, when we felt a ground shock and heard a large explosion. A great black cloud shot up from the houses and drifted away on the wind. This was, of course, the very same explosive, which had blown itself up through 'degeneration'. It blew out a corner of the Public Works' yard in the town, destroyed part of a workshop and killed two lepers who were asleep under the trees. I found Jones the Engineer and the Yard Superintendent looking at the wreckage and wondering what had been there before. The Y.S. said, 'I know now, it had a badly painted red door and I always thought it was a latrine, but never had time to look inside.' The arrival of the explosive must have been so secret that there was no entry in the stores ledger or in any handing over notes.

My long record of good health was spoilt in 1942. Small ulcers started to form on my legs and Nolan our M.O. treated them to no avail. They would start to heal and then break out again. In the end there were six large and small ones on one leg and foot and three on the other. In myself I was quite well and went on with my work; I even went to Fort Lamy in this sorry state, as I had to do. Finally Nolan gave up and I went into the hospital at Jos. There, after a few experiments, they decided to operate.* Five weeks later I was able to leave the hospital. However, during all this time important papers had been sent to me from Maiduguri for my approval, so I knew what was going on there. On my first night out I took the Senior Sister to the cinema and returned afterwards to find that my cherished white pigskin suit-case had been stolen from my room with all my clothes. And I then discovered I had not renewed my insurance.

Two days later, to our delight, Dorothy arrived in Jos. I had not seen her for nearly two years. The children were safely with Nanny at Tenbury Wells, a town in the centre of England, where the war made little impact. Wives were not allowed berths unless going to a job, and she got one because I appointed her to my Provincial Office, Bourdillon concurring. So we went back to Maiduguri together.

Before long we were back in Jos for the annual Residents' Conference. The twelve Residents of the Provinces and the Secretary (S.N.P.) met informally to discuss problems. It was always a splendid stimulant to breathe the good air of Jos. When it was over we decided to drive straight through to Maiduguri – a gruelling 365-mile trip.

*My thanks to Mr Lovat-Campbell for his skill.

Visitors

The next day at 6 a.m. a 'most immediate' telegram in cypher was handed to me with the early morning tea. My wife was the cypher queen and she sat up in bed to decipher it. Then with a startled cry she jumped to her feet and rushing into the bathroom and turned on the taps. The telegram began 'HRH Duke of Gloucester will reach yours fifteenth at 1430 hours travelling as [giving his alias]' and giving details of his flight and suite. The fifteenth was that very day: and we could so easily have stopped off on our way home from Jos, as we sometimes did.

The Duke arrived at 3 p.m. wearing general's uniform, and we drove to the Residency. It was desperately hot – nobody then had air-conditioning. We suggested tea but apparently they never had tea at home till four o'clock so we sat and sweltered and made conversation. The Duke was very good and kind and told us a lot about his life and his family. He thought it strange that he had a special ration of whisky.

Meanwhile, I had arranged to take him down to the city to see the Shehu's horses and had warned the Shehu that my guest was a very important person. Of course the car stalled as I drove it away from the house but the driver appeared as if by magic, through a minute gap in the henna hedge and got it going.

We sat down over the Shehu's gate house while horsemen galloped up to us in waves. I felt it only right to tell the old man who my guest was, and with the Duke's permission said to the Chief that this man was the King of England's brother. 'I knew that, of course,' said the Shehu 'his face is the same as the one on my medals.' So much for security. The next morning H.R.H. left early and we relaxed. He was on his way to the Middle East and India to inspect troops.

Other distinguished visitors at this time were Sir Stafford Cripps (passing through at the start of his momentous mission to India), the Kings of Greece and Yugoslavia, and the Australians R.G. Casey and Robert Menzies. There were numerous admirals, generals and air marshals. All this meeting of crowned heads and other important people brought official retribution. It must not be forgotten that I was still only acting as Resident: there was no substantive Resident, so I had no one to answer to and took all action on my own responsibility. This was all very well for a short time, but I had done it for many months and here were all these people coming to the airport and being met by a mere Senior District Officer. Kaduna opinion felt that it had to be changed. So E.K. Featherstone, a very Senior Resident, was sent to take over. He arrived and took over, but did not know what to do with me. Then he fell sick and as soon as he was better some crisis developed in Kano. Meanwhile I had been posted to Adamawa Province, our neighbours to the south, a place in which nothing ever happened, the most remote area available. Then Featherstone was transferred to Kano a post which fitted his rank. There he would also have a chance of meeting distinguished visitors. He went off at once and left me still in Maiduguri as Senior Officer. I would normally have taken over automatically, but by now I had had enough messing about: with my tongue in my cheek, I telegraphed Kaduna for instructions as to who should take over the Province. The Secretary wired back asking, in so many words, if I would do so, and I did. Soon afterwards I was promoted to the rank of Resident, and all was well.

All this time both British and American aircraft streamed through Maiduguri – Spitfires and Blenheims, Bostons, Kittihawks and Flying Fortresses, Dakotas by the score. It took two hours to clear the airfield every morning, at a plane every minute. Just before the Battle of El Alamein I counted seventy-five Dakotas on the concourse: I looked into one and saw it was full of small arms and ammunition, and you don't fly that kind of stuff round Africa, unless the situation is pretty grave.

There were a number of memorable aircraft incidents. Hurricane fighters used to fly from Lagos to Egypt in sixes, with a Blenheim as navigator and stores-ship. All was well in good weather but one day in bad visibility one of the fighters lost 'mother', circled about looking for her and finally ran out of petrol. The pilot did a crash landing in a field of guinea-corn. The plane was a write-off. The pilot said afterwards that he thought he was landing in a cornfield – as in a way he was – but when he sank ten feet through the corn he noticed the difference. In fact it slowed his landing and saved his life. The R.A.F. in Maiduguri were naturally in a great state about the vanished aircraft and were about to scatter everywhere looking for it, when the Emir at Potiskum cabled giving the name of the village nearest to the crash. When the rescue tender reached the point on the main road, they found a rough track cleared for five miles through the bush, and at the end of the track was the wrecked fighter. Beside it was the pilot in a grass hut which had been built round him where he lay. His broken leg had been set by the dispenser from Potiskum and the Village Head was fanning the flies off him. It seemed a shame to break up this idyllic scene.

Another time, a large U.S. transport plane went off course and came down in the bush east of Maiduguri. The D.O., Tupper Carey, and our Engineer went off as soon as a report of the location had been received – the grapevine works quickly in those parts. This time the plane was intact but short of fuel. The rescue team took a pair of forty-gallon drums with them; within a day a 800 yard strip was cleared through the bush and the plane managed to take off and fly back to Maiduguri. The U.S. Commander went into Tupper Carey's office one morning and reported that a Kittihawk had come in the previous night without a rear-wheel; he realised that there was little chance of its being found – and so on. Scarcely looking up from his work, Tupper said, 'Is that it in the corner behind you? They brought it in this morning from X [60 miles away]'.

We were fortunate in having few fatal accidents during this period, either in the air or on the roads. One day, however, two fighters collided at high speed over the airfield. The British pilot ejected and landed safely, but the American was killed. There was no one to officiate at the funeral, so the Americans asked me to do so. Surprisingly, they had no suitable flag, and we lent them a big Union Jack and they were deeply moved – so much so, that they treated it precisely as they treated the Stars and Stripes – it must not touch the ground under any circumstances.

The plain round the town was closely tilled farmland and there were hardly any trees. At least in Maiduguri, that is Yelwa, there were fine trees planted by the great Resident Hewby at the beginning of the century at the 'smart end' of the town. It was essential to plant more trees and we found that most of the ordinary ones failed. But we had a few *neems* brought over from the Sudan, and these had done well in their twenty-odd years of life. We set out tens of thousands of seedlings, planted in avenues in the town and round the outer hamlets, alternating with dry-zone mahogany, which grows slowly but well. I planted many myself and in four or five years a million had taken successfully. Sir Hugh Foot (later Lord Caradon), when Acting Governor, planted the millionth neem tree on a visit to Maiduguri in 1949, outside the Shehu's gate on the north side. The Waziri planted another to make sure that something would survive and the Forestry people planted two more again, as they were naturally pessimistic, so there were four 'millionth' trees. These trees have prospered and the climate of the area around the city has been noticeably altered. While I was there in the war, we planted fruit trees along the Alo bank a hundred yards or so deep, and allocated them personally to the Councillors.

At the time the neem trees were being planted, I set about laying out a new extention to Yelwa town between the Shehu's house and the Alo river. A great new road was built round the town to the north, called the 'Avenue of the Sudan', planted with a triple avenue on each side. The new area was laid out in blocks on a completely new pattern based on plots 50 feet by 100, a convenient size for African town-houses. The Council were so pleased with the arrangement that they gave it the name Gambaru, after the ancient palace of the Queen Mothers of the old House.

Before this development Forestry had had an uphill struggle. The so-called Forestry Reserves were tragic, though they had a few more trees than outside their boundaries. The demand for fire-wood for ordinary household purposes was alarming when expressed in 'acres of growth', so the neem plantations helped a lot.

It was becoming clear that the whole future of the war might depend on the Allies getting enough troops and supplies into Egypt to drive Rommel out of North Africa. The steady flow of aircraft was not enough, though by the time this trans-African route was closed, more than 3,000 Spitfires and Hurricanes and 1,000 Blenheims had been flown through with minimal loss, plus all the freight planes, and U.S. aircraft in great numbers. So Churchill appointed Lord Swinton Minister Resident in West Africa with Cabinet rank and in direct contact with the Prime Minister. He was furnished with an aircraft which, according to the official handout, would enable him to fly 'backwards and forwards' across West Africa, and was based on Accra. R.G. Casey's appointment to Cairo at this time as Resident Minister was on the same principle.

The British Army decided to build a highway across Tehad Territory to link up with the Sudanese road system, so that troops could be moved by road: a secret scheme called 'Marble'. We knew little about the terrain it would have to cross. For example, just beyond Dikwa, our road-head, the track entered a vast swamp about 70 miles across. Most swamps are level and stationary; but this one had a slight slope in it towards Lake Chad, which meant that the water in it was moving. If an embankment were to be built across it, that would turn into a dam, the water would pile up behind it and in the end it would be breached and destroyed. There had therefore to be bridges in it to let the water through. The British Sappers thought that if they mixed clay and sand in certain proportions they would get a 'stable' material for embankment building; all other things being equal, this was possible and it succeeded to some extent. They sited the first of these bridges about 30 miles east of Dikwa. The water rose as the rains progressed and the wretched Sappers were driven on to the embankment where they lived in tents and huts and worked on the bridge using pile-drivers and great baulks of timber. The work meant that spikes and clamps had to be driven under water. They dived into the muddy water; then they had to feel for their spike by hand, hit it and re-surface. This they did repeatedly. There was no diving equipment that I ever heard of, and their daily courage and endurance filled us with astonishment and horror.

One day I went with Swinton to see Lapie in Fort Lamy. We had a good reception and an excellent lunch and returned in the afternoon, having cleared up a lot of problems in two languages. I had told Swinton all about this bridge-building and he wanted to see it for himself, also the work being done on the road. He told his R.A.F. pilot to fly low over the road all the way to Dikwa (a hundred miles or so). When we came to the long embankment section, there it all was: the bank stretching across the face of the water like a pencil with a great gap at the bridge site, and the tents and huts of the Sappers in a miserable row.

Swinton held a special meeting at the Maiduguri airport of all those concerned with 'war works' in the neighbourhood, including the U.S. commander, our Engineer and the O.C. Troops. We went through the jobs, of which the most important was the extension to the main runway at Maiduguri to two miles and a new control tower. The road to Fort Lamy was under a different works team. all the work was considered as of the highest urgency. Swinton told me that I should communicate direct with him in Accra and by-pass my Governor, though I was to keep him informed. Anything we wanted was to be asked for through him and he would see that it got priority. I was to use all my authority to urge on the work, and then he uttered the famous words, 'If anyone asks you why you are doing such and such, just say "Lord Swinton said so".' This became a catchphrase among us, even on rather dubious occasions. As we left the meeting, the U.S. commander asked me if Swinton was one of our Cabinet Ministers. When I said that he was, the American remarked 'We're going to win this war.' He had indeed filled us with zest, and we were clear of the ridiculous frustrations that had dogged us in the past. Swinton was well served by his staff: Folliott Sanford, the top civil servant (later Registrar of Oxford University); Harold Evans, his publicity man (later to serve Harold Macmillan in a similar capacity); and Butters, his A.D.C.

When the North African war was over, there was no more need for our installations and the forces folded up. We thought we would gain needed stores left by the Services but not a bit of it. Our own R.A.F. treated us as if we were hostile territory. They moved a great many things, but what they left they destroyed, such things as refrigerators, which would have been most valuable to us, were put out of action by pickaxe blows through the casing. They never asked us if we could do with any of the things. The commander had his own light aircraft – this he took up one morning and, baling out, let it crash. The

Americans carried off all movables in their transport aircraft for use elsewhere, but, for example, they left us the electricity cable (5 miles) to the airport and a generator. They gave us the chance of buying what we wanted, there was a terrible haggle with Kaduna over the £3,000 required. Finally, Eric Thompstone, who was Resident after me, bought the lot on his own responsibility. This did not please Kaduna at all, but when he said he would dig up the cable and sell it to the French, Kaduna capitulated and issued funds.

Just after Christmas 1942 we went on leave after an unheard-of thirty months' tour – eighteen months was the maximum in normal times. I had had, all things considered, a heavy tour in Bornu, but despite the strain, it had been fun. I was just forty-four, with twenty-one years' service. I often had to take great administrative risks which paid well in the end: but our Native Administration system justified itself admirably.

There were two ways of going home on leave. One of them took two or three months by sea. The other was the 'quick' way: by flying boat from Lagos Lagoon to Gambia, then nineteen hours in the air to Trinidad, and from their via the Bahamas to Baltimore. The journey continued by train to New York, where we waited for three weeks in bitter February cold. Finally, our 'fast' passenger ship, in a five-knot convoy via Greenland and the north of Iceland, took a month to reach Swansea. Out of the ninety-six ships which set out with us from New York, thirty-six, mostly tankers, were sunk.

XII. Lagos: Public Relations

I went back to Lagos in the late summer of 1943, having been brought in by Bourdillon to set up a complete Public Relations office, late in the day as it was. There had previously been an Information Officer with a small office in the Secretariat, who had lived a frustrated life almost alone on the job, and was anxious to go on his leave. He had received little support from the Secretariat, and consequently had achieved little. There was a mass of propaganda material from London, but no adequate way of distributing it.

My appointment was to create a separate organisation, quite clear of the Secretariat. The first thing was to find an office, then furnish and staff it. There was not much money. A native-built two-storey house in Campbell Street was leased. We managed to acquire staff, especially a good 'number two' in H.C.B. Denton, a Southern officer. We had an excellent Czech photographer, Francis Uher, who had bicycled all round West Africa, and a Swiss called Huber, an expert on radio. The Post and Telegraphs found staff for our redistribution stations, who did the maintenance while we supplied the local programmes and mobilised local talent. We picked up B.B.C. news and issued our own local news, general Nigerian news, local music and talks.

While on leave I had spent three months with the Colonial Office and the Ministry of Information (then in the Senate House of London University) to learn about 'information'. I did not learn much but saw enough of the Colonial Office to deter me from ever wanting to go there again. I started as P.R.O. alone but my wife came out to join me.

The Ministry of Information in London sent us a mass of printed material, much of it unsuitable for the unsophisticated people. For example, there was a superb photo of an aircraft-carrier taken from the air. I was admiring it in my office when a Northerner on my staff came in. He asked what it was, and I told him. Then he asked, 'What sank it?' I said it was not sunk. He said it must be: there was sea below it and sea above it, and that could only happen when the ship was under the water.

Some of the most intelligent ladies in Lagos, black and white, came to join us to do all sorts of jobs in the office. We also had some Lagos ladies of the kind that the others called 'Been-tos' – i.e. they had 'been to' England for education. We imported our own two white block-makers who made the blocks from Uher's photos – the first time that had been done in Nigeria.

We printed and published two weekly papers as well as a number of pamphlets on Nigerian subjects. All the soldiers from Nigeria in the 81 and 82 (West African) Divisions in India and Burma received a weekly news-letter giving up-to-date news of their home towns. For economy this was printed in very small type, difficult to read, but this had no effect on its popularity. In the other papers we tried to explain the war to the Nigerians and the Nigerians to the white strangers who came to us in uniform, unused to our ways. Our 'Sunrays Club' boasted 20,000 tiny members, all of whom had at least one birthday a year to be noted.

By this time there were large numbers of white Army officers and N.C.O.s (but never any white other ranks) in the country, for the Nigeria Regiment had turned itself into a great service of all arms. Indeed a pamphlet was issued called 'The Regiment that Became an Army'. The Army lent us two men: one was a cockney infantry corporal who had been a journalist in civilian life. His accent was strange to the African staff, but they would imitate him precisely. The other was a gunner officer, Captain John Stocker, from the battery at the harbour mouth. An experienced journalist on provincial papers in England, he helped us immensely and was eventually transferred to us, becoming P.R.O. himself in later years. Then we had a shopping service for people up-country. This was officially frowned on, but gratified letters from the bush were our reward. In those days it was only in Lagos that one could get many daily requisites.

We had a beautiful house just back from the Lagoon. The casuarinas sighed in the wind and we sighed over our difficult garden. Good gardeners could produce flowers in quantity and Government House had gorgeous beds of scarlet cannas with dark bronze leaves. We only produced periwinkles, and anyone could grow them, they kindly said. There was much entertaining, and prices had gone up. I was on £1,200 a year (Resident's pay) as P.R.O., but it did not go far, with two daughters and a nanny to maintain in England. However, we never overspent.

Alexander Grantham, the Chief Secretary, told me to prepare estimates for what I thought would be necessary to put the office on a good footing for the future. My total came to more than £25,000, then an enormous sum. A great part of it was capital expenditure for reading rooms in the larger towns. I pointed out that it was no good sending out masses of our literature without supplying some proper centres in which people could read in comfort. There were to be three grades of these rooms, from the very simple mud huts at £250 each to the better types at around £1,000. I also said that I must be supplied with good hard news from the provinces and departments. Nothing trickled through to me unless something had gone wrong or had come in for heavy press criticism.

Sir Arthur Richards had arrived as Governor by this time in place of Bourdillon. He had been governor of three territories before coming to us and was not easy to deal with. I was summoned to a meeting before him, the three Chief Commissioners (all close friends of mine) and the Chief Secretary. Sir Arthur then tore my proposals to shreds with much sarcasm, and innuendos of megalomania (mine, not his). These important officials sat by like dummies and raised not a voice in my defence, although Grantham had agreed to all my proposals and had actually recommended them. In the end I asked for a personal interview with the Governor and he approved most of my proposals. It was tense while it lasted. After that our relations were good. Richards was a most able Governor, but no one could describe him as cosy or approachable: he was angular in person and blunt in speech. He took on where Bourdillon left off in the way of constitution-making, but his had to take concrete form.

Every Thursday morning I had an interview with the editors of the three Lagos dailies – Dr Azikiwe (later first President of Nigeria) of the *West Africa Pilot*, Akintola of the *Daily Express* and Thomas of the *Daily Times* – and the one weekly. They would walk very cautiously into my office. They had reason to be apprehensive. I had in my desk drawer what I called the 'editorial of the week'. I would keep it back for a while and then take it out, very carefully. By this time they were on the edges of their chairs, but when they could see from the type the paper in question, the others would sit back looking smug. Then I would pull the editorial to pieces – in the kindest manner, of course – and invite the editor's comments and explanation. I was always ready to explain our attitude and would invite a head of department to be present, if they had been sniping too near a departmental target. I am sure that these meetings did real good. Akintola eventually became Premier of the Western Region and was shot down in his own office in Ibadan on that terrible Night of the Ibo Majors in January 1966.

During the war we had a number of fast Royal Navy coastal motor-launches, moored off the Marine Wharf near the Secretariat. One afternoon a Hurricane fighter, being tried out after assembly, lost control and came screaming down out of the skies; it plunged into the harbour, missing one of these motor-boats by twenty feet. The stern of that craft had just been reloaded with depth-charges and, had it been hit, a considerable slice of Lagos could have been wiped out. I happened to be on the Secretariat verandah at the time and saw the huge column of spray shoot up high over the house roofs, followed by a great black cloud.

There was much activity by German U-boats along the coast during that period and many merchant ships were sunk off Freetown. One morning in Lagos harbour the big dredger the *Lady Bourdillon*, was working between the moles attending to the 'bar', when it was blown out of the water by a tremendous explosion. Very fortunately the tide and river were running sharply and so the wreck was not only drawn into deeper water but also slewed round; it was not long before the passage was once again usable.

By this time (1943) the army command had risen to that of a major-general (Hugh Hibbert) and there was a proliferation of relatively senior ranks below that – 'colonels, half-colonels and palm kernels', as used to be said. By then, too, the defence of the harbour had become a matter of such importance that the Lagos Defence Force – which had been started in 1916 and later lapsed – had been reactivated, taking responsibility for posts on the 'training bank' and the extreme end of the Apapa wharf. The defence of these points was entrusted to two Vickers heavy machine-guns with volunteer detachments, from sunset to dawn. I was a corporal in the Force at the time and had sole charge of the Apapa gun on my nights of duty from sunset to dawn, but came under a sergeant when on the 'training bank'. These two guns were to deny access to the Harbour of any enemy craft rash enough to attack. What was to happen to a daylight attack was not clear: it would certainly have succeeded. Surprisingly, there were no troops in Lagos beyond the Household Guard; the R.A.F. were inland at Ikeja and the Navy was not geared for field defence.

Burns told me that in the 1918 war Lugard, as Governor, had a train permanently available at Iddo to evacuate essential staff and that files were kept bundled ready for instant despatch by it, in case of an enemy attack on the port.

Later, two six-inch guns were sent to us from Freetown and mounted in a battery on the seaward side of the West Mole, with British gunners to man them. General Hibbert had a beach hut on the far side of the battery: to reach it you had to go through the battery position and check in at the guardroom en route. We were with the General there one Sunday morning when he was signing the guard book. I saw him going purple and I looked over his shoulder; just above his own signature were those of Hitler, Goering and Goebbels.

Lagos and the rest of the country was under strict rationing (applicable to those normally eating food of the European type) and my wife had a fine time in the Lagos Colony Office running a food section; here the ration cards were issued to the public. Imported goods were rationed, especially flour, sugar and drinks: one bottle of whisky per head a month was pretty grim. There were, however, a number of people who never drank it, and the Roman Catholic Sisters, for example, acquired a sudden and to them bewildering popularity. Cigarettes were made locally and a brisk trade developed in locally made cigars – now and again you came across one that could be smoked right through.

The period when I was P.R.O. was one of the most interesting of my service, being so very different from anything else I had done or was to do. It meant that I could go to all the places I had never visited, especially in the Eastern Region. It was on one of these journeys that I actually visited Okigwi, the station to which I had been unavailingly posted in 1921, twenty-three years before. It was, as they rightly said, a pretty place, but it seemed rather backward to my experienced eye. The only place I did not go to on my P.R.O. tours was the Southern Cameroons.

The Campbell Street house soon became too small for us, and we were lucky enough to find a large building, just back from the Marina, and overlooking the open-air cinema – it had been a three-storey hotel, to put it at its most complimentary. There were many small rooms on the top of the three floors, ideal for offices, and an immense room on the first floor which could easily be divided up. We had much more room and I had an office large enough to take my secretary and myself.

I thought that the Government of Nigeria should interest itself in a little culture, so I used funds I had to buy works by local artists. They were innocently charging ridiculously low prices, and the highest we paid for a picture was £50. And so we acquired early works by Ben Enwonwu* and Lasekan, among others, and fine wood-carvings, and specimens of the exquisite 'thorn carvings', including a complete chess-set, then very rare. The Office mounted an art exhibition in which these people exhibited their works in an excellent wooden hut on the Marina waterside, which we used for all sorts of exhibitions and so-called cultural purposes. There was then no museum, although I pressed for one, and for a zoological garden: the people of Lagos had never seen any of the beautiful wild animals to be found in their own country. I had urged years before that land be acquired behind Ebute Metta for this purpose, when it was readily available, but was greeted with derision.

Richards' new Constitution came into effect in 1946. For twenty-four years there had been no constitutional change, yet the country had gone ahead fast in every way. The Governor still legislated for the

*One of his early drawings is on the cover of this book.

North 'Under his own Hand' and Northern matters were seldom mentioned in the Chamber. They certainly could not make any comment on Northern Native Authorities.

Richards increased the number of elected African Members representing small areas or interests in the South, with some white Members to do the same. The Regional representation also changed. The senior Resident in each Region (though they were not yet called Regions) and four of the great chiefs came into the new Council. Richards had his tongue well in his cheek when he decided a substantial unofficial majority in the Chamber. It looked very well. If the Government had been defeated by a vote there would have been no alternative Government to take over. So far as I can remember there was never a division. In most matters the Northern members would, in practice, have voted with the Government and so ensured a majority.

In all, Nigeria had five constitutions between 1946 and Independence in 1960, and we spent a lot of time working on drafts to see that the maximum progress that could be given was properly expressed in the British Orders-in-Council. The fact was, of course, that we ourselves were so bound up in Nigeria, and it was so integral a part of our lives, that we were more Nigerian than the Africans themselves, and we knew very much more about the country than they did. The ignorance of the ordinary African about his own country, and indeed even about the next Province, never failed to astonish me and my friends. Naturally, there were some well-travelled and well-informed people, but most were not like that.

We must accept the cold fact that this lack of political advancement scarcely mattered at all to the ordinary people in the bush. Not until the very final changes did they begin to realise that something was happening, that the flags had changed, that the white man was no longer in power, and that they had to deal not only with their own people but with black people who came from other parts of Nigeria. These people spoke languages that were strange to them and their understanding of local affairs was sharply limited: they were also much more difficult to cheat.

My tenure of office ended in 1945 and we went home on a Dutch ship. We were sorry to leave Lagos – I was never to serve there again. After our leave, we returned to the 'holy and undivided' North.

XIII. Kano: The Residency

On my return from that leave I was posted to Kano as Resident. Having previously been D.O. there gave me a working knowledge of the Province and an understanding of the background to its problems. It was difficult to come as Resident to such a place without this start; you could learn it, but that was never quite the same. There were always areas of uncertainty. I had this great advantage not only in Kano but in Bornu and rather less in Jos. The post was one of the best in the country and by far the easiest. You could of course worry yourself into decline, but there was little need to do so. The machine ran very smoothly.

Now that I look back, I see that the Residents of the three great Provinces along the northern frontier – Sokoto, Kano and Bornu – were in most respects more powerful than the Colonial Governors of all but a handful of major territories. They had substantial statutory powers under a large number of Ordinances, and, if they worked closely with the Native Authorities, they had vast indirect influence. They were entirely alone and the decisions they took were their own. They had no corps of advisers and there was no legislature to worry them. While they could not actually post staff to themselves (or hold on to good staff indefinitely) they could beg to be excused if an unfavourable posting was to be made.

Of course, they kept their Lieutenant-Governor informed of important incidents, but much information could be conveyed informally. After all, it was their job to carry out the general policy of the Central Government, but they had a voice in framing the policy and often used their own discretion on how it was to be applied.

In these important Provinces the District Officer did not deal direct with the ruler: this contact was exclusively in the hand of the Resident. There was a weekly meeting between him and the Emir and Council and the District Officer went with him; they would sometimes take an official who had some special message. The business in Kano was conducted in Hausa, for all the administrative staff were bilingual; although many of the Councillors spoke excellent English, it was better for us to speak Hausa as we could convey the exact meaning much more easily and could understand the nuances of their speech. A scribe kept notes of the points decided but no minutes or records: we might make an entry of a decision in our files, but that was all and even that was not always done. Record books were later, reluctantly, introduced.

There was a desire to be frank, but the Hausa, as one of the politest races in Africa, had a tendency to say what they thought would be

197

agreeable. a flat denial would be rude and most unusual. The Kanuri of Bornu, on the other hand, and the Pagan councils always said what they actually thought, the latter rather more bluntly than the former.

There were always matters concerning the Emirate to be discussed and often subjects were referred for opinions from the Lagos Government. Sometimes the arguments were difficult and took time, but in general the meeting did not last more than an hour and a half. The venue alternated. One week we would go to the town for a meeting in the Emir's throne room – it took a long time to get the Hausas to sit round a table on the level with the Europeans but it came in the end. On the alternate week the Council would come up and visit the Resident, in his drawing room at first and later, as papers proliferated, round the dining room table. The Emir would come up to tea from time to time, and at long intervals we would go and have an evening drink of lemon in his own house.

Early in my tour in Kano I saw the Emir privately and said that while some Europeans had 'spies' who reported on what was supposed to be going on in the town and the Emirate, that was not my practice. If anyone claimed to be my secret agent, as happened from time to time, he was lying. The Emir smiled and expressed pleasure: he said he knew all about the spies and could name them readily. He was often astonished at the stories that were told to the Europeans and at the fact that they were believed. He said, too, that people in the town would give the spy completely wrong information with a view to securing someone's advantage or discomfiture. We agreed that there should be complete understanding between us and that he would say exactly what he really thought and let me know developments himself.

It was easy to suppose that in these Provinces there was only one area that mattered. Beside the great Kano Emirate there were three small ones. Kazaure, part of the Kano Division, often seemed neglected, having only an A.D.O. who sometimes did not know what he was meant to be doing there – the D.O. was far too busy to guide him. Gumel and Hadejia formed a Division to the east. When I say 'small', they were still much larger and wealthier than my first N.A., Koton Karifi, and even Kabba, which was not insignificant. Hadejia is in the complex of waters that leaves Kano and eventually fails to reach Chad, under the later name of Yobe. It was, in the past, a favourite spot with D.O.s, off the beaten track and unsupervised. I found it depressing when I visited it, but then I was not interested in the local beauties or the wonderful though exhausting shooting in the swamps.

Gumel was under a very go-ahead young Emir, a real Fulani with all the looks and grace of that people. He knew everything that was going on in his Emirate and was always anxious to improve things for his people, a large population with not much money. One day he wanted to show me a new market which he was constructing almost on the northern frontier, desperately hot without a breath of wind. The market seemed to consist entirely of deep fine sand. The people of those areas have a passion for the most pungent spices of all kinds, for their foods and for rubbing into their fine skins. There must have been many tons of them on sale, of every type and colour and effect. It was picturesque but suffocating. This active young ruler walking at a high speed, urged me all the time to appreciate this and that. I became more and more exhausted as the spices entered my lungs like a mephitic cloud, and thought I should never reach the car and the comparatively purer air alive. It is difficult to convey the friendliness and enthusiasm of these simple people, so far from the great world and so ignorant of its possibilities and horrors. We enjoyed them and they enjoyed us.

The Resident would go on tour sometimes to these places and it was a pleasant change from Kano, though obviously rather strenuous. Katsina (in its own Province) was 106 miles away on an excellent road and we went there quite often. Talking to the Emir there was always a tonic and the general air of intelligence was striking – after all, had it not been the university town of the Hausa long ago?

The Residency compound had superb mahogany trees, forty or fifty feet high, with two tennis courts and a big vegetable garden. Right round the whole compound ran a wire fence and inside that a thorn hedge, neatly clipped and, six feet or so inside that again, a henna hedge, also finely trimmed. Henna has a sweet almost sickly scent when fully out.

This once produced a social dilemma. The Governor (Sir Arthur Richards) was dining with me and as it was a very hot night the long table was laid outside the house. One end of the table was near to a small henna hedge in flower, while the other was, as it were, in the open. At this end the Governor was sitting next to me, while at the other was my D.O., Guy Money, A large fat man. We had as our main course a real sirloin of rare and excellent quality. Money suddenly got a strong whiff of henna and turned to the Private Secretary, David Physic, next to him and said he thought the meat was 'off'. The P.S. instead of getting on with his dinner, moved quietly round to the Governor to whom I heard him say that H.E. should be careful of the meat. Sir Arthur played with it for a minute and put down his knife and fork. I finished mine with enjoyment and no after-effects.

At one end of the Kano Residency, in a corner of the verandah opening out of the dining room, was my office, which was not only hot but impractical for lack of space. Telephone conversations could be heard clearly along the verandah into the main house, so secrecy was non-existent. One day there was an odd incident. A European woman official came in to see me. She was about thirty-five and had pleasant but not remarkable looks. I was sitting behind my desk, in a small bay between filing cupboards and a telephone table. She was on the other side of the desk, and was talking about a project their department wanted to set up in Kano Township. I had expressed general agreement with the idea; it seemed good if they had the staff to run it. Then she stood up and, in one slow motion, raised her simple cotton dress to her shoulders. She wore no underclothes. She then slowly lowered the dress, smiled quietly and sat down. She had taken a tremendous risk as messengers, with silent feet, constantly came in and out with papers and my secretary would also come in without warning. She talked for a few more moments and then shook hands and walked out of the office and the Residency.

Not unrelated is the story of a certain Resident who went to lunch with a young administrative officer and his attractive wife far away in the bush. The Resident wanted to wash his hands before lunch and the young officer showed the guest the bathroom and said, 'While you're doing that, sir, I'll slip over to the office for some papers I want you to see.' After a while he heard a movement and turned to find his lovely hostess bare to the waist and about to undress further.

He thought fast. The young man had a motor-bike he was proud of which he always used, even for short distances, but the Resident had not heard it start up. Had he really gone to his office? The Resident turned and wrenched open the door of a huge cupboard, and there was the husband ready to burst out upon them in wrath. It was an uncomfortable lunch and the career of that couple in Nigeria came to an abrupt end.

Just before the war, aircraft of Imperial Airways came to Nigeria from Khartoum and an important stop was Kano. At first they landed their little planes on the Kano polo ground but a new airfield was already being developed when the war started, two miles north of the City. This gradually grew and at the height of the war large numbers of planes were landing and taking off. The runway was extended to 8,000 feet – the ground was entirely flat for a long distance.

The war brought to Kano many people who in ordinary circumstances would never have heard of it. As at Maiduguri there was a constant flow of service personnel, and many enjoyed the hospitality of the Residency or the District Officer. One such had an unusual sequel. A very important Belgian politician stayed a night or two, and the Resident was able to help him out of some difficulty. Months later a Belgian ambassador was passing through and he too stayed at the Residency; the Resident by then was not the same. At breakfast the next morning, the visitor handed a packet across the table – an appreciation from his Government he said. The Resident, who was Featherstone, opened it and found the neck badge of the *Ordre de la Couronne*. He explained that he himself had never had any opportunity to be of service to the Belgian Government and that it would be difficult to find out for which of his predecessors it had really been intended. The ambassador told him not to disturb himself: he should accept it on behalf of the Nigerian Administration. And so reluctantly, for he was a shy man, he did.

Within the year a 'drawing room' plot moved me from Kano. It was in fact quite a fair arrangement but I would have liked to stay longer, uncomfortable as the climate was. At that time Eric Thompstone was Resident of Bornu Province, and it was becoming clear that he would be the next Chief Commisioner of the North at Kaduna when Sir John Patterson retired. Unfortunately Thompstone had never served in Kano, an experience which was considered a *sine qua non* for this high post. I knew Bornu only too well and was the obvious one to go there. We were not pleased. When, three years later, we were offered Kano again we chose Jos, but that was because we wanted to be comfortable for our last years in Nigeria.

XIV. Bornu, 1948

In 1948 I was once again Resident Bornu. There had been changes. The American camp had virtually disappeared, so had the mud buildings for the R.A.F. There were some new official houses and many more staff. A bungalow had been converted into a club, with a small swimming pool. The most striking change was the disappearance of the old mud Residency, which was now a heap of rubble – I planted it as a garden. A splendid new house was near completion on the same site.

Thompstone had planned and brooded over it; he loved brooding over new buildings in the afternoon and good often came of his apparently glazed and unconscious stare. This house was specially designed for its purpose. Built in the good Bornu brick with a corrugated iron roof, and entirely covered with a thick thatch, it was impressive and cool. There were various devices to give good or restricted ventilation, as required.

A small entrance hall led into a large, elegant sitting-room, beyond which was the Resident's home office. A good dining-room could comfortably seat twenty or more. All the woodwork was in fine *sida* (the finest of the Nigerian furniture timbers) wood and the floors were of *sida* parquet, highly polished; so was the staircase. On the north side was a good verandah for sitting out and beyond that lay the original terrace with a new flight of steps leading down to the lower slopes. I spent time laying crazy pavement paths round the great lawn and bisecting it.

Upstairs were a very large owner's bedroom and bathroom, from which opened a deep sleeping-porch with the unique feature of part being under cover: beds did not have to be dismantled if rain should come on during the night as it might at the change of season.

The Public Works used a new form of shutter for this house. Called a *brise-soleil*, it was made up of a series of overlapping ceiling-board blades about five feet by ten inches set on end, pivoted in the centre, top and bottom, and joined together by a transverse bar. It was possible to close it completely or set the blades to catch the wind. It had the great advantage of being successful.

In extreme heat you lose salt fast. I noticed one morning in my office at Maiduguri that there were strongly marked white parallel lines on my bare forearms: out of curiosity I scraped a bit off and tasted it. It was pure salt. After that I took a teaspoonful of salt followed by half a glass of water as soon as I got home before lunch at about 2.30, and found that all feelings of exhaustion disappeared in a few moments.

Round the interior of the terrace wall we had gay beds of verbena
and petunia and huge cannas of every shade. There were flamboyants
in the lower part and the vista to the river remained as before. Over to
the left rose a great circle of high trees, in a nearly complete circle
about forty yards across, which had a strange origin. It was said that
these trees grew from the stakes to which Colonel Moreland's horses
were tethered at his camp by the water side. It was he who had
commanded the small British column that came to Maiduguri in
1902. There was no fighting and the whole march, after an incident
near Bauchi, was entirely peaceful.

While we had been away, water supply in Maiduguri had
improved and there had been a steady programme of well-sinking in
the districts with differing results. In many places so-called 'surface'
water was as far below ground as three hundred feet. In a deep well
the weight of the rope was so great that just over a gallon of water in a
leather bucket could be raised at a time. The 'ropes', of plaited
ox-hide, got water-logged and broke off, falling into the well. It is
impossible for people living in developed countries fully to understand the hardship caused by having only a bucket of water at a time,
perhaps after a mile or more of walking. No one can wash all over in
those conditions. At the beginning of the rains it was quite common to
see respectable Muslim women, normally very prudish, strip and
wash in the big pools of fresh rain water at the roadsides. The chance
of a bath after six months' abstention banishes modesty.

Why not use pumps, one may ask? A good question, but there are
two difficulties. The first is that the maintenance of the pumps in the
deep bush is difficult since they must be serviced constantly. Well-
intentioned amateurs with spanners can do much harm – ill-
intentioned they can ruin them. The second point is that if it is easy to
'overdrain' with a bucket, how much the more is it easy to do so with a
pump? There was a further difficulty when 'thugs' got hold of the
well-tops, as they did from time to time in a 'weak' village. Then they
would sell the water and deny its use to those who could not or would
not pay.

Every evening, if you were by one of the lower-class town gates in
Yerwa as the sun was setting, you would see , through the dusty haze,
shot with its dying rays, the head of a column of hundreds of goats.
They came in briskly with their nimble pattering feet, raising more
dust as they came. With them came the day's goatherds striding
among their charges. The owners of the goats would come out of their
alleys and stand in little groups. The goats accelerated as they came in
and the tempo of their bleating rose. Then they would catch sight of
their owners. A stampede carried them across the open space straight

to their masters or mistresses, and the bleatings became excitement and appreciation. And they streamed off to their several homes like children from school.

Driving one morning in the northern part of the Province, very sandy and 'duney', I was in a light kit-car with my own driver. After miles of sand, we came round a large sand-dune and the driver stopped, of his own volition. He was a splendid driver, a man of few words and one who never expressed any emotion, except when nearly killed by overladen lorries. Before us, in all this sand, lay a vision of heaven. There was a longish curve of the bluest water, sparkling in the sun; there were palm-trees and great tamarinds casting their heavy shade; there were fine green patches of maize. Little white huts were happy in this setting, sheep and goats wandered in the reeds by the water's edge and in the distance was the laughter of children. The driver pushed his little cap back on his head and said, 'You could live to be an old man here, and never would you go without water.' He knew that water was a major problem for the strong – for the aged it was a luxury.

The French Mission

When Sir John Macpherson* had previously visited Maiduguri, we discussed the possibility of building a railway from Jos, or Kano, to Maiduguri to bring this huge area into direct touch with the sea. Denis Woodward, then general manager of the Railway, had come on a visit to us and I had raised it with him. He was greatly interested.

The Governor's discussions opened the possibility of a railway east to Fort Lamy and even beyond. There had been a scheme during the war to link up with the Sudan Railways at El Fasher: had the North African campaign dragged on longer, something of the kind might have materialised.

Some time after this the Macphersons were invited to visit Cornu-Gentille, the French Governor-General in Brazzaville. Our conversations in Maiduguri were remembered and I was invited to go with the gubernatorial party. It was believed that my knowledge of French was better than it was. The party numbered about ten from Nigeria, including the French consul in Lagos, his pretty wife, and the Lagos Attorney-General. My wife was at home in England with the children.

We flew to Libreville, the capital of Gabon, a country which we

*Succeeded Sir A. Richards as Governor. He had served as P.A.S. in the Lagos Secretariat in the 1930s.

found to be the most unspoilt piece of Colonial stagnation that could be imagined. We were received by a guard of honour of a black infantry company. Cars took us up a steep hill to an old-world Government House where the old-world Governor of Gabon received us with old-world courtesy and plenty of modern whisky and good food. After a brisk drive round this depressing place, we were put back on our plane – for Pointe Noire, a new town of fine houses and trees and roads, circling the obviously thriving seaport, crowded with shipping. We had been puzzled too by the French insistence that we should go by train from here to Brazzaville, which is far in the interior. We thought it would have been better to fly there in a couple of hours.

On landing this time the Governor was received by a larger guard of honour, a whole battalion with armoured vehicles, very smart and warlike. The Governor of the Lower Congo, gave a tremendous party for us, and we finished up on the very hospitable French mail-boat then in port.

We enjoyed the usual drive round the town the next morning and were then taken to the Railway station, a splendid building with marble floors and fine fittings, apparently designed to resemble a château. There stood the Governor-General's own beautiful train to take us to Brazzaville. The Macphersons had a suite to themselves;and we had fine cabins and there was a proper 'drawing-room' coach. The sensation was the dining-car, a standard restaurant car stripped of its fittings, carpeted and refurbished to seat twenty in comfort, with elegant dining chairs. The party had now grown to this number, for the French Governor (who spoke no English) and his wife and staff had joined us.

Shortly after leaving Pointe Noire, we understood why they had wanted us to go by train. The country started to become hilly. We followed charming river valleys, plunged through tunnels and emerged into fresh beauty, we followed other valleys, steeper and steeper, with rushing mountain streams, rocks and great trees, and wild isolated stations. All the rest of the day the train toiled up the steep climb to the central plateau.

That evening, over dinner on the train, the men of the English party had a vital discussion – what to wear when we arrived the next day at Brazzaville, the Governor-General's capital. Our Governor was then wearing a peculiar khaki costume that had, it seemed, been approved for his rank, with red hat-band and tabs but no military insignia, a kind of major-general *manqué*: he thought it would do for him, and that lounge suits would do for us. I said no to both propositions, knowing the French habits. I had persuaded Macpherson to bring his full (white) dress uniform and he had instructed us to do the same:

this seemed to be the time to wear it. In the upshot uniform was agreed, and that the ladies should dress in their best – and just as well too.

At the station we found Cornu-Gentille, with the whole of the senior official French population, drawn up in their white uniforms and medals and so we looked all right when we alighted. Through the great ticket hall, all imported marble and trimmings (imitated from the station at Deauville), and out into the *Place*. Here was another spectacle: a formal guard of honour of the Brazzaville garrison, two infantry battalions, a battalion of white parachutists and again armoured vehicles. As the last company went by, Macpherson turned to me and said 'What a sight! What do we do when he comes to Lagos? All *I* can mount under King's Regulations is a Guard of 167 men and a colour.'

We spent three days in Brazzaville and had long and complicated bilingual meetings in the Palais de Gouvernement which reached no particular conclusions, though a number of 'avenues were explored', and some mutually satisfactory positions were discovered (almost). My conclusion was that although there was great enthusiasm for an international railway, nothing would be done, nor has it been since.

There was a dance at Madame Cornu-Gentille's invitation and everyone turned out in their varied 'best'. We saw the sights. From the town you could not see much of the mighty Congo, but at the Chief Secretary's residence, where some of us went for lunch, there was a fine view. The river, though wide, was not smooth – there were many rocks and rapids. One afternoon we were taken on a *promenade de fleuve* in a big launch. Across the water, at least a mile wide, was Leopoldville, 'Leo' to the locals. It was as much anathema to the Brazzavillois as Guernsey is to Jersey. No one admitted ever going to that other place, '*là bas*', if it could be avoided.

It was with regret that we flew back to Lagos, crossing the Equator for the second time on the trip, and feeling a certain sense of hangover. I flew on to Maiduguri and sat down to write thank-you letters in my best French.

United Nations mission

Dikwa Division – 'Dikoa' when the Germans ruled it – was first a Mandated Territory under the League of Nations, and then a Trust Territory under the U.N. The change of status made no noticeable difference to the life and manners and well-being of the 50,000-odd people who lived in that particularly inaccessible and inhospitable country. It made little difference to us either: we continued to administer it and worry over it. But our real worry started when it was announced that a United Nations Mission was coming to inspect the area and scrutinise our administration and that of the French next door. We had no precedent and did not know how to start. There were six members of the Mission. The Chairman proved to be a Mexican of great charm and greater intelligence and the Secretary was Chinese. They all spoke excellent English and had polished manners.

The first thing was obviously to make them as comfortable as possible and not expose them to any hardship while at the same time showing that it was a pretty ghastly place for us to live in. In fact by that time Bama was a charming place: the neems planted by Warren had all grown quite large, indeed there were veritable woods, so that on that score we had nothing to be ashamed of. The difficulty was that there were no suitable houses for them. After all they were high-powered people, doubtless used to luxury in five-star hotels. There was no time to build a five-star hotel, and the expense of building even a single-star one would not have been justified. there was just one 'permanent' guest house – that is to say it was not built of mud alone – and a good D.O.'s house. We decided to build a complete new village for them between these two buildings. An existing tree-lined road at that point furnished the axis of the site, on each side of which large huts were set up made of straw and matting on bush poles, but well constructed and well furnished. They were of new grass and smelt like hay, which was fine, so long as no one suffered from hay fever. We used the Rest House as a mess – it had a nice view down the Yedseram river – and the D.O.'s house as a 'centre'. Furniture and bedding were brought in quantity from Maiduguri on loan from the Public Works and hospital.

Lighting was another problem, lamps and candles would have been dangerous with so much straw. The answer was electricity. By chance the Works had available some old generators left behind from the war, and three of these were mounted on trucks and brought over. Then the whole place was temporarily wired, with the generators set up some distance away to avoid too much noise. It all worked perfectly (2 on and 1 in reserve) and as we had constant electricity the Mission were deeply impressed, and that did us no harm.

They arrived by plane at Maiduguri, and we gave them an official reception at the airport and again at the Residency. The baggage went on and was ready in their rooms in Bama when they arrived. It was very hot in Maiduguri, and the afternoon run to Bama quite trying. However they found their shady camp agreeable and welcoming. They were received by the Emir and his councillors and given cold drinks – kerosene fridges had been specially brought over from Maiduguri.

The Mission had a set programme for their inspections and sight-seeing, and in the evenings horses were available and they could ride wherever they liked. The food was good, supervised by our own fine cook. There was plenty of good fish, duck and turkey, vegetables and fruit. We took them to Dikwa to show them the conditions there compared with the new capital at Bama. They had conferences with the local people through interpreters, in which the field was left wide open to them. They were a little disappointed, I think, that no crowd of complaints attended them to inveigh against the brutalities of our administration. The local people, apart from the councillors and the more intelligent staff, had practically no idea what the whole exercise was about despite our prior endeavours to explain it to them. Indeed on all occasions it was stressed that the Mission were different from other Europeans in Nigeria.

We arranged an excursion into the high hills, 25 miles away from Bama. We drove them to the foot of the hills, then started off up a good path, a trade route. This was the tense part of the visit, with the possibility of trouble from these very sensitive people who disliked strangers. It was essential that everyone should behave, and members of the Mission were sharply warned by myself before we started not to leave the path. If there is trouble, the first sign is a flight of poisoned arrows from an invisible foe.

When we were about half way up, I saw a young pagan girl in a 'farm' about 150 yards from the road. She was farming quietly and apparently alone and, like all of them, quite naked. To my horror a South American member of the party left the road with his camera poised. I shouted to him to come back but he did not hear. Unfortunately the girl looked up and let out a high-pitched, shrill scream that rang through all that valley and up the great terraces and continued steadily. My messengers rushed out and got him back, and our invaluable local District chief, a prince of diplomats, reached the girl swiftly and calmed her down. I watched for the arrows, but, by the grace of God, nothing happened. We went on up the steep path and had lunch in the rest house below the saddle. We got home tired but contented by sunset. At the end of the visit we drove the Mission to the frontier and handed them over to the French. I am glad to say that we got a very good report, which we richly deserved.

We had visitors but not like those of war-time: now they were mostly local. Once or twice we had the Chief Justice visit from distant

Lagos, but that was rare indeed. The Residents of Bornu received a Commission giving to them personally the full powers of a Judge of the High Court, whether or not they had legal experience. Most of us had some. I used these powers seldom. Once was when two bandits killed a man in an ambush in Fika Emirate. I sentenced them to death: the case went to the West African Court of Appeal, and on purely legal grounds my judgment was set aside. The men were brought in and told of the Appeal result, but on leaving the Court they were at once re-arrested and charged with highway robbery. For this they got fourteen years: they fell on their faces and begged (as others had done) for death rather than such a long sentence in far-away Jos Prison. I could not give them their wish. In practice there was little crime that came to us. The Native Courts were more than capable of dealing with all that arose, only in the smaller (like Fika) they did not have the full powers of death and life imprisonment.

An incident took place concerning taxes at that time, which was amusing to both parties. In Potiskum a few men had got quite rich as a result of the war and clever trading. The Chief – Mai-Fika – wanted to make them pay a reasonable tax. They were then paying about £25 each, which was large compared with the taxes of the ordinary people. We had a consultation, went into some estimates and guesswork about their probable income, and arranged a plot. The chief would assess them, as he could, at £1,000 (which we thought was well below their rightful deserts). They were then sure to rush to me, as they were entitled to do, and appeal. This duly happened and one morning three men were ushered into my office in Maiduguri. They were ragged and travel-stained – part of the ordinary routine for making tax-appeals – and said that a dreadful thing had happened to them. Mai-Fika had gone quite mad and in his insanity imposed on them a tax of no less than £1,000 each. I asked vaguely, how much they had paid in past years. Oh, they had even then been over-taxed. They were poor people – yes, they had lorries, but everyone knew these ate up money and no one ever made anything from them. In spite of their poverty, they had had to pay the appalling sum of £25. And now this new disaster had befallen them.

I was sympathetic. It did seem an enormous jump – from £25 to £1,000 in one year. I said I wondered whether it would be fair to decide on £600 each for this year. They instantly agreed and rushed from the office before I could change my mind.

XV.   Towards Mecca

Maiduguri was the clearing house for Nigerian pilgrims. The Koran lays down, in so many words, that the devout Muslim must carry out the Holy Pilgrimage to Mecca at least once in his lifetime. He must prepare for the journey, both financially and spiritually: he goes in an aura of peace. At any given time there used to be at least 50,000 Nigerians on the Pilgrimage. A very large number of them have settled in the Sudan, either permanently or to save for their return. At one time much Government work in the Sudan was carried out by Nigerians – the huge Gezira cotton scheme depended on them. Many never came back: many did not want to.

They had to traverse 800 miles of French territory and then the entire width of the huge Sudan. About half way they could board the train from El Obeid to Port Sudan, if they still had the money for the tickets. Because of the French passion for personal papers, a special passport was evolved. This eventually had tear-off coupons to cover the Railway ticket, the Steamer ticket each way across the Red Sea, the Customs dues, and so on, and a final coupon which entitled them to an amount of money, to be handed to them at the conclusion of the Pilgrimage in Khartoum. These passports were signed personally by the Resident of Bornu. In the description, against 'eyes' the scribe always wrote 'red'. I asked him why. 'Eyes, sir,' he said, 'are always red.' No more to be said!

All this had taken some organising. When Eric Thompstone was Resident of Bornu, he went on the first official visit to Khartoum and I went a few years later to clear up difficulties and improve the passport. Besides a stay of three days each at Cairo and Luxor to change planes, the tour took me to Jeddah and along the road to Mecca to the barrier which prohibited passage to all but the Faithful. Jeddah, with its towering six-storey houses and jalousies of finest Malayan teak brought by the pilgrims over the centuries; the tight religious control (the British Ambassador, with whom I stayed, had to disguise Evensong in his drawing room as a 'late tea party'); the secret showing of quite innocuous films on embassy roofs; the smashing of Muslim-owned radios by the police with axes; the ugly but essential distillation plant – Jeddah had no fresh water.

For hundreds of years the Pilgrimage had been on horseback, by ship, by camel or on foot, but in the early 1950s B.O.A.C. started to run pilgrim planes from Kano to Jeddah. This was considered by some, who felt that the Pilgrimage should be a form of endurance test, to be unsporting. The Saudi Government had already brought 'comfort' by supplying, through a subsidiary company, motor buses and cars to carry the hundreds of thousands of pilgrims on the short journeys that had to be undertaken on the day of the Pilgrimage or immediately afterwards theoretically on foot – thus they too had queered the pitch.

The late Sardauna of Sokoto gave his blessing by using the air-route quite early on, and thereafter almost every year. The pilgrims were not used to air travel. On one flight a stewardess found to her horror, behind the rear seats, a very old man setting alight a small pile of dried sticks he had brought with him to cook his supper.

Once at Mecca, at the time of the Haj, all men are equal: prince and wealthy commoner set aside their finery and the poor their rags, and all assume the simple pilgrim loincloth. The Sardauna brought back a photo of himself and some of his ministers in this simple garb.

Before we leave Maiduguri, there is a unique incident that I feel should be chronicled. Rumour reached the D.O. that a man in the market could print Nigerian pound notes on ordinary white paper. This seemed a remarkable claim and we investigated it carefully. The man had a very crisp negative, like X-ray film, showing the face of a pound note. He took a sheet of plain white paper and clipped it to the negative. This he dipped into a bowl of good well-water. He covered the bowl with a cloth, removed the cloth and, hey presto, there was a fine clean Nigerian pound note attached to the negative.

Now he was clever, for he did not attempt to sell a counterfeit note; what he was selling was the negative. The price was about £60 (in 1950) and a number of people actually bought them, convinced that they could print money at will. This man came unstuck when he tried it on a Councillor, who at once observed that the negative was for the *face* of the note only: how then was the reverse printed? The trick was that genuine pound notes were thickly coated with some kind of white-wash: as soon as they were immersed in water, the white-wash disappeared and there was the good note. We could not charge him with any currency offence but he was found guilty of obtaining money by fraud. He had done pretty well out of it.

We left Bornu for the last time early in 1950. It had expanded greatly. There were numbers of officers of various departments; the trading community had grown in numbers if not in competence; the Native Authority was much more sure of itself; the general income had gone up and although many hundreds of villages were still far from any motorable road, the place seemed more closely-knit. Bornu's relations with the rest of the North were good – when I went there, Hausa was a forbidden language, few people went to Lagos, and even fewer to the United Kingdom.

XVI. Plateau Province, 1950

The Residency

I found it strange that I did not go back administratively to the Plateau Province for twenty years. I had been constantly passing through or visiting Jos, in my long years in Bornu. It was an obvious place to visit; it was on the road to Kaduna, a place of meetings and a good shopping centre, and of course had a wonderful climate and provided scenic refreshment to the eyes.

In the latter days of my official service, about 1950, when Bryan Sharwood Smith, my senior on the list, became Lieutenant-Governor of the North, Kano of which he had been Resident was vacant and so was the Plateau. Kano was by far the most important province in the whole of Nigeria. The job was tempting, but the climate was tiresome, and Jos seemed to have all the advantages. Why have an uncomfortable ending, when one could go no further?

The Plateau had far more problems than Kano. First, there were the Native Administrations, of which there were well over a hundred. Some were tiny, some quite large, Jos itself being the largest, with a revenue of about £30,000 a year, a shaky federation of smaller units. The pagans of the region were the second problem. In the early days of British Administration they had been viewed rather as 'pets' by the Europeans, with their endearing comic streak, but now they were educated – up to a point. They were particularly upset about mining and miners and things like dams and new roads; also they did not care for Forest Reserves. I quite agreed with them on many of these points but they tended to be obstinate and unreasonable and so lost sympathy. The women had little education.

The third problem was the Europeans – as miners and as individuals. They could be nearly as tiresome as the pagans. However, I was able to deal with them, as I had known the Minesfield twenty years before, understood mining law, and knew a lot they did not know.

The fourth problem was the telephone to Kaduna. It was a poor line but it was a nuisance because of a regrettable tendency on the part of those at Government Lodge to ring up and ask for explanations before a matter was complete.

The real temptation about Jos, apart from those I have mentioned, was the Residency. Out of the twenty-four Residencies in Nigeria this was easily the best. It was a 'house' and had a real living presence. Macpherson would come in and say 'When I come into this place I feel it is a "home" and not an official residence.'

212

Up a short drive off the Bukuru road and hidden by trees was this long low house, nestling into the rocks behind it – typical of many mining houses on the Plateau. The walls were of rough-cast and the window frames were black, again like the mining houses. Over the front door was one great gable, veiled in a tumult of yellow rambler roses.

On the other side of the house, the east side, was the great garden. This was the 'view side', so the windows were big, sheltered by verandahs. Visitors, when they came in daylight, were spellbound by the spectacle.

The climate on the High Plateau was seldom extreme. The sun was not excessively hot in the dry season and the rains were not severe. But thunderstorms – we called them tornadoes – were sometimes sensational: we were told that the area around Bukuru had the world's second highest 'electrical potential' – the highest being Venezuela. In the bush an excellent storm covering was used, made of two fine mats sewn together along a short side and a long side; worn over the head and back-to-wind it was effective. The girls with their skins rubbed with vegetable oils seemed impervious. We had severe hailstorms too. One that travelled across a strip of country about a mile wide stripped all the leaves from the trees and killed a man.

My way of life was to work from seven to nine in the house office. No one was allowed to ring up, unless a real crisis was brewing. There I worked on the papers I had brought back with me from the office, and if we had a free evening, I would often do this after dinner. I would go down to the office (a mile away and four hundred feet below) at 10 a.m. and look at any papers my secretary had put on my table that morning. When she arrived at 10.30 I would dictate the drafts I had prepared before breakfast and, if we were lucky, would be ready for interviews from 11 onwards. These would often continue until 2 p.m.

The Resident's office was a large room on the upper floor of the Provincial Office. In my time we built on a new wing which nearly doubled the office space by absorbing the administrative staff, whose removal left the old building to the departmental officers.

The District Officer in charge of Jos Division was on the ground floor in the same building with his staff. For most of the time this post was filled by a Senior District Officer, the grade below Resident. There were quite a large number of African clerks in our combined offices and the Mines Section. This latter must not be confused with the Mines Department, also in the building, composed of its own Inspectors and Senior Inspector under the Chief Inspector of Mines. They were responsible for the legal control of the Minesfield and advised the Government on technicalities. At one time five of them averaged six-foot-two, and by merely rising to their feet they could intimidate the toughest miner – including the one with a sense of humour who entered their office waving an official letter and demanding which of them was 'my obedient servant'. Among others in the old building was the Treasury Officer. The Police, Surveys and.Public Works had their own offices and considerable staffs. The Government was in general very well represented.

Outside Jos were the Forest and Agriculture officers, with Veterinary Headquarters at Vom 16 miles away. Finally there were the Prison Service and the Posts and Telegraphs. The Station Magistrate (an administrative officer) had his own office and Court.

The Resident was not 'in charge' of all these talented people, but he was expected to know what they were doing and planning, and whether they were likely, by any misadventure, to worry the local population. If they did, it would be his business to clear matters up.

To say exactly what the Resident's responsibilities were is not easy. He was, in his Province, the representative of the Nigerian Government, not of the Crown, as was often wrongly believed. He was responsible, through the Native Administrations, for the peace and for law and order, for the smooth administration of the area, for the administration of justice in the dozens of Native Courts of all sizes, and for Government expenditure in his own field and that of the Native Authorities. He was also responsible for the personal (and sometimes also the official) conduct of all Government staff, to ensure that 'Government' should not be brought into disrepute and that the people should receive their just dues and treatment at their hands; and all that without seeming to interfere.

Almost all development either started with him or came to him for advice and comment. He was the Government's adviser on 'political' matters, e.g. on the conduct and appointment of the chiefs and the high N.A. staff. He commanded and received the utmost respect from all in his Province. Under more Ordinances than one cared to think about, he held legally enforceable powers and duties, but the unwritten powers were greater and more varied: there was what the lawyers called an 'inherent authority', a phrase with a wide interpretation.

Among these duties was that of Registrar of Marriages. Most Christian Africans were married in their own churches under licence; and Muslims of course before the Iman and the Congregation. All whites, Christian or other, came to me for the purpose. The legal ceremony lasted 35 seconds and its final words were 'shall be guilty of bigamy'. I used to offer the bride any prayers she wished from the Prayer Book – usually she left it to me. Only one – a hard-faced woman who married a dredge-driver – refused.

Years later after Independence I was in the same office visiting my successor, a Muslim, on a Saturday morning. He said in Hausa: 'I have an odd thing to do at noon. I have to marry two Europeans and I a Muslim coloured man.' I said I was sure he would do it well. Then he said 'I do not like the legal words alone. These people are entering a new state of life and such words are not sufficient.' Then he added, rather humbly, 'Do you think they would mind if I offered a little prayer, invoking the blessing of Allah?' I said I thought they would appreciate it, if it were explained.

As an outward sign a Resident within his own Province flew a Union Jack on the bonnet of his car, as well as on his official house. Towards the end of British occupation this was an obvious mistake, we should have flown the Nigerian flag, for by then the royal writ ran but faintly. Indeed I feel now that we should have brought in a territorial flag much earlier than we did, with proper territorial arms, such as came with independence, and a local 'national anthem' would not have been out of place much earlier too. These small, but immensely important points could have made the way to independence easier.

Visitors

I have said that there were many interviews. Almost everyone of any dignity coming to Jos had something to discuss with the Resident, and vice versa. Every newly posted officer was brought in and presented by the officer he was about to relieve.

Everyone was expected to sign the 'book' at the Residency gate and most did. This was valuable to us as it showed who was about. The fact of having signed did not mean that one was thereby entitled to a meal with the Resident – a popular misconception; but it meant that those who did not sign would not be asked to any entertainment.

Entertaining was quite a problem. Not only were there all these visitors, but the local people had to be taken into account – not to mention one's personal friends. At that time Nigerians, excepting senior officers, judges, doctors and the like, did not expect to be asked. We found that two dinner parties a week, of at least twelve people covered requirements, plus a larger drinks party from time to time. I brought in a new idea to cover those who would not 'normally' be asked to dinner – the Nigerian Government Service had two recognised groups, of senior and junior officers: the latter did a mass of useful and in fact indispensible work. So in Jos we used to ask them to lunch on Saturday, a half-day.

There was an incorrect belief that the Resident was paid an enormous entertainment allowance. The fact was that in 1950 there had been no alteration in the salaries of anyone in the Service since 1922, although a revision was on the way. The Government Estimates showed that only three Residents received an allowance: mine was £300 a year which just covered one dinner party a week, plus something for drinks.

We did the 'canteen' shopping – groceries and the like – ourselves by car, while the 'market shopping' was done by Cook. His 'float' was made up each Sunday morning, when he brought in his purchase book, totalled for checking. This was also an occasion for discussion of 'common interests'. One Sunday I mentioned a new organisation that had appeared in Jos. Holding the position he did, Cook was obviously a likely target for bribes, and I thought he might be interested. If he took anything, it was probably not very much, and he never pushed any special person or idea in my direction. This body was called the 'Bribe Scorners' League'. Cook was most interested and said that on Monday he would find out the terms of membership. The following Sunday I asked what had happened. He said indignantly that he had found the Secretary of this League, and this bastard (I had never before heard him use strong language) refused to give him membership particulars except against a payment of twenty-five pounds cash.

I have mentioned an Archaeological Service – this developed over some years. At first we had no representative in Jos, but later an excellent little museum was built by Kenneth Murray, with the primary reason of housing the Nok terracottas. I well remember one day when Bernard Fagg, an administrative officer who had become deeply involved in archaeology, came into my office holding a small cardboard box. This he opened and took out a strange terracotta head about 6 inches high. It was unlike anything I had ever seen – quite distinct from the terracottas at Ife. The characteristic feature was that the pupils, ear-holes, mouth and nostrils were deeply indented by what seemed to be a kind of stylo; the modelling had a remarkable crispness and precision, and it was well preserved, considering it was probably 2,000 years old. This feature is found in all of them (cf. Fagg's book *Nok Terracottas*). Here in my hand was the very first of these terracottas. It had been found at the remote village of Nok in Jema'a Division, stuck on a reed as a scarecrow.

With a large 'unofficial' white population, the Resident was often asked out to parties and dinners. In other stations, he seldom went out, and then only to the D.O. or the Doctor. There was much drink at these Plateau entertainments, and the miners were determined, as kindly as possible, to get the Resident 'under the table'. We used to take prophylactic doses of oil or biscuits piled with pâté, to 'line the stomach' and resist the alcohol. We were never once even slightly tipsy, to their great disappointment. It was always fun to get away from the strictly official circles: the miners were different and intelligent, and scarcely any 'shop' was talked.

Talking of interviews, there was a rather important one about tin. The then Chairman of A.T.M.N. (Amalgamated Tin Mines of Nigeria, by far the largest of the mining companies), out on an official visit to the Minesfield, came in with the local General Manager, Eric Wilson. He had scarcely sat down before he launched into an attack on the negligence of the Government in the matter of tin-stealing. Indeed he said that he would take it up personally in London with the Secretary of State (naturally a 'personal friend'). What did I propose to do about it. I said, 'Nothing at all.' And waited for the explosion to subside. When calm had been restored, I explained: 'Any house-holder is responsible for the primary protection of his property. That applies in Nigeria as anywhere else. When your people tell me that you have done everything humanly possible to protect your tin, and losses still occur, then I will confer with the Native Administration and the Police and see what more can be done. But until that happens I will do nothing at all. We will of course deal with cases of theft actually notified to us.'

I knew, and he should have known, that the greater part of this tin-stealing was from the unprotected sluice boxes. These were long metal channels, usually in groups, down which the tin was 'washed', the ore, being heavy, settled behind transverse wooden slats, whence it was scooped out from time to time, and locked up in the tin stores, where it was fairly safe. But at night these sluice boxes were open to any who wished to help themselves. What the mines really needed were night patrols moving quickly and silently and without any fixed programme.

I pointed out to the Chairman that the mines did not pay their people enough: a man in charge of an area producing many hundreds of tons of tin a month was only getting £1200 a year, a man running a half-million pound dredge about £800. My visitor explained that the mine was very generous about leave pay, housing and furnishings – and he added, almost with emotion, 'including soft furnishings'. I said that you could not eat all these delightful extras and that children at school in England could not be maintained on soft furnishings, however soft. At a ball in Barakin Ladi, in A.T.M.N.'s southern area, a few days later I was not really surprised to hear the great man say that the Company had decided to grant substantial pay increases all round. I held my peace, and was interested to hear subsequently that there had been a definite drop in the estimate (for this is all it could be) of tin-stealing.

The really profitable stealing was done after the ore had been cleaned and bagged ready for transport to the Coast. This required special effort and ingenuity. Tin ore was a valuable commodity, and of course, the grains could not be identified; thus tin stolen in one area could readily be sold to a miner in another. An ingenious way was to get under the railway waggons in the sidings and run spears up through the gaps in the floor boards: these slashed the tin bags and the tin ran out into the pans arranged below. Tin ore is like a black sand, some of it very fine indeed, and it runs easily.

One gang, bolder and more ingenious, merely detached complete wagons fully loaded, from a made-up train, and pushed them to a distant siding. There a waiting lorry was quickly loaded with sacks of pure tin, the size and appearance of sand-bags. It was said that a £5 note would afflict a Station Master with temporary blindness, but that always sounded rather cheap.

As Resident one of my aims was to run a good government team, and to secure this I continued an idea I had used elsewhere. Every Thursday all the senior officers of each department came in and sat down round my table at 11 a.m. The whole thing was quite informal: no agenda, no minutes. I would start by giving out any bits of information that I thought they should all know, and would then ask each one if he had anything to say. The idea was that they should explain any new plan or policy that their department might be thinking of or set out any difficulties they were encountering. At first it was not easy, the whole idea being novel; they all tended to work in their own little watertight compartments. But when it caught on they all talked and people from different spheres helped to solve each other's problems. The Posts and Telegraphs and the Prisons were the most sticky – they thought it a waste of time and had nothing to contribute – but after a while they found that they wouldn't miss these sessions for anything. Men leaving the Province would bring in their reliefs and they would then not only have a chance of meeting all the top people locally but would come in on a rundown of what was going on, unintelligible though some of it might be at that stage.

I had a somewhat similar meeting about once a quarter to which 'unofficials' (like the mines managers and important traders) and the Chiefs would be invited. These discussions were even more valuable and gave a sense of unity and purpose to those in the Province. We called it a Development Council: it had no teeth but lots of brain.

Market

During my tour as Resident Plateau, my administrative staff and I managed, with much difficulty and endless discussion, to reduce the number of Native Authorities, so that where there had been (in one case) twenty-seven, we merged them in a single federation with a common treasury and common central African staff and departments, such as health, police, prison and so on.

The Jos Division was by far the most difficult and the Birom, the largest of the local peoples, were not only unco-operative but also noisy and sometimes even rude, which in Nigeria was unusual. I did not blame them very much since most of the mining development had worked against their interests. At the first tribal meeting I attended the noise was loud and the language (as translated) offensive. I walked out and refused to go back till they improved their manners. This upset them gravely but I did not return till two years later.

Jos was a place of unexpected difficulties. For example, I was told one day by the District Officer, Tupper Carey, that a nasty fracas had broken out at a remote Birom village. We found that the trouble was over a Forest Reserve. A local farmer had gone in on his own initiative and started to farm, unlawfully and knowingly. The Forestry Department had persuaded some misguided Native Authority to send in a couple of N.A. policemen. Blows had been exchanged. This was the kind of incident I always dreaded. Many of the Reserves were quite old and had been established when our administrative line of thought was rather different from what it later became. In the best agricultural land, their existence meant that the local people could no longer farm or even set foot there. The Forest Department had omitted to plant these areas with good timber. This neglect did not help farmers to appreciate the value they were supposed to be gaining from this policy of conservation. The D.O. went off to see the situation for himself. The Forestry were very indignant and demanded instant reprisal on the villagers – who being obstinate people, announced that the farming would become widespread.

I then earned the dislike of the higher authorities by saying to the top Forestry people (the Government Forest Department, not to the small forestry units of the Native Authority): 'Supposing these farmers carry out their intention, do you expect me to clear them off by force? I shall have to send in Nigeria Police, as it is clearly beyond the scope of the N.A. Police. The Nigeria Police will naturally be armed. Someone is bound to do something silly and hostile and in the end the Police will have to open fire. Someone may then get seriously hurt or, if the worst happens, killed. Do you expect me to take action which is likely to lead to such grave consequences? Is your Forestry Reserve really worth the lives of the villagers?' While they were digesting these thoughts, I added, 'if you manage to get Government authority for the Police to go in over my head, you will understand that any casualties will be laid directly at your own door and will be *your* responsibility.' In the end they saw the point and the matter was dropped.

It was not enough to have settled this incident; the future had to be taken care of as well. So I got the Chiefs together with the Forestry officers and we worked out a new policy. In future we would agree to the creation of almost any amount of Reserves *on the hillsides*, where the erosion was bad and farming nil, provided that the Forestry Reserves on good land were reduced or opened to controlled farming. This was accepted. The Forestry had a strange aversion to planting trees. They were all for conservation, even if there were no trees for them to conserve.

But to go back to Native Administration. However insignificant these Authorities might have seemed to us and to those used to greater institutions, to their own people they were the Government, and thus objects of respect and even some devotion. I have always thought that offices play a large part in creating the right 'image'. Kano had its splendid offices matching in dignity the Emir's lofty gate across the Square. The Bornu offices matched up. Dikwa's were charming, so were those in Potiskum. The Jos offices were pretty poor but were greatly improved by a small tower.

The other three N.A. centres were given (at their own expense) well-designed granite buildings, quite small but effective, with public clocks. Such buildings, I felt, gave the people a focal point, and on such a basis it was possible to create federations out of the small units. It may seem silly, but it worked.

Another problem was Jos market. This was a very large collection of tattered huts and tumbledown little mud-stalls and stores, occupying a valuable site in the centre of Jos and doing an enormous business. People came to it from all over Nigeria and beyond. There was a startling variety of goods on sale, old and new. Something had to be done to improve it and justify the charging of proper market fees, apart from stimulating local trade. Policing, too, was almost impossible in the far from charming confusion. No one actually got killed, but trouble of all kinds was rife.

The solution was unexpectedly simple. A middle-aged white man was shown into my office – my staff said he had something rather special that might appeal to me. He had been an administrator in Kenya and on retirement had become interested in a construction company called Acrow. He cleared a little spot on my desk and set up in a few moments a scale model of a steel-framed shed. All the parts were there and could be assembled in the same way as full-scale members. It was simple and strong.

I reached for the telephone and was fortunate to catch the Engineer, Effion Jones, in his office and asked him to come over. After studying the model, he asked technical questions and examined the specifications. He then said he thought it excellent technically and financially. The sheds could be joined together indefinitely, lengthways and sideways, and could cover a large area. But we had a problem posed by the irregularities in the floor-level of the market area; further, there were well established trees, an important matter in that area because we could not afford to cut any of them down. This chap said that if we sent him an accurate plan of the area showing the contours correctly and the position of the trees, his firm would send out by air plans of shed arrangements to cover the greater part of the space, together with detailed specifications and a firm estimate, with a promise of delivery in three months. It all sounded too good to be true.

The plans duly arrived and the estimate, with all freight and handling costs, came to just under £40,000, an enormous sum in those days but well within the reserves of the Jos Native Administration, who were most excited and readily agreed to release the money. Our estimate was that the N.A. would take £10,000 a year in fees. Maintenance would be cheap as the structure was so good, and we would pay for the whole thing in five years. As things worked out, the time was even shorter.

We had notice that the steel frames were arriving by ship in Port Harcourt. Knowing full well the delays and pilferage that were likely to take place en route, I sent an A.D.O. specially to disembark the goods and load them on to trains. This he did with great ability and energy and three special trains puffed up the mountains to Jos. I gave him (let us call him Stewart – you will see why I cannot name him) the job of erecting the sheds according to the manufacturer's plan. Once the local artisans had got into the way of handling the sections, they went up like magic. The only difficulties were that strict levels were required and an absolutely correct lay-out.

Then Stewart suddenly disappeared. This was surprising, as we knew that his wife was coming out by sea and would be arriving in a couple of weeks. The next thing was a telegram from him in Lagos, apologising for his absence and saying that he and his wife would be with us soon. When he appeared, the only reasonable course was to forget about the irregularities since the couple were obviously so devoted – he had flown to Freetown in time to join the boat there! He now completed the market buildings.

A week or so later, we had just finished dinner at home when one of my staff came unannounced through the open front door, 'Excuse my butting in, sir,' he said, 'but I thought you should know that Stewart is trying to kill his wife.' He had tried to strangle her but my informant and a colleague had got her away and locked her in their bathroom. The Senior Medical Officer sorted out the immediate crisis, and we flew the wife home to England soon afterwards. Stewart himself was persuaded that retirement 'for personal reasons' would not be out of place. The affair never appeared on any official paper.

Hospitals and accidents

Besides the Government Plateau Hospital (later 'Nursing Home') and the 100-bed General Hospital in the town, there was a fully-equipped hospital belonging to a wealthy missionary society. Several doctors and at least three and sometimes four white sisters were on the staff – the two Government hospitals together seldom had more than four sisters. This particular mission hospital was for white people and seldom had patients. The Government Hospital Sisters had a busy life – socially as well as professionally – and it was a grievance among them that when they were short-staffed and over-worked, the mission sisters would never give them any kind of help.

The attitude of the Missions to the Government staff was in general un-Christian. They always seemed in fear of contamination if they came into social contact with people who were not obviously religious and who 'drank'. I could never get the heads of certain missions to accept invitations to my parties, because it was an established fact that we 'partook of alcoholic liquor'. I felt particularly annoyed at the negative Missionary attitude when, by my efforts, the tiny Jos church of St Piran (the patron saint of tin-miners – it was they who built this church in the first instance) was more than doubled in size. I frequently took Evensong myself when there was no one else to do it. Above the altar we erected a large new cross of the finest streaked ebony given by a Baptist, designed by a Polish atheist, edged in fine brass by a Methodist, polished by a Jew, and paid for by an Anglican.

The climate at Jos was considered by all to be good and easy for Europeans, yet almost every month there was a white burial in St Piran's cemetery. Some Europeans came up in a bad state from the plains and, arriving too late, died among us. Other deaths were due to accident or worse.

For example there was a couple with a distinguished English name. They had tried tin-mining without much success; they went into transport and failed; they tried other things and got nowhere. One night the wife – we presumed she had made her husband drunk – put a stick of gelignite under their pillows, lit the fuse and quietly waited till it went off: we always said that of the two she had the guts and brains.

There were other very strange deaths. One of my D.O.s, a pleasant and able man called Haddow, had the Pankshin Division, a posting which was highly coveted among administrative officers. The road out of the town to the east passes not far from Amper, where General Gowan was born. It then forks right to Shendam and left to the small town of Dengi, the seat of its own small Native Authority. One day Haddow went down there on a rare visit to look at their Treasury books and talk things over and stayed the night in the Rest House. He had left his wife behind in the comfort of Pankshin. I stayed in this rest house myself shortly afterwards and there was nothing odd about it. It had none of the eerie feeling you got in some places – however, the next morning Haddow was found dead on the floor beside his bed. His body was brought into Jos and I arranged for an autopsy by the reliable and experienced senior M.O. and his Deputy. He was found to have been absolutely fit and sound in every respect.

We had had certain little bothers over post-mortems. In one case a Nigerian had died complaining of violent headaches: the Ibo M.O. certified death from natural causes, but when they were washing the body for burial, someone noticed that a four-inch nail had been driven into the man's skull.

We were determined, therefore, that in this unfortunate Haddow case nothing should go unnoticed, but absolutely nothing was found. In the end they thought he must have died of fright, yet we could find no cause for it.

At that time the Mau Mau was flourishing in East Africa, there were not lacking those who expected it to break out in Nigeria, though the situation was entirely different; and who thought that the Plateau with its variety of races was a likely place for an outbreak.

One night I was rung up in Jos by the Superintendent of Police who said that a white man and his wife had telephoned from an isolated mining camp miles away to the south, and it had sounded as if they were surrounded by raving crowds and were in a state of siege. He had sent out a riot unit and would let me know what it found. After breakfast he rang again. The Unit had found the white couple barricaded in their house with all their weapons loaded: the compound was clear and there seemed to be no one about. However, there was a loud noise of banging and shouting from inside the tin store where the Police found two ancient night-watchmen sitting against the door.

The night watchmen, it appeared, had been off in the bright moonlight looking for food, and when they got back they had found the store door standing open: they guessed what had happened, slammed the door, and locked it. The thieves inside – there were only two – started the pandemonium which caused the panic. So much for the insurrection.

We had one odd consequence of the kind of apprehension which was spreading at that time. The wife of a middle-grade white mine employee was about to have a baby in England. To while away the time, it seems he went into the 'native town', and walked into the African Club, which was of course purely for Africans. The members were mostly very staid clerks of some standing. He sat down and demanded a drink. The staff asked whether he was a member, knowing that he could not be, being white. He said that did not matter, and took out a revolver and placed it on the table. 'That', he said, 'should deal with the problem of membership'. Wisely a boy brought him a large beer and in due course he left. To impress the public, he fired a shot from the pistol over the club building. He was intensely surprised when three policemen, including a white police cadet, fell on his back and marched him off to the lock-up.

The next morning they told me about it and the man's remarkable statement that the General Manager of his Company had instructed his white staff to carry loaded arms. In the Nigerian Criminal Code the bearing of arms of any kind 'to cause fear' is a punishable offence. He was accordingly charged.

I sent for the leading General Managers and at first they denied that such an instruction had been given, but when the position was explained, they admitted it. I pointed out that I alone was responsible for the peace of the Province and that when I thought it necessary for arms to be carried I would say so. After a little time the head of the Company involved rang up and said that he felt that the man in question should be sent home, but that he was engaged in an accounting enquiry that would last a week or so; would I agree to his remaining for that time? So the situation had been much graver than it appeared, and it was just luck that in the state in which he found himself, he had not shot someone. Further, the general bearing of arms would inevitably have produced a sharp reaction among the Nigerian people.

Coronation

You will have realised that we of the Colonial Administration had to turn our hands to anything that came along. One of the most taxing situations arose from the deplored death of King George VI. Obviously something special had to be arranged for the day of the funeral and we knew that many and various people would attend such an occasion. Where to hold it was a serious problem; the largest covered area was the cinema, but with its fixed seats and awkward stage it was not suitable. We had not yet started building the Provincial Office extension, so the west end of the old building was still a blank wall and below it was a cemented expanse. This was the best we could do. The blank end of the office we covered with a huge purple drape, lent to us by a Lebanese firm: and on to this the ladies put a dominating white cross above a temporary altar.

I took a very simple religious service and the great crowd of black and white people sang the old hymns. I gave a brief address and there was a genuine and powerful emotional feeling in that strange setting so high up in the Nigerian air. Many sobbed quietly.

Early one morning in May 1953 I arrived in Kano off leave in England to go straight by local plane on to Jos. The acting Resident of Kano, Douglas Pott, came out to the airport to meet me, an act of courtesy which in this case was uncalled for since I was not stopping off. He was an old friend and I said, 'I have seen the new moon through perspex – don't know what it may signify – but you are the first person I have shaken hands with, so if there is any ill-luck connected with this sighting I am passing it on to you!' He said, 'I think it is already starting: as I came along the road I saw Ibos sharpening their matchets. I think there is something in the air.'

There was indeed. That morning the Ibos launched serious attacks on the Hausas round them (or possibly *vice versa*). Most of these people lived in a 'reservation' allotted to Southern peoples. I had always been opposed to this survival of the intense antipathy felt in the early days by senior white officers in the North towards Ibos and Yorubas, especially Ibos. By the 1950s these places housed some thousands of Southern people. Normally they all lived together in peace, and of course worked together in their offices and the trading companies. In time a few Northerners came to live amongst them.

The trouble had really started during the previous three months over a self-government motion in the Lagos House of Representatives. Anyway, on that morning the Southerners started laying about them and the first Hausas they came up against were the very tough group living near the Water Gate. Battle raged across a large open space outside the city walls. Nigeria Police formed a line across the ground to keep the combatants apart: the combatants respected the police and during the entire riot, none was seriously hurt. However, they used the police as cover and lobbed missiles over their heads.

The riot went on all day and dignified Yoruba women stalked through the mob as they went about their trading concerns, unscathed and superior and not without loud comments. Lorries for Katsina went through, for the main road traversed the battlefield, and all was well until the driver of one truck took fright and inadvertently swung off the road, charged into the rioters, and overturned. After this, the road was at last closed. The evening brought the end of the first day's fighting, but next morning they were at it again with much the same programme. I had hurried to Kaduna to preside over a special Assembly meeting called to consider the so-called '8 points' (see p.249) and, like others, was bemused to see that these riots were in danger of becoming a way of life. For example, a special inter-service committee was set up in Kano and met twice a day. On the third morning, however, a flash of intelligence appeared: barbed wire was spread right across the ground between the combatants, and the riots stopped. Thirty-one people had been killed and 241 wounded.

But all was not evil in those three days. There were heroic rescues by Hausas of their Ibo friends and the other way round, and people of one side concealed those of the other side being hunted by furious mobs demanding, and sometimes getting, blood. But no one who was not a Hausa or an Ibo was injured or even put in fear, and no child was hurt – I was told they ran unconcerned among the rioters.

Kano was not a place of bloodshed and terror; usually it was peaceful, quiet and industrious – which, considering the huge population and the tiny police force available to deal with trouble, was just as well. But as in other places the peace was firmly in the hands of the village and ward heads and their elders. We got very few complaints, and there was nothing to stop people coming to us: walking or riding through the villages, we talked to the people in their own language and were sensitive to any 'upset' feeling. The Emir sat outside his gate every fine evening before and during sunset and was available to any person. He did not have alarming numbers of 'courtiers' hedging him about; his people could come to him and say what they wished to say. This was the way it had been for generations.

To celebrate Queen Elizabeth's Coronation appropriately, we had arranged a gala day for the children, and there was to be a great display of fireworks in the evening. This was just after the Kano riots broke out and Kaduna was convinced that something similar would occur with us on the High Plateau, with our explosive mixture of

Hausa and Ibo (about 40,000).

My Nigeria Police officers firmly believed that trouble would break out under cover of the children's sports. I found it difficult to swallow much of this, and my administrative staff likewise. I could never understand where the police got their information from and why it was so often wrong. Anyway, there was much worried coming and going and the disquiet of the Police reached its height on a Sunday evening when I was having a bath before going to church. Alcock, the Police Superintendent, called wishing to see me. When my wife, who was outside heading the roses, said I was in my bath, Alcock said he would wait and she replied 'I don't think that would be much good: he will hurry off to church as soon as he is dressed.' 'To church at a time like this?' he cried. My wife, after saying that there was no better place to be at such a time, suggested he should ring after 8 p.m., and Alcock withdrew.

To assuage the police, and just in case they turned out to be right after all, I had some Bailey bridging that lay to hand for the Shendam Road brought in to Jos. It was erected in a day across the Canteen creek that ran down the west side of the 'native town'. The Works built one of the quickest sections of road ever laid in a couple of days. Using this route we could move police from their barracks into the 'native town' within a few minutes and thus outflank any move potential rioters might make by the normal route into the Government station. The police gleefully ran lorries full of men back and forth along this new route to impress this fact on the populace. The road was closed to ordinary traffic as the light surface would soon have been ruined.

I had a dramatic conversation with the Kaduna authority on the telephone. I was told that I was going to have bad riots on my hands and was offered a complete infantry battalion. I said that this was the very thing calculated to incite a riot – which was not well received, though the truth of it was obvious enough to me. I was pressed to say what they could send me to deal with the riot, which had not started. I said that if they really wanted to send something, a mile of barbed wire could, in certain eventualities, be used to separate the combatants. I then said that if a riot did break out, it would be *my* riot and nobody else's and that *I* would deal with it in my own way. If they thought I could not do so, they should at once send someone else to take over from me. This was received in pained silence, and the conversation ended. The barbed wire duly arrived by special plane.

Meanwhile we went on with preparations for the grand gala. The children were timed to move from the 'Native Town' at 2.30 p.m. By lunch time the police were still confident that a great riot was inevitable – I felt they would be upset if it did not happen. They formally advised that the procession should be called off. I went down to the Provincial Office half an hour before the time it was due to start and there found an anxious group of white police officers, still dead against it. I wondered what the senior African police felt on the matter, but was not able to find out. Because the police were so obviously worried, I felt I should meet them half way, and said I would drive around the 'course' in the 'Native Town' where great crowds were known to be assembling, and from which they would debouch into the Township and on to the golf course. When the Superintendent kindly said he would send police cars with me, before and behind, I said that this would destroy the whole experiment. If I got through on my own without any adverse sign, it would clearly be safe to let the procession start; if I did not return in a reasonable time they could rescue me in whatever way they thought fit.

I set out in my little Morris car – not the big official Buick with its driver – driving myself, with a Union Jack on its tiny bonnet. It was with some apprehension that I found myself in the first of the streets between solid crowds composed of all the diverse races of Nigeria. However, as soon as they saw me, a roar of delight burst from them, and all the way round I received a tumultuous reception – the Coronation had got them. When I got back to the ashen-faced police, they said 'Thank God you're all right, sir – when we heard the noise we thought it was all over and we would be too late.'

So the proceedings started and ran their length with great success. No one who saw it will forget the astonishing sight when the head of the children's column appeared from among the houses and burst into the open – ten thousand children of all sizes, waving at least ten thousand Union Jacks: a cheering, noisy, delirious stream of youth coming down the slopes to celebrate something that was happening thousands of miles away in a country they could not imagine, concerning people they knew little about. The Police would have stopped it and so spoilt their day: it is nice to be right sometimes.

At some time in this period Lady Macpherson issued an appeal to the country at large to encourage and develop Red Cross work. Nigeria was badly off for charities. There were a few efforts to raise funds in the large towns of the South but hardly anything of the kind in the North. During the war successful appeals were made for the Red Cross and for the Spitfire Fund. This appeal was passed on to Residents by Joan Sharwood-Smith, and it was decided to raise funds both for local Red Cross purposes and, specifically, for the provision of stretchers. The great proportion of our villages were distant from motor-roads, as is probably still the case, and so sick people could only be brought in for treatment at the cost of great discomfort to them and difficulty for their friends.

It was agreed by many of the Native Authorities to levy three pence per tax-payer towards the fund. This was cheerfully done and a large sum was collected. By the time I left Jos it had reached more than £10,000. To make sure that all were associated we bought about two thousand steel stretchers. These were of strong wire-mesh on tubular frames and were solid, not too heavy, ant-proof and even, to some extent, fool-proof. A huge concourse assembled one morning in Jos. People from every village appeared, and every village-head was called up and personally presented with his stretcher. They were accepted with astonishment and people trooped off rejoicing. What happened to the stretchers is another story.

In Kaduna in later years I became chairman* of the Northern Red Cross and we raised quite a lot of money, much of it by raffles with large prizes like motor-cars. My wife and I gave a cup for a Red Cross team-competition: the contests held in Kaduna were excellent, but were mostly between Southern people. The Northerners, though generous to their own people, were not very co-operative in this respect. Umaru Gwandu, the Clerk of Assembly, was an enthusiastic supporter and took over from me as chairman when I left Kaduna in 1962.

There were two road projects on the High Plateau that I was determined to achieve. The ten miles from Jos to Bukuru, perhaps the most used section of any road in the north, followed the original trade route. The first three miles were good, then it went off in a curve and came on to the railway. In the early days, when money was tight there were no funds for a road bridge over the Ngell River, the headwaters of the Kaduna River (several other great rivers rose near Jos), and so the road used the Railway bridge. This might have been reasonable but as the two tracks approached the bridge on different curves, it was difficult to see a train approaching from either direction – like the rest of the railway it was single line. At night, with the odd Minesfield lights visible in the landscape, it was almost impossible to distinguish the headlight of the engine. Further, the railway gradient down to the bridge, from either side, was steep, and with its rather poor brakes the train would have needed a far longer stretch of track to pull up than

---

*The British Red Cross kindly appointed me a Life Member of the Third Class. The qualifications for the Second and First Classes must indeed be remarkable. It reminded me of a continental country's Order of Chastity of which a visiting British admiral received the First Class while his wife was accorded only the Third Class.

was available. There were no gates on the road or railway. As a result, there were both horrible accidents and startling escapes. Some lucky drivers managed to get away from the train by accelerating just in front of the engine, but it was not recommended practice.

We were always pressing the P.W.D. to build a road bridge and the extra few miles of new road that would be involved: many were their reasons for not doing so. Finally, one night twenty-five people were killed when the train collided with a lorry. I wired to the Director of Public Works personally and told him this. I ended 'grateful you indicate how many people must die before you start new bridge construction.' The reply was remarkably humble and promised action. In fact they started so quickly that we had difficulty in dealing with the inevitable compensation to the miners and farmers, two quite separate considerations. The result was an excellent wide structure with straight approaches and a general improvement to the road. Now people got killed through speeding, but that was their fault and not ours.

Shendam road

I have mentioned the awkward road that went to Shendam by way of Pankshin far down below to the plains of the Benue. I had always wanted to build something direct across this huge arc.

The problem about getting to Shendam was how to descend the 3,000-foot drop on a more direct route. I had a retired officer, Lieutenant-Colonel Hollington-Sawyerr, assigned to me for special duties and I sent him along the escarpment to find any possible and direct way of descent in the direction of Shendam. He fortunately found a deep cleft in the hillside and thought it worth exploring more closely. I invited him to mark a possible route with stone cairns, white-washed. He took a football with him, and whereever he stopped he taught the local youths to play; as soon as he came in sight of a village he blew a whistle and everyone would be kicking the ball about before he had got his loads down.

The direct distance was about 20 miles, in practice twice as much. When he reported completion we chartered a small aircraft and skimmed over the trees as we followed the line of the whitened cairns. Effion Jones and I saw that the line was practicable.

A few weeks later, after the construction had started at the top end from the village of Panyam, Jones and his wife, the D.O. Pankshin, my wife and the colonel set out to walk along the upper part of the line. The beacons went gently down hill until we came to a place on a line of extinct volcanoes. At this point there were no more cairns in sight. The Colonel took us to a precipice and pointed down to a cairn visible a hundred feet below; he explained that he had worked up to that point from the plains and down from Panyam to where we were standing. I asked if he had any idea how to get the road down to his lower beacon. He said he had thought a lot about it but was 'quite foxed'. Effion Jones and I looked at the country ahead of us and found it was pretty steep. Jones looked gloomily at the descent. To my question whether men could work on it, he pronounced the dogma, 'Where a man can stand, he can work.' So that was that. In the end I laid out the descent myself to join up with the Colonel's route. Beyond that section, then far below us, was a gorge 400 feet deep, and on its further side rose a 1,000 foot volcano: later we worked with its grey ash when we were forming the road surface. For the road I bought, on behalf of the Pankshin N.A., a lot of Bailey bridging, and including a whole Bailey suspension bridge which I planned to put over the Shemankar river nearly on the plains level. However, after I left the Province the Works lost heart and built an ordinary bridge lower down. The whole new route saved forty miles on the journey.

I must say a word about Pankshin. It was a coveted District Officer's station. Seventy miles from Jos, it was the right distance from authority, and yet not isolated for there were mining camps round about and there was always 'company' if you wanted it. But the climate was the thing. The ground level here was a little higher than Jos – about 4,200 feet – and there were undulating plains, split with high-timbered dells and pierced by great rocks, crowned with proud villages. The people were delightful, intelligent and determined, but without the tiresome and blinkered obstinacy of the people round Jos. East of Pankshin the ground fell steeply away into the first of the steps down from the Plateau and here the scenery was utterly different: far horizons and glorious cloud-effects.

The Government station itself was on a knoll about 200 feet high, with a steep motor road up it. It was in its way a fortress and you felt that a drawbridge could be pulled up. The illusion was carried on to the house, which was impressive, furnished with substantial remains of numbers of devoted D.O.s all determined to improve it for their successor. The garden had plants and shrubs of every kind, a real horticultural paradise – the only 'private' garden in the North maintained by two gardeners paid from Government funds. In the winter it was bitterly cold and there was a great log fire in the baronial fireplace and even one in the rest house for the visitors. One could see for twenty or thirty miles in every direction from the look-outs round the hill, which were joined by a sentry-path, a souvenir of the days when a small W.A.F.F. garrison was stationed there. In fact the whole place seemed removed from the Nigerian world.

Of the private miners, most of them did well. The majority were white men but there were some Nigerians amongst them; indeed my cook was a member of a syndicate that owned a mining lease. They used to bring the tin in weekly and I would find them late at night dividing the ore up in correct proportions on the kitchen table.

Some private miners lived in fine style; they all entertained very graciously and used to ask us and of course we gave parties back. Their houses were beautifully and comfortably furnished. It was always a pleasure to go to them, and a pleasure to get away from 'official' conversation, which could be exasperating, specially where someone thought he could 'get a quick one through.'

We were fortunate too, in our District Officers of the Jos Division: Gordon Wilson, Mike Counsell, Christopher Reynolds – their wives always ready to help – and Kenneth Maddocks, then still a bachelor. They were all of high calibre and I could not have asked for better people to support me. I cannot say that I always took their advice, but having said their say they carried out the final decision with skill and discretion. We were a very happy family as a Service and it was a delight to work with such people.*

It came to pass that the end of my administrative service in Nigeria, fell in 1954. We were all expected to retire at fifty-five, and could not receive more than two-thirds of our final salary as pension. The plan was that I should stay on for a little, but it was discovered that I had already over seventy weeks' leave on full pay due to me, from wartime accumulations when full leaves could not be taken and this would put me well beyond my pension limit. So I went rather unexpectedly. By selling everything we would not want in England, I was able to pay my bills.

My wife had gone ahead and I faced alone the horrors of the farewell. A large crowd assembled at the airport and I shook hands with nearly a thousand people and so held up the take-off quite a while. It was all very emotional and moving. Mike Counsell made a charming speech and I a sad reply, though I would probably still continue as President of the House of Assembly. My real service would be over, and that was that.

*Maddocks became Governor of Fiji and Counsell Deputy High Commissioner in Calcutta.

XVII. The New Kaduna

After we left Kaduna in 1932 I do not think we even visited it again until the end of the war. The appointment of Eric Thompstone as Chief Commissioner in 1948 made visits easier, and the start of the new constitutions made consultations on them inevitable. John Patterson's tour as Chief Commissioner of the North (he took over in 1943) was distinguished by the intensity of the work and care that he put into everything personally. It was told and re-told that he passed through the big hall in Government Lodge and caught sight of his wife sitting in a chair sewing. He clamped his hand to his jaw, a characteristic gesture, and said, 'Elsie, how long have you been here?' and she replied quietly, 'Just three weeks, Jack.' Another time he went into his office and found on his engagement pad the simple message '8.15 a.m. Interview with Lady Patterson'.

After the war Kaduna changed dramatically, from a small country capital to a bustling city. An industrial area was opened to the south of the Junction station. The first to arrive was the textile factory, covering six acres. This was the beginning of a Government enterprise aimed at making as much of local produce as possible; Nigeria grew plenty of good cotton; why send it to Lancashire to be made into cloth for subsequent reimportation? To train local people a dozen real Lancashire mill lasses were brought out for a tour, with unnecessary trepidation on the part of the authorities; they succeeded in teaching their craft to advantage. When they left there was great lamentation among the African staff. The factory soon doubled in size and output.

The Government departments expanded too and new staff houses and offices had to be built. Areas we used to walk over were now built up. We even had a Bishop in the North, Bishop Mort from Worcester: appointed (among other qualifications) because he was a bachelor. It was not surprising that a Judge appeared; later, with 'regionalisation', the post was raised to Chief Justice. We had, however, lost the Army Commandant, now a Major-General with headquarters in Lagos; a brigadier commanded the Kaduna area. Two more banks appeared on the scene and the old British Bank of West Africa was in a new smart building where it should always have been near the 'Native Town'.

A Kingsway Stores, on the Lagos model, had replaced the dirty old 'canteen'; where the goods were sold at strikingly high prices. There were British building contractors now to take work from the P.W.D. and two motor firms to explain why they could not supply you with the spare part you wanted. The Government built a fine new post office, in which delays were guaranteed over the simplest transaction beyond the mere purchase of a stamp; it seemed sometimes as though sections of the African public actually lived either in the Post Office or at the Railway Station.

The 145-mile road from Kaduna to Jos had been built by the P.W.D. For the first two-thirds of the way, it was very dull and then it began to run through hilly country. There was no spectacular climb on to the High Plateau, you just felt that you were getting higher and, as you neared Jos, the air, the grass, the people – all were different, and fine distant views were visible in the clear air. Over the years peasants came to live on the road. Originally it ran through almost virgin country and there were few villages, but in time new villages sprang up and with them farms, many of them with excellent cotton, but there was never much traffic. This was one of the purely 'administrative' roads, which did not follow a trade route.

Government Lodge ran to a sharp time-table when guests were present, but at other times meals depended on bell signals. We sometimes took our daughter Jane with us on visits and she once precipitated a crisis. Thompstone enjoyed his drinks before lunch: at least three pink gins and soda, sometimes more (he was never the worse for it). One day he had had a couple and asked Jane to ring the bell near her seat for the third. The signal for a gin was one ring of the bell and no more; she being rather hungry and always impetuous rang three times. That was the ineluctable signal for lunch or dinner, impossible to reverse short of calling in the Army. The whole Government Lodge machinery swung into action; a boy came in, bowed and started to collect the glasses, the great double doors into the dining room were slowly opened, the white-robed head boy entered, bowed, and announced that lunch was served. Reluctantly the Lieutenant Governor hoisted himself to his feet and, with a nasty look at Jane lumbered dutifully into the dining-room.

This Government Lodge was comfortable for the privileged guest, who had a charming private sitting room and bedroom. Breakfast was served in your sitting room according to what you had ordered the evening before; you were not supposed to join the household till lunch. You would find a seating plan for lunch or dinner on your dressing table, with short notes on the other guests. It was considered rather unsporting to take the list down with you.

One day, in a regrettably frivolous mood, I casually mentioned to Thompstone that I had overheard two Secretariat men saying that they were putting a snake in one of the despatch boxes. Only he had the key to these boxes: they had the special Whitehall spring locks and he had to open them himself. He would not do so, as he refused to believe that I was joking. The boxes mounted up and the Government ground to a halt. They ran out of boxes in the Secretariat and finally Sir Eric was persuaded to let the head messenger open a box, with two colleagues standing by armed with heavy cudgels. It contained a canvas shoe, three squash balls and some mouldy mangoes.

Clothes often confused guests at Government House (the name changed to 'House' when the office became a governorship). In the daytime we were usually formal. Some wore light suits – I used to wear brown cord trousers with a shirt and tie – always a tie – and an oatmeal linen jacket. In the office we took coats off unless important people were coming; when I was Resident I expected everyone who was coming in to wear a coat and I believe that a communal coat was kept in the outer office by helpful A.D.O.s.

On tour I wore shorts and stockings, and those whose jobs involved physical activity like the Engineers wore shorts all the time.

The French, who were slack in some ways (e.g. shaving), invariably wore fresh white uniforms with gold rank badges in their offices. White drill was not really sucessful, as it creased so quickly.

In the afternoon, after the siesta and tea, one wore some kind of 'sporting' gear consonant with what one was going to do. In the evening everyone dressed for parties (men in dinner jackets). For cocktail parties and receptions it was always lounge suits. The Northerners scored because their clothes always looked impressive though sometimes cumbersome.

Two Labour M.P.s visited Government House in Lagos in the Bourdillons' time. They came into lunch, after going out shopping, wearing shorts and shirts with no ties: all the other men were smartly dressed in suits. They were overcome with confusion, but put at their ease by the genial Governor. In the afternoon they came down to tea with Lady Bourdillon under the great tree, wearing immaculate suits and ties and found everyone in shorts and loose short-sleeved shirts. As they went away, one muttered to the A.D.C. 'We shall never get the bloody thing right. What do we wear for dinner this evening?'

In the early years the white ladies had to cut and trim their own hair or get others to help them. I was able to cut my wife's hair fairly successfully and to trim and 'thin' it, but offers to help others were frowned on! The absence of this feminine amenity must have been a serious deprivation for many of them. Even in Lagos there was only one man who could cut hair of either sex, and there was lamentation when he went on leave. In places like Jos and Kano, individual white ladies of experience set up little salons to help others. They charged little, not being out to make money. This enterprise was good for morale and people living in the bush made the most of their occasional visits to headquarters to get tidied up.

Thompstone was replaced, on his retirement in 1951, by Bryan Sharwood-Smith who had been concerned mostly with Sokoto, Niger and Kano, while I had always been on the other side of the country. Both had first-class people in the Secretariats to help them. H.R.E. (Phiz) Browne, who helped me in Lagos (page 166), was a tower of strength, and if he ever made a mistake I have still to hear of it. Peter Guillam Scott was another very able man, though a little prejudiced in some ways and a great financial secretary. I had had him in my office at Jos and he was excellent. Petra Browne, Phiz's wife, had a genius for 'running' things but in such a friendly way that everyone could not help rallying around.

There was much ceremonial inevitably connected with this office. For example, guards of honour – that popular British institution – abounded. Even as a Resident of a Province you had to keep an eye open for a guard of honour when you visited a public place on a formal function. They could vary from tiny children or girl guides to police, with or without bands, which might consist of anything from tin whistles and tin drums to bugles and side drums. Also you had to watch out so that you would recognise familiar music, like the British national anthem or popular hymn tunes, that was being dubiously rendered.

Strange things happened when the guards were inspected, as once at Zaria fairly late in the British period. Carrow, who was acting Lieutenant-Governor at the time, had a very nervous Private Secretary, and it was one of his accident-prone days. After the guard had been safely inspected, Carrow got in to the back seat of his car in the approved manner. The P.S. rushed round to get into the car from the other side both were wearing white uniforms with their trousers tightly strapped under their insteps. The door being held open by some underling, the P.S. dashed at it, caught his foot in the sill, and fell flat into the car across Carrow's legs. The far door at this moment flew open and the P.S.'s white helmet shot out through it, to the delight of the onlookers. Carrow, already testy, said in a strangled voice, 'This is no time or place for humour.' It was always difficult to move with these tight trousers, but eventually the P.S. worked his way out backwards into the open air. Meanwhile, the Guard Commander (they were regular soldiers this time) standing stiffly with a drawn sword, was astonished to observe the while helmet rolling over the ground and coming to rest at his feet. How do you pick up a helmet with a drawn sword? Is it correct to do so at all? In the end he stooped down, still holding his sword in the proper position, and picked it up, marched in a brisk, soldier-like manner to the car and handed the helmet through the window. The car drove off and another page in Nigerian Colonial History was turned.

Investitures can produce their problems too. a Governor pinned a medal to one worthy and turned away to the next in line only to find that he had pinned his white glove to the breast of the first one. The man was standing to attention and the unexpected viceregal pull nearly upset his balance. To save himself, he clutched at the Governor, who pushed him back again. The A.D.C. struggled with the pin, and in the end the glove was taken off and left hanging on the man's chest with the medal. Another Governor pricked his finger on the first medal-pin, and left a tiny rosette of the gubernatorial blood imprinted on the uniform of each recipient along with the medal.

Twice during my duties at Jos I had to break off and go down to Kaduna to take over as Lieutenant-Governor. Working as a Resident, though that was impressive enough, was as nothing to being in the very seat of Government. First of all, you have a large office with a special staff (the Secretariat) devoted to seeing that you have as little to do as possible and that your efforts are confined to writing 'yes' or 'no' or even simple initials at the foot of a minute. Further your personal staff rotate round you running the large house and all entertaining and movements, specially when you go on tour. There are several official cars and a comfortable special train of two white coaches, one containing a drawing room and a dining room seating a dozen people, the other with two bedrooms with real beds and a bath room with a long bath, as well as a composite coach to take the staff, a wagon for stores and furniture and the like and a flat for five cars.

Soldiers and others

Not far from the gates of Government Lodge and by the railway was a large military hospital, a post-war feature, with a number of Army doctors and sisters. We gave them a two-storey house for the Sisters' Mess: Majors in rank. At times we found this unisex-title system confusing. One evening a Colonel Williams was among the dinner guests at Government House. When my wife and I went down just before zero hour, we were met by the P.S. Hugh Patterson who, with a sideways smile, said 'Colonel Williams seems to have come a little early, sir.' We went into the great lounge and could only see a handsome and well-dressed lady. It took a moment or two to realise that was the Colonel – a doctor.

When the two West African Divisions came back from Burma after the war, they had with them, of course, scores of white officers who had never been in West Africa, knew nothing of it and seemed to care less. They treated themselves more or less as an 'Army of occupation' and had nothing to do with the people of the country, black or white: they had their wives and children with them and mostly they never spoke to those they regarded in a superior way as 'civilians'. The Sisters' Mess have a dance one evening and we were asked, being neighbours and having entertained some of them. I was dancing with a young Captain and she suddenly remarked – 'Are you a civilian? I suppose you must be.' I said I was, and she said she had not spoken to a civilian for six months. 'Odd, isn't it?' she added, 'are there many of them here?'

One night in Kaduna I was asked (it was the first time) to dine with the 1st Battalion – because we had staying wth us not only the friendly General Sir Lashmere Whistler, who was the G.O.C. British West Africa, but also General Ingles the G.O.C. Nigeria. After dinner I found myself making an impromptu and unconsidered speech. We made a stealthy and tiptoed entry back into Government House rather late, and the next morning Whistler said, 'That was a jolly good speech you made last night – I enjoyed it a lot.' I said, 'Thank you very much, but can you tell me roughly what I said?' 'Haven't an idea,' he said, 'but it was a good speech.' Then General Ingles came in and said, 'Jolly good speech last night, sir, very enjoyable.' 'What did he talk about?' asked Whistler. 'Haven't an idea,' said our G.O.C. I could only remember starting off by saying something about the use of troops in support of the civil power.

General Feilden, the Adjutant-General in London, came on an official visit from London and stayed with us for two or three days in Kaduna. One day before lunch I said I hoped his inspections had gone without any disasters. 'Disasters,' he replied, 'I have had a dreadful morning: something went wrong at every unit. I know they're good chaps, I know they're efficient and that a general's visits have a special menace of their own, but I have never known a round of inspections where there was some kind of trouble at every unit.' He took a deep swallow of restorative gin, and went on: 'I thought I'd give them a real chance to score at the last unit I saw. When I got out of the car, I said to the Colonel, "What day of the week is it?" Without hesitation he said "Thursday, sir".' (It was a Friday.)

In Kaduna, we had authors in search of copy and people in search of notoriety: Elspeth Huxley was one of the most pleasant (she wrote the book *Four Guineas* about this visit) and the South African Stuart

Cloete the most incisive. We had the heads of great firms, bishops and archbishops, politicians of all sorts and Service chiefs (even admirals, far though we were from the ocean) – they all either stayed with us or made their way to our table. The most unfortunate was the well-known journalist Eileen Ashcroft (Mrs Hugh Cudlipp), who not only had to push the car sent to meet her at Jos, but had money stolen from her handbag while she was in the Army pool. She bore it all with good humour.

In addition to the Private Secretary we had excellent shorthand typists – very different from the days in Lagos when we had a single stenographer. There was a lot of correspondence in spite of the work turned out by the Secretariat. One of them, Sybil Llong, successfully took over as Private Secretary. It surprised people on tour to see a woman doing the job, usually done by a male A.D.O., such as opening car doors on formal occasions.

One of the attractions of the 'Acting' periods was that one could go on tour by road, train or air. There were always places to visit and we managed to go to areas we had never seen in all our years in the country. There were schools and hospitals to see, workshops to inspect and all sorts of people to meet and talk to about their work and problems. All this stimulated them in a benign way. When difficulties arose it was easier to journey over to see the people concerned and the actual place they were talking about, than to write letters. Where you knew the place yourself, the person at the other end could be invited to Kaduna to discuss it face to face. I also made a point of visiting (not inspecting) institutions in Kaduna so as to meet the staff, to see their background and discuss difficulties. This was unusual, and was appreciated.

In the course of the two 'Acting' spells, we managed to get to most of the provinces. I admit that some of these visits were because I was curious about changes and 'development' in places I had not seen for some time. One of these was Lokoja, where I had not been since leaving it in 1926. We flew there and landed on an alarmingly inadequate airstrip just behind Patti. There had been a little expansion but most of Lokoja seemed unchanged. Cedric (Foxy) Cole, the Resident, and his wife Margaret met us and put us up. On the second day he arranged a motor trip through Okene and Kabba and back by (my) road. We found them much expanded with charming little African cottages – not huts any more – in shrubs and greenery, the kind of houses to be seen in the South.

From time to time it became necessary to travel to Lagos for meetings of the House of Representatives, of the Council of Ministers in its early stages, and of *ad hoc* committees. The journey could be by train, if there was any time and if some place en route needed to be visited, or by air, which only took an hour or so.

While I was acting in Kaduna, Jos was in the hands of my excellent seconds-in-command, Gordon Wilson for my first absence and Mike Counsell for the second. They kept in touch by phone if anything interesting was arising in the Province but otherwise I left them to their own devices since we had a good mutual understanding. It surprised me, on the other hand, that Sharwood-Smith did not expect endless letters between us while he was away. The morning he went off on leave for the first time, he came into the Government House guest room at breakfast and merely put two keys on the table, saying, 'That is the Northern Region – it's all yours.' One was the key of the office safe. I signed nothing and took over no instructions.

There were weekly meetings of our Executive Council in Kaduna. The L.G. still presided; in the next spasm of constitution-making the chair passed to the Sardauna of Sokoto as Premier. A fine new office was being built for this body at the back of Government House. Executive Council could be very interesting when the Ministers were themselves sometimes interested in the subject before them. If they were not they would just let it go by default. If the matter was awkward and complicated, there was a simple technique: to have it put back to the next meeting. Of course, it then came up as first item, and they merely said that they had discussed it among themselves and did, or did not, agree to the proposal. The white members* had no time to argue about it and found the thing settled before they could express an opinion. There was a way of dealing with that but it did not dawn on us for a while.

We brought down our own boys and cook from Jos and Sharwood-Smith's lot went off on their holiday. There was a caretaker paid by Government who jealously guarded every fork, spoon, pillow-case and rug, but he also gave a hand at parties. All the officials and many others signed the book (for us) in the Guard Room by the main gate – if they did not, they would certainly not be asked in without special reasons – and the A.D.C. kept a card-index of the signatories showing what parties, if any, they had been bidden to attend. As in Jos we had about two dinner parties (only more were invited than in Jos) a week and more, if we had house-guests. The food was very good and the drink up to standard. The boys enjoyed it and my head boy, Yaro, must have done well in tips. But he came into my office just after one

---

*At first these were the Civil Secretary, the Attorney-General and the Financial Secretary. As the Ministries took over, the two Secretaries dropped out, leaving only the Attorney till 1960.

guest had left for the airport, and said 'Master, did you say that was a *big general?*' I said he was. He opened his hand and showed a single shilling piece; he grinned and went off muttering ' a very big general!'

The catering and ordering came mostly under the Private Secretary, with my wife's assistance; it was not cheap and at the end with all the allowances, I only just came out even each time. I found that quite a lot of people who 'deserved well of the state' never got asked into the house. So I started Saturday lunches on the same plan as in Jos. The guests saw the house in daylight and they had a nice lunch, and above all could say that they had been asked in. That of course was the whole point.

I was glad that I had only one riot, and that a minor one, to cope with in my time as acting L.G. and that it called for no special effort on my part. I mention it as it had strange features. An Ibo man died of heart failure in the market in Kaduna. He happened to be that unusual combination, a Muslim Ibo, and when the Ibos took the body up for burial (presumably by Christian rites) the Muslims swooped down – he had been a well-known character – to bury him in their way. Blows were exchanged and a nasty situation developed. In the end the police got the body away from both sets of contestants and locked it in one of their stores. By the next morning feelings might have subsided and some rational arrangement could have been arrived at, but in the meantime the trouble went on intermittently. Sharwood-Smith seemed rather to like controlling action in such situations himself; I did not, but preferred to let people do what they were trained to do, and only come in later if the situation got worse. Following precedent, therefore, the Commissioner of Police rang up and asked if I had any special instructions; I said, 'No, thank you very much, but please get the riot under control as soon as possible.' (I am not sure that it was *his* business either; he had a Superintendent presumably in charge of Kaduna area.) We went to a film at the Army cinema that evening, and the riot came to an end. But when the Police store was opened the next morning to hand over the body to a now docile crowd, there was no body. And it was never found.

In the North there were only two Government prisons – in Kaduna and Jos respectively – strictly for persons convicted in the High or Magistrates' Courts. These had white Superintendents and were considered superior to the N.A. prisons, some of which at times held 1,200 prisoners. There was a memorable case concerning a prisoner held in the Government prison in Kaduna. The Superintendent of the Jos Prison rang me one morning and said he was in a fix. He had received a parcel of prison clothes through the mail without any message or covering letter: what should he do? I suggested that he

ring Kaduna Prison. He did so and was told that a prisoner whose
name was written on the clothes had escaped from a working party
and they were looking for him. I said we had heard nothing from the
native Authority, and it was possible that he might be following his
clothes. Sure enough in a day or two he turned up at the Jos prison
and knocked at the great entrance door. He said he did not care for the
food and amenities in the Kaduna Prison and understood that things
were better in Jos, and so here he was. He had, he added, come 140
miles in mufti and on foot to avoid recapture. For the sake of discipline
he had to be sent back to Kaduna, but before long some hard heart
melted and he was formally transferred to Jos.

Sudden death

Considering the risks they incurred, the number of Europeans who
were murdered in Nigeria during my long service was small. There
was a D.O. in the South who was shot by a lunatic policeman during a
pay parade: a miner was killed by thieves on the Plateau for the pay
packets of the labourers to be issued the following day: I have already
mentioned the death of Barlow in Shendam Division, and there was a
strange case in Kano after my time as Resident.

Many years ago the Nigerian Railway built a 'Railway Guest
House' just across the tracks from the station. It had a central lounge
and dining room, behind which stretched wooden bedroom blocks,
each containing about a dozen austerely furnished bedrooms opening
off mosquito-proofed corridors, with lavatories and bathrooms at the
ends. In the middle of each corridor was a mosquito-proofed doorway
leading onto a sandy path that ran along the space between the
blocks. They were single-storeyed and rather low-roofed.

One Saturday a P.W.D. white man from the Kaduna Works
arrived on a week-end visit and went to bed at a reasonable hour.
Some time during the night he heard a noise, probably the opening of
the drawers in the dressing table, which were still open in the morning. He woke and found a thief in the room. He grappled with him and
the thief broke away into the corridor. Here he pulled out his knife and
stabbed the white man; the wound was grave but not immediately
mortal. The struggle continued and they broke through the double
mosquito doors out into the open, where the white man finally collapsed and died. No one heard this struggle which cannot have been
conducted in silence. It was a Saturday night, but even so, few people
would actually have been drunk.

The hotel boys going round with the early tea found the body and reported to the European manager. The manager had either not read any detective stories, or took the good name of his hotel a little too much to heart. The body was picked up and put into the bedroom, and staff at once started to clean up the room, while a gardener raked over the path. All traces of the crime were thus removed. However, a Nigerian policeman was passing by and noticed a commotion. He heard something of what had happened and without reporting back to his headquarters went direct to the nearby house of the Chief Superintendent and told him that a man was dead in the hotel and no one had reported anything about it.

The Superintendent, Bill Ford, had no reason to think that a serious crime had been committed until he saw the body and realised that the man had been killed. An autopsy was held at once and the cause of death by stabbing was established. There was at this stage only one clue – the sheath of a wrist-knife with a broken strap. The Superintendent showed it to the Madaki, the Councillor, in charge of the City Police, who said at once that it was a Shuwa Arab knife from Bornu. So they spoke by telephone to the Bornu police and an expert was sent down. He smelt the leather and confirmed not only that it was a Shuwa knife but – from the smell of an oil which that people rub into their skins – that it had recently been worn by a Shuwa. The police looked through their old lags' lists for recently released criminals likely to be violent and found two possibilities: one of them was in Shuwa. It was proved that he could not be involved in this case, but he was charged with being a vagabond (which he undoubtedly was) and got three months – he would be handy if needed. The policeman from Bornu had discovered meanwhile that this man had been associated with another Shuwa, an address in Jos seemed to give a line on him and they asked the Jos Police to search his hut. They found a cloth, the kind men wrap round themselves at night, with a big bloodstain. This was laughingly described by its Shuwa owner as a stain of cow blood. He was brought down to Kano and examined at some length through an outside interpreter, the police having no one who could translate from or into Shuwa Arabic. His Hausa was very poor. After a few days he volunteered a statement. So the Superintendent and the officer in charge of the C.I.D., with a special and completely independent witness, a learned scribe from the School of Arabic Studies in the City, went along. The man told what had happened. His narrative was as expected, save that he maintained that during the struggle the white man held his throat and things started to go black. It was then that he hit out with his wrist-knife. The strap broke and so the sheath fell to the ground.

So far so good: there were no tape recorders in those days but it was all taken down very carefully. But Bill Ford was not satisfied. There was no shred of corroborative evidence: the knife had not been found, and even if it had been, it would have been difficult to link so common a tool indisputably with the crime. He thought about this for some time and then remembered that another object had been found at the scene of the crime – an ordinary two-battery electric torch. He looked at it and no inspiration came. Idly he unscrewed the base cap and tipped out the batteries. One of the batteries bore the perfect impressions of a set of upper and lower teeth. Nigerians have discovered that a moribund battery can be stimulated for a short while by biting the battery casing. The impressions were excellent. He asked the best available dentist in the North to make casts of the suspect's teeth, top and bottom, the suspect cheerfully agreeing. The dentist by using his clamps, produced a deep bite in a similar battery. On comparison they were identical. The case was proved.

The hearing of the case suffered delays, during which the suspect was learning from others in prison. When he came to give evidence, he denied every word of his statement to the police. He said that the Superintendent had tied a rope round his neck when they were questioning him and had threatened to hang him then and there, and the C.I.D. man had nearly dislocated his arm. The police, who had fallen over themselves to be fair and who indeed had not pressed the charge until the clinching evidence of the batteries was produced, were amazed. But the accused had forgotten the learned scribe. His independence and his dignified and unshakable evidence disposed of the accused's new claim.

The man was found guilty and was hanged. The scribe many years later became a Judge of the High Court of Nigeria.

XVIII.   The Assembly

Constitutions

Soon after the war, in 1947, Sir Arthur Richards brought in the new Constitution named in the public mind after him – this was the first change in government structure since 1922. The intention was that each group of Provinces should have a Council of elected representatives, which would be able to discuss legislation and the estimates of expenditure affecting the area. Motions could be brought before them and they would elect representatives to go to the expanded Legislative Council ('Legco') in Lagos. These were all definite steps forward, though tentative and experimental.

The first hurdle was to settle who was to choose these members. There had never been an election in the country, apart from ones of a very restricted nature in certain Southern areas; there were no political parties and no candidates. The problem was solved by expediency and with democracy. So far as the North was concerned, the people most likely to launch the scheme and those with the most to offer were the members of the non-elective Native Authority Councils. So selected councillors gathered in each Province and selected one member to go to Kaduna – Kano and Sokoto, being large had more than one. The elected members for the North were fifteen, for the West eleven and for the East ten. In the North, six other Africans represented certain interests like trade (and one for 'educated elements'!); in the other two Regions, the number was five. With them sat officials: all the Residents of the Provinces, the Secretaries, Crown Counsel and the Directors of Works, Agriculture and Education, totalling eighteen in the North and thirteen in the West and East. The Works made a little desk for each member – well made but, maddeningly, just too small for the papers we had to spread.

In the North, each Resident sat with his Provincial Member, while Kano and Sokoto sat between theirs. The idea was that the official would guide these new members on procedure and on how to say what they wanted to put to the meeting. I had the Wali (later the Waziri) of Bornu, for I was Resident of that Province at the time. One of the ablest of the Bornu people and certainly the most eloquent, he was nonetheless terrified by the whole thing and completely tongue-tied. I had to urge him to speak on something he knew about: I felt it vital that the difficulty be broken or we should be forever stuck. He wrote his paragraph, about ten lines, and brought it to me to look at. I smartened it up a bit and made it easier to say. When the time came he shambled (there is no other word) to his feet. He trembled so much

I thought that he would fall flat, and as his hand shook he couldn't read what he had written, but fortunately memory came to his aid. He recited the words in a whisper that could scarcely be heard, and sat down in a collapsed state. In other words, he had gone through the ordeal endured by so many thousands of public speakers at the start of their careers. The next time he was better and before long he was fluent and convincing. He became an excellent Minister.

We officials suffered nearly as much, for we were equally strange to the game and we had to take our part. We were, of course, all working together – there was no matter of 'opposition' or even of conflict of opinion. The proceedings, fortunately, were far from Parliamentary and indeed were almost cosy. The President's* rather dingy pith helmet – he was one of the last to wear them – lay on his desk before him, like a strange symbol of office.

These early meetings were held in the Trades Centre – the centre for teaching 'trades', that is, not for trading – and were always known thereafter as the 'Trades Centre Meetings'. It was not a good hall – long and narrow, it reduced the public to two rows of seats, but the 'public' were completely indifferent to the public birth of democratic government.

Meanwhile, the Chamber for the Regional Legislature was being planned in Lagos. Although we did not know it at the time, the Chamber at Stormont in Northern Ireland, was taken as a model. Thompstone spent a lot of time on the plans. I found him one day in the great lounge of Government House spread about with photos of famous domes he had had looked out for him. We settled down to discuss them. It was obvious that the dome must be the main feature of the new building, that it could not cover the Chamber or the latter would have the wrong propositions; and it would have to be impressive not only at a distance but also close to. It is well known that St Peter's in Rome suffered gravely when the nave was lengthened, so making it impossible for the dome to be seen properly from the ground in front. In the end we decided that the drum should be heightened by six feet — the whole thing is of course quite small. This gave space for a room under it, used as a library-store. The result is the structure that sits so serenely on the centre line of the former King George's Way. The P.W.D. finished it in 1953.

I was at this time a member of the Executive Council ('Exco') for the *Region* – the name assigned to each group of Provinces in the 1951

*G.B. Williams, the senior of the Residents at the time, then Resident of Adamawa at Yola. Later Presidents were Thompstone, Sharwood-Smith and myself.

constitution. They then were given their own Excos, while Lagos now had a Council of Ministers in place of the Exco of colonial times.

On the Constitutions of Nigeria I must go back a little way. When I was in Bornu, I wrote it all out in a book called *How Nigeria is Governed* (Longmans 1948; three editions were published in ten years). I sent the MS for approval to the Governor, Sir John Macpherson, as in duty bound and it came back unaltered with the words, 'Thank God I know at last'.

The Richards Constitution had been so successful that in 1949 Macpherson started discussions on a revision. What I think impressed everyone was the way in which the members of the new Councils played their part (in spite of limited powers) and the skill and knowledge they brought into discussions of really very recondite matters, hitherto unknown to them. On local affairs, of course, they were completely at home and therefore excelled. But it was their shrewd common sense, so well known to us, that surprised the unaccustomed. Throughout 1950, proposals were discussed all over the country, in many places down to village level, and in mid-1951 there was a conference in London attended by all the Africans concerned – and very few Europeans, as was quite proper. New Orders-in-Council were issued under the King's hand to authorise a new constitution.

Under this arrangement, the Assemblies were increased in size;* the African vote was now supreme. The Northern Executive Council could be between 10 and 15 members with between 3 and 5 officials. The unofficial members of Exco were for the first time called Ministers, though their actual 'Ministries' were rudimentary. The Lieutenant Governor presided over the House of Chiefs of fifty Chiefs with four other members. I took over the House of Assembly as President, under the rule that the office should be held automatically by the Senior of the Residents of the North, and that was me.

After a session of one constitutional committee – there seemed to be scores of them in those days – Sir John Macpherson turned to me and said, 'Rex, I am never going to be forced into decisions I do not like by screaming mobs round the gates of Government House and in our flower beds. I will always be one jump ahead of them and in our direction, not theirs. I hope you agree?' I did, of course. The whole great complicated epic thus went smoothly across the Nigerian stage

*	North	East	West
Elected	90	80	80
Nominated	10	3	3
Officials	5	5	4

in the years of the changes.

It will have become clear that our Legislative Buildings needed to be of good size. The interior was superb in polished woods with green leather seats, and a floor of some green composition, so highly polished that it looked like water and made the whole place cool. The acoustics were excellent, and ordinary conversational tones would carry into any corner. There were a few offices and lounges but there was no provision for long sittings. Very soon open wings had to be added to shelter the hangers-on of members, who would otherwise sprawl about in untidy groups. It was rightly called Lugard Hall.

The original custom was that the House of Assembly did its business and then a few days later the Chiefs came into the same Chamber and did theirs, only more quickly than the Assembly. Eventually it became desirable for both Houses to sit simultaneously, so the old Chamber was assigned to the Chiefs and we designed a new and larger chamber. The late Sardauna of Sokoto (then Premier) and I sketched it out one day in 1957 on a sheet of foolscap paper, to provide all the accommodation we thought would be necessary and the arrangement that seemed best to us. This was translated by the Public Works architects into the present splendid group of buildings. The new chamber for the Assembly was of course much larger than its predecessor and had extensive public galleries; it backed on to the old chamber. The whole building cost half a million pounds and was no doubt cheap at the price, though we thought it rather costly. The general finish was as fine as in the earlier building, and rather more attention was paid to decorative detail and comfort. For example one wall was covered by a huge mural – we had not thought of such features ten years before.

But I have digressed. The 1954 Constitution brought in fuller Regional Government with a Federal body in Lagos in place of a Central Government. The Regions were given much more power. They could pass their own laws and administer their own funds. In fact they became sovereign legislatures. The Northern Assembly was made up of 131 elected members, which was increased in 1960 to 160.

This Constitution came about as a result of a strange chain of events. At the Budget session of the Lagos Chamber in 1953 a Southern member moved that Nigeria should receive self-government by 1956. This did not suit the Northern book at all; they knew they were not ready and could not be ready by that date, only three years away, and they feared, with some justification, that self-government before they were fully ready for it would result in Southern people getting the best jobs in the North, if they did not actually dominate it. All they would vote for was self-government in due course. The Southern members were infuriated, and walked out of the Chamber. Outside the building, jeering crowds met the Northern members, and when their special train left Lagos station (Iddo) they were jeered and booed through the suburbs, and at every railway station on the long route northwards crowds (predominantly Southerners) demonstrated against them.

At this time the Members of the Lagos House were also members of their Regional Houses: thus the thirty members of the Kaduna House represented a third of our entire strength, and included the Premier and some Ministers. They reached Kaduna fuming after this tiresome journey.

The Sardauna demanded a special meeting of the Assembly and officially presented a motion that became famous as the 'Eight Points' motion: this virtually demanded independence for the Region. He and his ministers had been determined on secession, but the main difficulty was the absence of any sea-port through which goods going to and from the North could pass. The Niger was an international waterway but its use was sharply restricted by seasonal water levels. I remember very clearly discussing the problems with the Sardauna and studying the large-scale maps to see whether it would be possible to get the French to build an extension of their Dahomey (Porto Novo) railway either to Mokwa, just north of Jebba, or to Sokoto. Secession would of course have implied that the North would take over the Northern Division of the Nigerian Railways. It certainly seemed feasible but difficulties would be great.

Among the consequences of this 'Southern' demonstration were the riots in Kano (see p. 225) which broke out at this time and were actually in progress on the first day of the meeting. I had just got back from leave and hurried from Jos to preside over the first meeting, which was promptly adjourned. After three anxious days of discussion, the Ministers decided on a compromise. They wanted full Regional control over everything but defence, customs and foreign affairs, with virtually no central government, just a series of central standing committees to represent the Regions for co-ordination of various activities. The House re-assembled and I presided over this remarkable debate, which was conducted with much vigour but no acrimony. It was a morning I vividly remember. When the debate was concluded, in accord with our procedure, I read the long motion, which did everything but demand secession, before putting the question. I was of course still Resident Plateau, a paid government servant, but at the same time the servant of the House. As I read it in English and waited for the Hausa translation, I reflected on the oddity of the situation. The high officials of the Northern administration, from the Governor down, were horrified at the whole idea but could do nothing about it. They felt, in some way which was not disclosed, that I should have prevented the situation developing or that when it had reached that point, I should – again in some unspecified way – have stopped the proceedings. Anyhow the question was put and the ayes had it unanimously.

This raised a nightmare for the Colonial Office, who, though by now powerless in practice, still had the legal supervision of Nigerian affairs. The resolution was taken with the gravity it deserved. The Sardauna was pacified by Macpherson's promise of an immediate new Conference in London to give the Regions real authority in their own areas and to reduce their links with Lagos to the most slender that were practicable. This, of course, pleased the other two Regions, which saw possibilities of earlier self-government for themselves by this new turn in events.

I had, at one stage, an informal discussion with the permanent head of the Colonial Office, Sir Hilton Poynton, about this matter of Regional autonomy. I suggested that the only way to make the Regions really feel satisfied that they were on their own in all the 'subjects' that they could justifiably claim, would be for them to have their own Governors with all the trimmings of that exalted office. If so, he asked, what about the present office of Governor of Nigeria? Well, that could only be a Governor-General, repeating once more the position at the Amalgamation in 1914. And so it came to pass. The Gold Coast copied this as 'Governor-Generalship on Independence', which was not the point at all, and the idea spread all over the Commonwealth.

It became necessary to introduce a formal parliamentary form of Government to replace the glorified committee pattern that we were following in the Assemblies. On one leave, I spent all the time I could spare in the House of Commons studying procedure and learning from their staff. The Westminster system is very complicated, having grown up over the centuries, and it became clear that it was quite unnecessary to bring all of it into use at Kaduna. The Northerners were not 'parliamentary' creatures as were the Southerners, and were unlikely to appreciate the more recondite features of the House of Commons. Hence in practice I cut it down a good deal. The two Southern legislatures took parliamentary procedure in their stride, as did the House of Representatives in Lagos: many of their members, it must be remembered, were lawyers and to the manner born (or educated). The Lagos House was presided over by retired Clerks of Parliament, who were sticklers for identical procedure. The Westminster experts did not care for my methods, so David

Lidderdale, later Clerk of the House of Commons, came out and watched part of a Budget session. In the end he agreed that my methods were suitable for the circumstances in which we found ourselves.

No one could guide me as to how to start off a full-size legislature from scratch. You have your 'duly elected' members: how are they to be taught their part in the machine? How are they to learn the Rules – and *what are the Rules*? The obvious line was to take the Standing Orders of the House of Commons, and issue them with some local variations, to the members in English and Hausa – the translation was not of the easiest – and let them read them through. So far so good, but how were they to have the needful binding force? I started the first full meeting by saying here were the Standing Orders from London and would they treat them as a draft? During the course of the meeting, I suggested, we would note anomalies and bring in amendments if needed, at the end of a reasonable period, and meanwhile use them as the guidelines for the running of the business of the House. They accepted this suggestion, and all was well. I believe that in the South there was a good deal of argument about the Orders. As it happened, at the end of our meeting there were no suggestions for amendments, and so at the beginning of the next meeting the Standing Orders were put and formally approved. They remained unaltered during the life of the House until it was suspended in 1966. We did not use all the provisions of the Orders, for as I have said some of them were superfluous in our position.

One of the most awkward and potentially embarrassing points was the 'ruling out of order' of a member for the first few times. Obviously it hurt a member's pride to be told that he was 'out of order' and could not proceed on a particular line. And if it hurt the pride of members, how much more did it hurt Ministers, conscious of their new dignity? However God was on my side and all was well. Quite early in the meeting Hedley Marshall, the newly created Attorney General, said something that was out of order and I ruled accordingly: he sat down looking stunned he later agreed that I was right. The African members were delighted: I had ruled out an important white man, so they would take the same treatment themselves. The white members numbered five – the Civil and Financial Secretaries, Mr Attorney, a member for trade and another for the minesfield. At this time the Regions received their own Chief Justices and Courts.

Robes and procedure

To bring dignity to the proceedings it was decided that the President should have robes and should not just sit there in a lounge suit, however fine a piece of tailoring it might be. The Southern Presidents wore the usual robes of the Speaker in black with wig, court-breeches and stockings. This seemed most inappropriate and of course very stuffy in that climate – especially in March, the usual period of the long Budget session. A more important consideration was the high probability that my successor would be a Muslim. Muslims could not possibly wear wigs, and the rest of the garments also would be quite unacceptable.

I therefore went to Ede and Ravenscroft, the well-known robe-makers in Chancery Lane, London and put the question to them. We went through their astonishing collection of robes of all kinds and colours then in use for ceremonial. Finally we came to a compromise based on the type of cloak used for the royal orders of chivalry, but joined at the front and not open as they are. We put a great fullness into the skirt, and the directors of the firm gazed with awe at a velvet embroidered cloak sent for guidance by the Sardauna. To make the robe even more impressive, there were to be gold trimmings and big white satin shoulder knots. The colour was emerald green and the material a fine velvet specially made in Germany, with an uncrush-able pile, so important in that climate. The lining was of white satin and it reached the floor with plenty to turn up for larger men. The velvet robe was to be the full dress – it cost £120 (the 'standard' black full dress cost £800) – and an alternative was required for daily use, so we chose a fine dark green barathea: this too was closed with hooks and had a high collar at the back. With it I wore white 'bands' like a barrister and heavy white cuffs on a fine wide-sleeved silk shirt. I did not wear a coat under either costume. For the full dress there was a splendid lace jabot and fine lace cuffs.

Ede and Ravenscroft also created a head-dress, a beret with a brim, they called it, in a strange Tudor style, with gold cord round the crown. One was in velvet and the other in barathea. Like the Speaker I did not wear a hat in the House; I carried it for the naming of a member, a matter that did not arise. In the sun on outdoor occasions the hats were useful. For the Clerks at the Table we designed black robes in corded silk for full-dress and stuff for ordinary. On the back and shoulders was the badge of the Assembly, the gold loops of the Northern Knot. They wore gold turbans for special occasions and black skull-caps for ordinary business. It all looked impressive and distinguished.

I was much better treated than the Speaker at Westminster, who sits in a splendid throne-like canopied seat but has no desk or table for his papers or to support his writing; he can unfold wide leaves on his arm rests for this purpose, but they look inconvenient. I had a great canopy rising behind me from above a display of the Royal Arms. I doubted whether this display could be justified and was relieved when it was replaced by the arms of the Northern Region, newly issued by the London Heralds, the shield supported by two savage red horses. I sat in a heavy high-backed chair with big arms; and before me was a large desk on which was a plan of the Chamber with members' names against their seats. It could be moved away for ceremonial occasions such as State openings.

A step below, the black-robed Clerks sat at a similar desk and below them, at a table, were the interpreters. Having discovered that it was impossible to attract the Clerk's attention without shouting, I had a switch installed to flash a red light that only he could see. When he put papers over it, he could not see it either. Here too we were better off than Mr Speaker.

The chair was too heavy to move easily so the Works put it on castors. They were very good castors, and no one warned Bryan Sharwood-Smith of this fact when he was presiding over the Chiefs; he gave the chair a sharp pull, whereupon it shot forward and nipped his thumbs against the desk. And when I myself leant over to reach a fan-switch in the floor, it overturned on top of me. I have never seen Ministers move so fast to help.

Of course, we had to have a Sergeant-at-Arms. We could not emulate Westminster with their high-ranking retired Service officers, so we compromised with an ex-Regimental Sergeant Major, a huge man of the greatest dignity and the necessary slowness of movement. He had a magnificent silken robe of many coloured stripes. Ede and Ravenscroft would have had a seizure had they seen it, but the members loved it and the public were impressed.

A badge or device was required for the Legislature, just as the Palace of Westminster has the Portcullis, and we wanted something striking. We worked on this with the Chiefs, and after much thought the 'Northern Knot' was suggested. This knot was much used locally in embroidered patterns on the elaborate rigas of the great men, a simple design of two flat loops interwoven. This now appeared on all uniforms, stationery, fittings and other articles of the Houses. It looked good. The flippant described it as 'two crossed paper-clips rampant'.

The Sergeant-at-Arms had to carry something – which was not an alien concept, for those who preceded Chiefs bore spears or official

staffs of office. But what was this article to be? Someone remembered
that a mace had been ordered for the Tiv N.A. in Benue Province and
that, probably because of the almost continuous unrest in those parts,
it had never been presented. It was a grand object, shiny and apparently of silver; though I believe it was really stainless steel. We took it
over and used it, but there was a catch: one end was shaped as the
royal crown and therefore terminated in a cross; at the beginning of a
new session the cross had been discreetly removed. Later the Kano
Chamber of Commerce gave us a splendid paddle-shaped silver mace
emblazoned with the arms of the North.

No meeting of a British legislature anywhere in the world ever
opened without the saying of prayers. We used those said every
afternoon and on Friday mornings in Westminster. In our Muslim
circumstances we naturally deleted references to Jesus Christ, but
they read well none the less. Some years later I was reading the
Prayers, as was my custom, in the English version – the Clerk read the
Hausa – when I noticed a change. The English had 'send down thy
heavenly wisdom *from above*', and so on; the new version simply read
'send thy wisdom', and there was a similar alteration later. I asked the
Clerk why he had changed them. He said, 'God is all-pervasive. He is
not "above" or "below". He is everywhere and in every place.
Therefore, He does not send *down* anything.' The three prayers
include the great invocation 'Prevent us, O Lord, in all our doings
with thy most gracious favour', which translated equally grandly into
Hausa.

Formal questions never had the liveliness of Westminster. Although Ministers were armed with answers to possible supple-
mentary questions, these were seldom asked. However, I recall one
new Minister not only answering the question asked but reading in a
monotone answers to supplementaries that had not been asked. I had
a copy of the answers on my desk and watched this unfold, powerless
to stop it.

One of the most difficult matters remained to be cleared up. This
was the reporting of the Proceedings. There were now quite a number
of shorthand writers in Kaduna, all more or less fully employed. Half
an hour each was enough to go on with. Then they went upstairs and
typed out their notes – and that took three times as long. I had two
A.D.O.s to supervise and 'produce' in the B.B.C. sense. The girls
could not always be sure who spoke and in what order, though the
speeches were all recorded: everything, just everything, was translated from English into Hausa or vice versa – even the interruptions.
From the start we had a seating plan and it was a standing order that
no member could speak except from his allotted seat. This was useful.

The Clerks kept a list of speakers, and so did I, for they were allowed to speak for not more than ten minutes (multiplied by two for the translations). All the speeches, once typed, were checked by the A.D.O.s and the stencils were then run off and clipped together so that each Member received his full copy of proceedings on arrival at the Chamber in the mornings. If anything was wrong in their speeches – naturally the first thing they looked at – they could complain and it could be amended later. The final result in English was printed and issued a few months' later. The Hausa version took much longer. All papers laid before the House had to be in English and Hausa, excepting only the Estimates. Fortunately there was no great difficulty in translating Bills into Hausa, but amending legislation was not so simple; direct translations sometimes did not fit. For example the simple English phrase 'for "and" read "or" ' appeared almost imbecile in Hausa. The Speaker was responsible for the correctness of translations both oral and written.

Like every other group of people the members, although elected from widely different areas and people and languages, tended above all to reflect themselves. Their interests were their own rather than those of the public but they were not – then at least – goaded to the same extent as a British M.P. If they were interested in a subject, especially roads, education (many were teachers) and native courts (many were members of courts), they would talk at length, if permitted, and there was quite a queue to do so. At the Budget free-for-all, many spoke eloquently of their local affairs and problems, of villages and bridges unknown to anyone else, of dispensaries in the wrong place, and so on.

When the Sardauna spoke, he always did so briefly and closely to the point. He had a dread of being 'ruled out of order' and would bring speeches to me to look at when he thought there might be a risk. His Ministers were not quite so careful but were also brief. There was one distinguished member from Bornu, who spoke only once towards the end of the five years; he received a tremendous ovation. It was possible that some did not understand all that was said. In the Lagos Chamber only English was used. Sir Frederick Metcalf, who came out to preside there, and had only a sketchy idea of the country, was astonished when I told him that at least three members of his House had no knowledge of what was going on beyond what their neighbours might tell them; they could speak no English at all and had only their natal Hausa. This left him with a problem which, to my knowledge, was never solved.

There was an Opposition of varying strength – the highest number it mustered was, I believe, eleven or twelve, and the lowest two.

Ibrahim Imam, a huge man from Maiduguri, seemed at times to carry almost the entire burden of Opposition on his own shoulders. Very able and brave, he never shrank from speaking against the tide and current. He was one of those who actually read the papers put before him and understood much of their contents. At one time he commanded a united, though small Opposition, and I awarded him the salary of the 'leader' at £1,500 per annum as set out in the Estimates. It was then a lot of money and to most people of the North an inexplicable waste of public funds. 'Why pay someone to criticise you?' they said; 'there are plenty ready to do so without payment.' Ibrahim Imam later lost his support and with it his salary.

Generally, discipline was good, but there could be a lot of noise when the Opposition was unduly tiresome. Once a member interrupted on a point of order. Would I instruct the members to moderate the noise, as they could not hear their friend speaking? I said that the noise was nothing compared with Westminster on an average day and added that it was up to the member by the loudness of his voice, the strength of his character and the wisdom and honey of his words, to persuade the other members to listen to him. This advice met with stunned silence.

As I have suggested, when they were interested they would talk and take notice. When they were not interested, little notice was taken. Once we had a new High Court Bill before us, to set up a High Court of the Northern Region, as distinct from that of the Federation: it contained at least one hundred and fifty clauses. The Bill was vitally important for the future – but not, it seemed, for the present. Hedley Marshall, the Attorney General, as in duty bound, rose to move the second reading. He spoke for some time – as usual, with great clarity – and was seconded on the 'bob-up' principle by a Minister. There was no discussion. Even the Opposition was silent or practically so. We went into Committee. A Minister kindly suggested that we take the whole bill, apart from the few Government amendments, in one gulp. I refused. It was too important to be let through on the nod. I made them take each small group of clauses and dragged it out as long as I could, but I doubt if the whole passage, including the Government amendments, took half an hour – and this a technically important Bill.

The Region Government gave me an honorarium of £800 a year in addition to my Colonial Service pension and a free house. Later, when the post was upgraded to Speaker, they increased it considerably under the impression that a Nigerian would soon occupy the seat – wrongly, as it happened. I went on, with their full concurrence, for a further two years. At first I used to stay at Government House but that was obviously improper; the President should not be in a position in which he could be suspected of being influenced by the Government. So when I retired from Government service, they built a charming house to my own design. It was built near the great mango trees that had grown up on the site of the old (wooden) Government House and I planted a vegetable garden and a clump of conifers there with my own hands. My former head boy, 'Yaro' Matthew, was installed as official caretaker and put on the Government payroll. He held the job until the anti-Ibo riots at Kaduna in 1966 (although he was not an Ibo), when he fled with his family. Later a new house was built nearby for the first Nigerian Speaker, Alhaj Umaru Gwandu.

During this time I was associated with a small private firm in Park Street, London, who were fortunate enough to have the licence to sell Bailey bridging in many countries of the world. Besides this they sold steel and hardware of various kinds. Chainmesh fencing, for example, went quite well in Nigeria. There were those who thought it *infra dig* for me to be thus employed, but it gave me something to do, and had the full approval of the Federal Government. At one time I went to Lagos to take over from the firm's agent there, and lived in strange conditions in the back end of Ebute Metta. The firm always allowed me to leave Lagos when my presence was required for meetings of the Assembly in Kaduna.

The curious situation was that the Northern Premier had to cable me in London to ask for a meeting of the House and I would cable back authorising the Clerk to summon a meeting. It worked very well and the Regional Government secured the services of a Speaker who was quite impartial to all influences and ignorant of the ins and outs of local intrigue and politics. I always travelled out by air, and my wife was given a free passage once a year for the Budget Sessions.

For eight years I sat in the chair of the Assembly and watched history pass before me. Often I longed to get out of the chair and have a go myself: things would be obviously going wrong for the Government – the outcome was not in question as they had an overwhelming majority, but some of the debates were unconvincing to say the least. Again, the small Opposition would ignore opportunities for attack left open to them by the Government.

Once there was real excitement. The Government brought in quite a simple Bill, called the *Fatal Accidents Bill* – a title which nearly became horribly appropriate. It was on the question of payment of compensation to the relatives of accident victims, and the House did not like it. The Members always sat according to their Provinces and the revolt started in Kano. They insisted that half-brothers and half-sisters (a local commonplace) should be inserted with some additional family variants. The Government, guided by the white

Attorney General, stuck to its guns. Finally, it was clear that there would be an adverse vote. I played the card I always kept up my sleeve and declared a tea interval: the Government had time to hold a hasty meeting and draft an amendment.

We had one other similar incident on a purely technical Bill, otherwise there was little excitement, except for a Member who laughed so much that he fell between two seats and had to be got to his feet by the united efforts of four neighbours. The House laughed very readily.

On a rather different note, an example of rather bewildering kindness. One morning towards the end of a meeting a messenger put a telegram on my desk. I looked at it with interest – I seldom got telegrams as Speaker. It was a cable from my wife in London saying that my father, who was well over eighty, was gravely ill and that I should come as soon as possible. I looked at the Order Paper and there seemed to me to be at least several days' more of work before us. There was an interval shortly afterwards and the Premier, the late Sardauna, came into my office to discuss a matter of procedure. I handed him the cable without saying anything. He read it through and then picked up an Order Paper off my desk. He said, 'Well, that and that and that need take little time, and I will see that no one speaks on that.' Then he paused, 'Ah, I fear this must have some debate – but we will keep it as short as possible. If you can get a booking on any plane tomorrow night from Kano, you can have my aircraft to take you to Kano in the afternoon. We will finish tomorrow about twelve-thirty.' And so we did.

I had time to finish my packing and have lunch and a short rest before taking off for Kano. A Sabena plane delivered me before breakfast at Schiphol airport (Amsterdam), a B.E.A. plane got me to London in time for lunch and the afternoon train took me to Torquay in time for supper. My father was still alive but unconscious, and died a few days later.

When I gave up the Speakership, the House elected the Clerk, Umaru Gwandu – a Fulani noble from Sokoto Province – to succeed me. He had been Clerk to the House from its inception and was a mine of information on procedure and conduct. Without formal higher education, he was well read in his own subjects. An intelligent man with a keen sense of humour and of correctness. He had supported me loyally and had controlled a large and rather miscellaneous staff in the maintenance of the building and surroundings – this responsibility continued when the House was not sitting. It was unusual for a Clerk to become Speaker, but the Constitution left it wide open for the House to select anyone suitable, not necessarily one of their own number.

XIX.   The Fierce Light That Beats. . .

The dinner

The most important and thrilling event for us before Independence was the visit by the Queen and the Duke of Edinburgh in the dry season of 1956. The excitement was naturally felt by the Europeans in the country but the people of Nigeria were, in the outcome, just as excited and gratified. The tempo with them naturally started fairly low but it built up rapidly as soon as the Queen was in the country. I was invited to fly out specially but my wife declined the suggestion.

They spent over two weeks in Nigeria, a long time for Royalty to spend anywhere. There had only been one royal visit before, that of the Prince of Wales in 1925.

The Royal party flew direct to Kaduna, and from there they toured the three Regions for several days each, before flying home from Kano. The programme allowed for three days in Kaduna and two in Jos. As inevitably the other great centres could not receive a visit, their representatives had to be brought in to Kaduna, and busy preparations went on for months before they came. The streets on the royal route were hung with the usual bunting and flags, but the arches were not usual and indeed were charmingly designed and built. An unsuitable royal pavilion went up on the Kaduna Race Course and two huge public stands with special lavatories that were never used. A great control tower like the Emir of Kano's gateway and coloured red to imitate Kano mud arose above the trees. Miles of wire fencing were erected where none stood before.

£20,000 was spent on Government House – nearly as much as it had cost when first built. The dining room was gutted and extended out of all proportion, and the charming spare room was ruined. Special baths were flown out at a cost of about £1,500.

The entire visit cost about £2,000,000 – of Nigerian money – but no one begrudged it. The Kaduna camp was enormously costly, as was the moving of the thousands of horses and men from the far ends of the Northern country.

The official programme of the visit was gorgeously bound in dark green leather, edged and heavily embossed in gold and printed in England. It had splendid portraits of the Royal couple – but none of the late Sardauna of Sokoto or any of his Council, or the great Emirs. There were some pencil drawings of 'types' of Northerners, but they were virtual caricatures and certainly not typical.

The Royal party in their travels in Nigeria must have met many hundreds of people and been seen by at least three million. It was a red letter day wherever they went: the schools shut and there was a general holiday atmosphere. The Police were worried that, with the crowds of people on the royal routes and with most policemen heavily employed, houses would be broken into and that there would be a general increase in crime. In fact, hardly any crime was reported at all. What the Police forgot was that the criminals were also human and they went along to see the processions with the rest. We called it the 'Queen's Peace' and it reigned over the country while she was within its borders. A Minister said to me, 'If she was here all the time, we could really get on with things without troubles and riots.'

In Kaduna security was fierce and with little justification. The 'peace' was naturally so strong Her Majesty could have gone any-where in perfect safety and comfort. In some areas it was almost impossible for the people to get near the routes, in others it was only possible to reach one side and not the other, so that enthusiastic crowds faced a blank area across the road. In other places there was no one at all except the people whose houses actually stood on the route. The place was bedevilled with passes and you were sunk without the right ones. I said to the Sardauna that I hoped he had the right passes. He said it would be all right as everyone knew him and his car – his bright green Rolls. And yet the worst happened. On the way to a rehearsal the Sardauna's car was stopped and he had not got the right pass. He pulled himself up to his enormous height and said who he was, in Hausa. The young constable refused to co-operate and said in English, with a happy smile, 'I am an Ibo, sir'. The Sardauna went off muttering, 'An Ibo, an Ibo.' He told me this himself.

The visit ran very smoothly considering its complexity and the large numbers of people involved. For example, among the horses at the Durbar some had been on the road for two months, and arrange-ments had to be made for their forage and the accommodation of their riders at each night stop on the many routes. Outside Kaduna a complete temporary town was built for 10,000 people and 5,000 horses, with food and forage, water and shade. There were special hospital arrangements and first aid posts on the same scale, with miles of new roads, pipelines were laid into what had previously been farmland, and electricity was brought in, with numerous telephones which no one ever answered. There were extra police, and troops and guns from Zaria. Still more telephones were wanted for officials and the press, and a complicated veterinary service was set up.

The royal planes touched down on time at the Kaduna airfield and in the Township we could hear the guns boom the salute. The last part of the route into the town was lined with horsemen and the chiefs sat under their great umbrellas, colourful in costume and turbans, and the wild drums throbbed. There had been drastic pruning in the list of those who should receive Her Majesty, and the President of the Assembly (myself) and Conrad Williams the Resident of the Province of Zaria, in which Kaduna is situated, found ourselves omitted. A special feature was the attachment to the royal suite of the first Nigerian to be commissioned in the R.W.A.F.F. – Captain Aguiyi-Ironsi, an Ibo of slow speech and powerful personality.* The Clerk and some ministers considered that the House had been slighted. He put chairs for us at the end of the east roadway into the Lugard Hall grounds and there we sat – Conrad and Helen Williams, Umaru Gwandu, the Clerk, myself, and Eric Wilson, the member for the Chamber of Mines. With us were the whole staff of Lugard Hall, from Sergeant-at-Arms sweepers and the caretaker, as well as quite a number of Members. Umaru had got a lot of small Union flags which he distributed to us.

A police car came by with a loudspeaker saying: 'The car behind us is a police car – behind that is the Queen in a big black car – she is sitting on the right' – all this in Hausa and not English. The Royal Rolls, with its standard fluttering, passed smoothly, with the Queen sitting 'high', holding a sun-shade and wearing a small hat. She smiled happily at the horses and the Duke waved. Behind them in an open Humber came the Governor and Lady Sharwood-Smith, looking gratified but anxious, with the Private Secretary. Then followed shining cars for Staff, and finally two coaches of press, looking as usual untidy and dishevelled and taking random photos out of the windows. We waved our little flags, and then they were gone.

That afternoon the Party went off to watch polo, while we in Lugard Hall had our final very full and detailed rehearsal with a white wife acting for the Queen: the timing was right and all of us fitted into our right positions. The royal Staff had to be shown the procedure and where they would be sitting and how they should move. Sir Michael Adeane, the Queen's Private Secretary, and the Countess of Euston, the lady-in-waiting, were helpful over detail. 'We leave the actual arrangements to you,' they said 'we are responsible for getting Her Majesty to you and back again, and making sure she is not asked to do anything awkward or undignified.' In the Chamber, the steps to my dais had been boarded over and thick green carpet was laid over all. We all knew where to go and when. Upstairs a brand new visitors' book stood on immaculate blotting paper with a pen and

---

*As Major-General commanding the Nigerian Army at the time of the military coup in 1966, he briefly became head of state and was murdered in a further coup later that same year.

shining ink-well.

The evening of their arrival saw the 'State Dinner' so long awaited and much discussed. There must have been at least twenty-four who sat down that night. The long line of arriving cars was held up for some time in the drive and then moved slowly forward. When we reached the door we found that Elnore Maddocks had brought the wrong gloves. A panic ensued and someone rushed off in a fast car. We were received by Brian and Joan Sharwood-Smith at the head of the entrance steps. All the white men wore shell jackets.

The Chiefs' and Ministers' robes varied from the superb to the very ordinary: one of them, Abba Habib, wore a transparent white nylon riga, causing quite a sensation. Their medals, which included C.M.G.s and C.B.E.s and the Sultan's Star of the British Empire, were often incorrectly worn; some ribbons were dirty and frayed, and pinned in the wrong places. No one thought of helping them on their arrival.

We were given drinks and stood around nervously talking – the Africans were just as nervous. The Chief Justice, Algernon Brown, and his wife, Brigadier Brown and his wife, Maddocks and Peter Scott, Hedley Marshall (Attorney General) and myself were the white faces, with the four Emirs of Sokoto, Kano, Zaria and Katsina, and the Sardauna and his leading Ministers. There were no unofficials. Our drinks were whisked away very abruptly and we were pushed into a semi-circle by the Private Secretary. At that moment Elnore's gloves appeared and though they were the right colour, they were the wrong length, but by now it was too late for further activity. The Governor entered the lounge with the Queen and Prince Philip. The Queen stood in front of the fireplace under a large photograph of herself by Dorothy Wilding – the contrast between the posed figure and the lively and most attractive person before us was startling.

We filed past her and were presented one by one, then went into the dining room to await their arrival. The Governor sat in the middle of the long table, with the Queen on his right and Prince Philip on his left. Next to her sat the Sultan of Sokoto, as the senior of the chiefs present. Beyond him was K.P. Maddocks. Opposite were the Emirs of Kano and Zaria and the Sardauna. The Makaman Bida, Minister of Finance, an intelligent and talkative man, was next to the Duke. I sat opposite with Elnore Maddocks.

When we had all sat down, the Queen looked round for people to talk to. She spoke to the Sultan on her right but his normally halting English had entirely disappeared. Opposite was the Emir of Zaria who spoke no English; next to him she found the Sardauna who, of course, spoke it perfectly. So she tried talking across the table. But that was not easy and she looked round again and found that Maddocks spoke good Hausa which was really the end of the dinner for him, as he had to translate for her to those in earshot. Our end of the table was rather gayer and there was a good deal of laughter.

The dinner was good. The salmon had been flown out from Scotland, and the turkey was local – there was no gravy with it and anxious looks over shoulders produced no response.

The discussion finally reached the apparently vexed question of what the Queen would wear at the Durbar the next morning, the first of the ceremonies in the North. Her Majesty was apparently inclined to an 'ordinary' dress and hat – if anything she wears can be described as ordinary. But the Emirs did not care for this: they said that the people were looking for a queen, not a lady who might be mistaken for an A.D.O.'s wife. The Queen said that if she was to wear the Garter she would have to wear full evening dress and was that really suitable for a parade on the race course? Then someone mentioned that there would be about 5,000 horses on the Durbar ground. That seemed to do the trick, and she agreed to dress up for the occasion.

The Regimental Band was in the garden outside Government House and played throughout the dinner. The Governor rose and proposed 'The Queen' and the band, by a miracle of modern telecommunications, managed to play the Anthem at the right moment.

The Durbar

The next day, the 2nd February, was the great Durbar, the first time since the visit of the Prince of Wales in 1925 when all the varied peoples of the North had attended a single event and taken part in a common display. Before the earlier event they had not only not been on speaking terms but had been actively hostile. By this time the passage of the years had smoothed away some of the difficulties, but the fact remained that the tribes were strangers to each other and to each others' religions: some of them lived 600 or 700 miles away from others and had no mutual contact. Their languages were as strange to each other as were their customs and beliefs, and yet there was no murmur of discord.

This was a full uniform affair, but I did not feel that my velvet was justified (it should not be sat on too long) and so I (as President) wore the dark green barathea with the new hat of the same, which attracted most favourable attention. The Chief Justice and the Judges flatly refused to wear their scarlet – turning up in lounge suits, they looked pretty dim. The Ministers were gay in their best *rigas* and the

Sardauna on the royal stand, was even more brilliantly dressed. The Sultan and the Shehu of Bornu were there also. When it came to the time for their contingents to march past, they descended and went off by car to join their columns. The Shehu managed to stay on his horse, a huge creature; we had a feeling that his closest attendants were holding his legs to steady him – he was very old and going blind.

Altogether, we thought there were more than 60,000 people round the ground; an enormous number of strangers had come to Kaduna for those days, and the white population had also doubled.

The R.W.A.F.F. band played the Guard of Honour on to the ground; the important people began to arrive and no one took much notice of them. The Governor and Lady Sharwood-Smith were the last, then the royal car drove right across the Race Course to the stand in stony silence. This was alarming to the strangers but was in fact an ordinary Northern way of showing respect; they would not have thought of cheering or applauding their own chiefs. The Guard presented arms, the band played the Anthem, and there was a gasp from the crowd as the Queen looking quite splendid in a blue-grey evening dress, with the Garter, stepped out. Prince Philip inspected the guard, which then marched off with the band. The swarm of pressmen burst over the area, to the astonishment of the population used to smartly dressed Europeans; generally they looked as if they had slept in their clothes and had not shaved for some days.

The march-past was by Provinces, some having very large numbers and some few indeed. Later I overheard a Hausa conversation between a minor northern Emir and a chief from my old Kabba:

Northern Emir: 'You mounted yesterday, I suppose?'
Kabba Chief: 'Oh, yes, I did.'
N.E. 'Borrowed horse, I expect?'
K.C. 'Oh yes, I had to: you know about our horse sickness?'
N.E. 'Yes, of course: borrowed from old Zaria, I imagine?'
K.C. 'You are quite right, it was he.'
N.E. 'Must have stung you properly, I'll bet.'
K.C. I'm afraid he will – haven't had the bill yet.' Sighs heavily. Exeunt.

In spite of this real conversation, the horses were mostly splendid and beautifully dressed: the hundreds of footmen made an ocean of glowing colours. This time the unruly pagans, nimble in their hoe-ing dances, were neatly loin-clothed, but their skins were well greased. There were tumblers, contortionists and snake charmers by the platoon, and the man who commanded his horse to die; he then stood on it, when it lay stretched out on the ground, waving a sword, till it suddenly leaped up and threw its master, to the delight of everyone in sight. The Emir of Kano rode by on a superb white camel, and the horses from Bornu wore trousers on their forelegs. Men stood on saddles beating drums and blowing bugles, pipes and trumpets, little hand drums with their soprano sounds, big heavy drums and the great deep camel drums. There was no nonsense about keeping time, but just a roaring, crashing tumult. In the midst of it all a group of Bornu Fulani wandered along, as though they were in the deepest bush without a care in the world, and their graceful bronze girls, with great calabashes of milk on their heads, walking with completely blank expressions. So they marched past for an hour and more – by Provinces and in the Provinces, by individual territory. It would have helped us greatly if there had been some nomenclature on standards or banners; the Emirs were difficult to identify, wrapped as they were in their robes and turbans – even the Ministers near me were confused at times.

Katsina Emirate stole the show with its disciplined, colourful ranks of horse and foot. The largest contingent was from Sokoto Emirate, with over 500 horsemen and 1,200 foot. Bornu was notable for the barbaric splendour of rich colour and waving swords under great scarlet banners, text-embroidered in gold, and black ostrich feathers waving round the spearheads. Then the columns turned into lines formed, without the footmen and performers, for the two great ceremonial charges. They charged faster and faster, straight at the Royal Pavilion – the scared pressmen clambered to safety islands. The old Mai Fika charged so fast and so hard that it looked as if he was going right up the steps of the Royal dais. But the lines pulled themselves up on their haunches in a great cloud of dust and a huge cacophony of salutation and simple shouting, spears waving in the air and thrust down into the ground in submission, drawn swords shaken and guns let off to the alarm of our senior police officers.

It remains in the mind how the Emir of Gumel stuck to his bucking horse while his turban and then his great cloak fell off – he remained unmoved; how in the first wave a rider's black turban started to unwind and streamed behind him like a pennant – he gathered it up in his spare arm as he turned at high speed; and how in the second wave a man fell off just before the end of the gallop – he lay motionless and all the horses missed him.

Never was there such a sight, and such a spectacle of friendship between people not so long ago bitterly hostile to each other: the slavers and the raided, the rich and the poor, purest of Muslims and pagans, plainsmen and people from the High Plateau, the men from the sandy wastes of Bornu and Northern Kano and the stalwarts from the steamy fertile valleys of the great rivers. All were there and all went home in peace with improbable, and indeed incredible, tales of the young Queen who wore jewels that glittered and flashed in the sunshine, of the people from other countries yet within the bounds of Nigeria, of the languages and songs they had heard, and the dances they had seen.

Lugard Hall

That afternoon there was a large garden party, at which there occurred what the programme coyly called 'presentation of certain guests'. These selected persons had been planted about the grounds, and stood in carefully casual attitudes concealing inward anxieties and sweaty apprehension. Their friends could not understand why they could not move away from the spots on which they had apparently been staked out, and they could not explain. I stood on a slope with unpresented friends and watched the progress.

Next morning we saw what in its own way was as good a spectacle as the great Durbar. This time it was the children's turn. Unfortunately many people did not realise it would be interesting, and the great stands were half empty. The Queen and the Duke drove round the Durbar ground and received the cheers of thousands of delighted children, who had not got the adults' inhibitions and let their enthusiasm go. There was a series of displays, quick and well performed, ending in a brilliant ballet by the technical schools. The key exhibit was a 'typical street in a Northern village'. In fact it was far better than that – a complete, beautifully constructed village had been erected on the Durbar ground after the horses had gone – constructed by inspiration, to half-scale; this was full scale for the children, who busily performed all the jobs that their elders normally carried out in a day's work. They showed zest and great acting skill. Her Majesty was fascinated and spent a lot of time walking round with the Minister of Education and asking questions. She was already late when she reached the West African Institute of Tripanosomiasis Research (anti sleeping sickness), and after listening to a long talk on the tsetse fly by the expert Tam Nash and being shown the Institute's animals by Dr Wilson, was even later in arriving at the 4th Battalion mess to meet the officers.

In the afternoon Her Majesty and Prince Philip came to see us in Lugard Hall, where a joint meeting of the House of Assembly and the House of Chiefs was to present a loyal address: this occasion was officially considered the culminating point of the visit. The members were all dressed, prince and commoner alike, in the most splendid of silks and turbans and the Queen again wore a beautiful evening dress, grey this time, with the Garter. The little procession formed up on arrival in the entrance lobby and the first small hitch occurred. Just as we started, the Queen, behind me, stopped and opened her handbag: she took out a small mirror to look at her hair and the tiara. Then we realised that there was no mirror anywhere: numerous ladies had been over the course, but not one noticed this. The entry into the Chamber was of necessity in single file but even so it was impressive. The Sardauna read the Address in English and Umaru Gwandu, the Clerk of both Houses, read it again in Hausa. The Queen replied in her crisp, clear voice in English and we filed out again. Then upstairs, to sign the new visitors' book. The pen-nib was new and there was trouble before it at last came to life for the Queen to sign.

On the fourth morning, a Saturday, the Royal party left us for Jos. Bryan Sharwood-Smith had hurried off to the Plateau to receive the Queen once more and it was left to Kenneth Maddocks and the Sardauna to see her off from the airport. It seemed lonely without her. She came back to the North on her last day and had a splendid time in Kano City. Security went by the board, and a quarter of a million citizens had a close-up view. The Royal party left that night for home from Kano airport.

XX. End of the Adventure in Africa

Bryan Sharwood-Smith left Nigeria in 1957, after five years in office. His departure by train took place at mid-day. It was particularly warm, and everyone was in full dress. Most Ministers were present, with the heads of technical departments and some Chiefs; and, of course, there was a full military Guard of Honour with the band. The programme was carefully worked out but unfortunately it ran quicker than anticipated and at the end of it there was a ghastly pause of ten minutes. There was some agonised and embarrassed conversation to fill in the time; Bryan and Joan were obviously deeply moved. No one could catch the eye of the driver, who was on the far side of the engine doing some oiling. At last a Colonel ran up the platform and got him into the cab and the Governor's white train slowly pulled out. We walked back along the platform. The Sardauna, who was with me, said: 'By God, we must now go forward!' I said 'Amen'.

Sharwood-Smith's successor, Sir Gawain Bell, was his complete opposite. He had served in the Sudan and Cairo, was a fine Arabist, and had commanded a battalion of Glubb Pasha's Arab Legion in the war. Small, neat and always elegant, he always had the right phrase, and always an understanding and friendly smile. He played polo well and shot duck and such efficiently. His wife Silvia was not only beautiful but kind and witty and a great addition to Nigerian society.

The post that Sir Gawain had to fill was quite different from that of the former Governors. They had had authority, but he, in spite of having all the trappings of Governorship, had no control. He received the Exco agenda and minutes but did not preside. The Premier, who did, had no legal need to consult him before decisions were made. In practice they enjoyed good relations and were in fairly close touch. For this new form of past not only was Bell personally ideal but, oddly enough, the fact that he was a stranger and did not know all the ins and outs of past Nigerian politics was of great assistance to him and to the country. It was hard for Bryan Sharwood-Smith to stand aside after he had lost authority and watch things take unexpected and no doubt unwelcome turns.

One morning, in November 1959, my telephone rang. I was surprised to hear the Governor's voice at the other end, there was usually some intermediary. He asked if it was convenient for me to come to see him for a few moments. I drove off leaving my wife convinced that I was about to get the sack. Before I could sit down in his office, Sir

Gawain asked me if I would accept a Knight Bachelor. Rather stunned, for it was the last thing I was thinking of, I accepted. The awarding of a title makes an enormous difference to a wife and in the Service we always thought it was the ideal way for us to repay our wives, if it lay within our power, for all that they had done and been through in the long hard years in the Tropics. We were in England on leave soon afterwards, and the reactions of friends varied from 'Why has it been so delayed?' to 'What on earth for?' (relations).

The Northern Region received local self-government in 1959 – the other two Regions had done so already – and the Federation became independent on 1 October 1960. A formal visit by the Duke of Gloucester was planned in the early part of 1959. I discussed the position with the Premier, saying that it was time for me to hand over the Speakership to a Nigerian; it would not do to have a white face presiding over the Assemby much longer. He said they had had that thought themselves, but had not wanted to raise it until I did, for they were well content with my Speakership. He asked when I wished to stand down, and I said I would like to be Speaker when the Duke laid the foundation stone of the new building, with the planning of which I had been closely concerned. So it was agreed that there would be a meeting of the House after the laying of the stone and I would then resign.

The Premier then asked whether I could get away from an arrange-ment which I had with a motor firm called B.E.W.A.C., and join his personal staff as adviser. I said it could be done. There were not wanting those who thought that I had wangled the whole thing but, in fact, I was very much surprised at the invitation. It was decided that I would be called a Commissioner for Special Duties, a title we had used before to cover indefinite appointments. I would have a sub-stantial salary and the house built for me as Speaker. I would, however, serve in Kaduna on ordinary tours of service with the usual leave, instead of living in London and coming out when needed.

This arrangement worked very well except that there was little to do. The Permanent Secretary of the Sardauna's own office and Head of the Civil Service, Bruce Greatbach (later Governor of the Seychelles), did not take kindly to the appointment. I did not blame him. First, he had not been consulted; secondly, he thought it would undermine his own position; and thirdly, he did not see what there was to do that he could not do himself. There he was almost correct. It was a pity that he did not make use of my time and knowledge since I offered to 'devil' for him on files and detailed work. But he never handed any to me.

I was given a free hand to go where I liked and look round. This could be interesting but was not ideal. Sometimes the Sardauna would say that I should go to a certain Province and just keep my eyes open and report to him. I could usually see what he was worried about, and it was obviously simpler for me to do this invisible inquiry than for Greatbach, for it would then have become 'official'. I used to make suggestions at times on bits of paper which would eventually become Policy – to the credit, quite rightly, of some Minister.

I wrote a draft of my memoirs – not this one – which did not see the light of day, and then the Sardauna gave me the job of drafting his own autobiography. This entailed going through piles of paper, all the Hansards both of Kaduna and Lagos to extract his speeches. There were all of 10,000 official photos in the Northern records, and I went through all of them and selected about a hundred for the book. The Sardauna would go through the draft and sometimes fill in blanks I had left where I was uncertain or particularly wanted his own impressions. This did not always work, and at one point it became clear that we were not doing well enough and he arranged a visit to Yauri, on the Niger. There my wife and I spent a happy three weeks in a rest house with all the equipment and furniture specially sent up from Sokoto. The Sardauna himself flew up and stayed for days at a time, and we really got down to the writing. The book (*My Life* by Sir Ahmadu Bello, Cambridge University Press, 1962) sold over 15,000 copies; it is believed that the royalties helped to build Sultan Bello's Mosque in Sokoto, a sentimental and devotional ambition of the Sardauna's.

We flew down to Lagos for the final Independence functions with the Emirs of Katsina and Kano and the Sultan of Sokoto. We were allocated fully furnished and equipped flats and a new car and a driver each. The last scene was on the race course. Princess Alexandra, in sweeping white, presided. Just before midnight the massed bands of the Army, Police and Royal Marines stood waiting. The Prime Minister and Sir James Robertson stood together at the foot of the special flagstaff. The British anthem was played and sung with enthusiasm by the great crowd. The lights went out, and when they came on again the Union Jack had gone and the new Nigerian flag fluttered in its place. The bands played the new anthem with which the crowd was unfamiliar. The religious leaders prayed in their several ways. Nigeria was Independent.

We travelled back with Sir Gawain and Lady Bell and Sir Algernon Brown, Chief Justice of the North – a complex character, simple and unassuming in some ways but very proud of his position and its dignities. In Lagos during the ceremonies we had occupied flats on the same landing, and had seen a good deal of each other. He was depressed by Independence, which he saw as a departure of the glories, not seeming to recognise their essentially ephemeral nature. He did not realise that for us veterans of the country the change was far greater than for him, but fully expected and accepted. His powers, after all, had been confined to his Courts and those brought before him, whereas mine had been over everything and everyone in my Province when I was Resident, and mostly stemmed from my own initiative. His gloom on the plane back was especially noticeable, and he told us that his application to do another tour of service as Chief Justice had been turned down and this tour, due to end in a few months, was to be his last. The next morning Yaro brought the tea at 6 a.m. as usual, but just before this we heard shooting seemingly from the Chief Justice's house across the road from us. My wife had clearly heard two shots; I, just waking, was only sure of one. Yaro looked worried and said briefly, 'C.J. shot himself' and disappeared in the direction of his house. It turned out to be true. It was all very sad and sudden, and seemed altogether unnecessary. We all had to retire, and most of us made a good job of it in the U.K. How had a man of sufficient calibre to become C.J. – there are not many such – collapsed in this way? Yet, considering the nature of the country and its climate, and the way in which things went wrong from time to time, it was perhaps surprising that there were not more suicides among British people in Nigeria.

I found the Sardauna easy to work with, perhaps because I had never been with him in his own Province and had not met him till he started to come up in the world, so our mutual respect was unclouded by the past. There is no doubt that he was the most dynamic personality in the North: he feared no man and was respected by all, though of course disliked by some. Like many of the Ministers he had been a schoolmaster but had had no higher education. His natural wit and quickness and his knowledge of the Koran made up for that. He did not care for European 'interference' and was naturally averse to white people who tried to tell him how to do things or to 'sell' him slick ideas.

The Sardauna's death was a disaster for Nigeria, for he alone at that time had the strength of character and the will to bring in reforms and to advance the people of the country. It was not to be: but did he have to be gunned down in cold blood against the wall of his house? And was it written that his head-wife should fling herself unavailingly between the guns and her lord? However, when we said goodbye in Kaduna in 1962, he was in fine spirits. I had said that we wanted no parties or gifts. At the close of forty years service, any speeches must be banal and inadequate, saying either too much or too little. The Sardauna said thank-you to us both and the Prime Minister, Abubakar, wrote a grateful half-sheet from Lagos. I did not want any more. The rest remained in the country. It had been a happy service.

INDEX

273